Wordsworth and Coleridge

# ANALYSING TEXTS

*General Editor: Nicholas Marsh*

*Published*

Chaucer: *The Canterbury Tales*    *Gail Ashton*

Aphra Behn: The Comedies    *Kate Aughterson*

Webster: The Tragedies    *Kate Aughterson*

John Keats    *John Blades*

Wordsworth and Coleridge: *Lyrical Ballads*    *John Blades*

Shakespeare: The Comedies    *R. P. Draper*

Charlotte Brontë: The Novels    *Mike Edwards*

E. M. Forster: The Novels    *Mike Edwards*

George Eliot: The Novels    *Mike Edwards*

Shakespeare: The Tragedies    *Nicholas Marsh*

Shakespeare: Three Problem Plays    *Nicholas Marsh*

Jane Austen: The Novels    *Nicholas Marsh*

Emily Brontë: *Wuthering Heights*    *Nicholas Marsh*

Virginia Woolf: The Novels    *Nicholas Marsh*

D. H. Lawrence: The Novels    *Nicholas Marsh*

William Blake: The Poems    *Nicholas Marsh*

John Donne: The Poems    *Joe Nutt*

Thomas Hardy: The Novels    *Norman Page*

Marlowe: The Plays    *Stevie Simkin*

---

**Analysing Texts**
**Series Standing Order ISBN 0–333–73260–X**
(*outside North America only*)

You can receive future titles in this series as they are published by placing a standing order. Please contact your bookseller or, in case of difficulty, write to us at the address below with your name and address, the title of the series and the ISBN quoted above.

Customer Services Department, Macmillan Distribution Ltd
Houndmills, Basingstoke, Hampshire RG21 6XS, England

---

# Wordsworth and Coleridge:
## *Lyrical Ballads*

JOHN BLADES

palgrave
macmillan

First published 2004 by
PALGRAVE MACMILLAN
Houndmills, Basingstoke, Hampshire RG21 6XS and
175 Fifth Avenue, New York, N.Y. 10010
Companies and representatives throughout the world

PALGRAVE MACMILLAN is the global academic imprint of the Palgrave Macmillan division of St. Martin's Press, LLC and of Palgrave Macmillan Ltd. Macmillan® is a registered trademark in the United States, United Kingdom and other countries. Palgrave is a registered trademark in the European Union and other countries.

ISBN 1–4039–0479–0 hardback
ISBN 1–4039–0480–4 paperback

This book is printed on paper suitable for recycling and made from fully managed and sustained forest sources.

A catalogue record for this book is available from the British Library.

Library of Congress Cataloging-in-Publication Data
Blades, John.
    Wordsworth and Coleridge : lyrical ballads / John Blades.
        p. cm. – (Analysing texts)
    Includes bibliographical references and index.
    ISBN 1–4039–0479–0 – ISBN 1–4039–0480–4 (pbk.)
        1. Wordsworth, William, 1770–1850. Lyrical ballads. 2. Coleridge, Samuel Taylor, 1772–1834 – Criticism and interpretation. 3. English poetry – 19th century – History and criticism. 4. Romanticism – England. I. Title. II. Analysing texts (Palgrave Macmillan (Firm))

PR5869.L93B55 2004
821'.708—dc22                                                   2004042103

10  9  8  7  6  5  4  3  2  1
13  12  11  10  09  08  07  06  05  04

Printed and bound in China

# Contents

# General Editor's Preface

This series is dedicated to one clear belief: that we can all enjoy, understand and analyse literature for ourselves, provided we know how to do it. How can we build on close understanding of a short passage, and develop our insight into the whole work? What features do we expect to find in a text? Why do we study style in so much detail? In demystifying the study of literature, these are only some of the questions the *Analysing Texts* series addresses and answers.

The books in this series will not do all the work for you, but will provide you with the tools, and show you how to use them. Here, you will find samples of close, detailed analysis, with an explanation of the analytical techniques utilised. At the end of each chapter there are useful suggestions for further work you can do to practise, develop and hone the skills demonstrated and build confidence in your own analytical ability.

An author's individuality shows in the way they write: every work they produce bears the hallmark of that writer's personal 'style'. In the main part of each book we concentrate therefore on analysing the particular flavour and concerns of one author's work, and explain the features of their writing in connection with major themes. In Part 2 there are chapters about the author's life and work, assessing their contribution to developments in literature; and a sample of critics' views are summarised and discussed in comparison with each other. Some suggestions for further reading provide a bridge towards further critical research.

*Analysing Texts* is designed to stimulate and encourage your critical and analytic faculty, to develop your personal insight into the author's work and individual style, and to provide you with the skills and techniques to enjoy at first hand the excitement of discovering the richness of the text.

NICHOLAS MARSH

# Some Important Events During the Lives of Wordsworth and Coleridge

1770 William Wordsworth is born, 7 April, in Cockermouth, Cumberland.

1771 Dorothy Wordsworth is born.

1772 Samuel Taylor Coleridge is born, 21 October, in Ottery St Mary, Devon.

1776 War of American Independence begins.

1778 Death of Wordsworth's mother.

1779 Wordsworth sent away to Hawkshead Grammar School.

1781 Death of Coleridge's father.

1783 Death of Wordsworth's father. William Pitt becomes Prime Minister.

1787 Wordsworth at St John's College, Cambridge.

1788 Birth of George (later Lord) Byron.

1789 Fall of the Bastille – French Revolution begins.

1790 During the long vacation Wordsworth tours France and Switzerland.

1791 Wordsworth graduates from Cambridge. Coleridge enters Jesus College, Cambridge. Thomas Paine publishes *The Rights of Man*.

1792 In Paris, Wordsworth falls in love with Annette Vallon; he returns to London alone in October and their child, Caroline, is born in December.
Birth of Percy Bysshe Shelley.

1793 Wordsworth publishes *An Evening Walk* and *Descriptive Sketches*.
Wordsworth visits Salisbury Plain and Tintern Abbey.
William Godwin publishes *Enquiry Concerning Political Justice*.

In December Coleridge briefly joins the army under the name of S. T. Comberbache.

1794    Execution of Robespierre; French wars begin. Coleridge meets Robert Southey and together they prepare plans for a Pantisocracy. Coleridge leaves Cambridge.

1795    Wordsworth comes under the influence of William Godwin's reformist ideas.

In August Wordsworth and Coleridge meet for first time.

In September William and Dorothy Wordsworth set up home together at Racedown, in Dorset.

In October Coleridge marries Sara Fricker and they settle at Clevedon in Somerset.

Birth of John Keats.

1796    Coleridge begins publication of *The Watchman*, a Christian journal.

Coleridge's son Hartley is born in September.

In November Coleridge begins to experiment with opium.

In December the Coleridges move to Nether Stowey, in Somerset.

1797    The Wordsworths rent Alfoxden House in Somerset.

Coleridge publishes *Poems* and composes 'Kubla Khan'. Begins *The Rime of the Ancient Mariner*.

In December Coleridge accepts post of Unitarian minister in Shropshire.

1798    Coleridge accepts Tom Wedgwood's offer of an annuity and resigns his ministry.

Wordsworth takes a walking tour in the Wye Valley and visits Tintern Abbey.

Publication of *Lyrical Ballads*.

Coleridge and the Wordsworths travel to Germany.

1799    The Wordsworths return to England and settle eventually at Dove Cottage, Grasmere. In France Napoleon becomes First Consul.

Coleridge meets and falls in love with Sara Hutchinson ('ASRA').

1800    Coleridge comes to live at Greta Hall near Keswick.

1801    Second edition of *Lyrical Ballads* (though dated 1800).

1802    Wordsworth visits France to meet Annette and their daughter.

In May Wordsworth marries Mary Hutchinson.

Third edition of *Lyrical Ballads*. The Peace of Amiens.

*Edinburgh Review* begins publication.

1803    Wordsworth and Coleridge make tour of Scotland.

1804    Coleridge leaves for Malta. Wordsworth completes 'Immortality Ode' and almost all of *The Prelude*.

1805    Fourth edition of *Lyrical Ballads*. In October, the French fleet is defeated at the Battle of Trafalgar.

1806    Coleridge returns to England.

1807    Slavery is abolished in the British Dominions.

1809    Coleridge edits his own newspaper *The Friend*.

*Quarterly Review* begins publication.

1810    Wordsworth and Coleridge in conflict.

1812    Wordsworth and Coleridge are reconciled.

1813    Wordsworth is appointed as Distributor of Stamps for Westmorland.

1814    Wordsworth publishes *The Excursion*.

1815    Napoleon's army defeated at Waterloo. Coleridge begins *Biographia Literaria*.

1817    *Biographia Literaria* published.

1819    Peterloo Massacre: in Manchester a public demonstration is dispersed by militia.

1827    Death of William Blake.

1831    Final meeting between Wordsworth and Coleridge.

1832    The Reform Bill, opposed by Wordsworth, is passed.

1843    Wordsworth is appointed Poet Laureate.

1850    Wordsworth dies on 23 April.

*For Anne-Marie and Lizzie*

# Introduction

Mr Wordsworth's genius is a pure emanation of the Spirit of the Age. Had he lived in any other period of the world, he would never have been heard of. ... He takes the simplest elements of nature and of the human mind, the mere abstract conditions inseparable from our being, and tries to compound a new system of poetry from them. ... Hence the unaccountable mixture of seeming simplicity and real abstruseness in the *Lyrical Ballads*. Fools have laughed at, wise men scarcely understood them.

(William Hazlitt, *The Spirit of the Age*, 1825)

[Mr Coleridge] . . . the sleep walker, the dreamer, the sophist, the word hunter, the craver after sympathy, but still vulnerable to truth, accessible to opinion because not sordid or mechanical.

(William Hazlitt, 'The Letter Bell', 1830)

Hazlitt's comments on Wordsworth's 'genius' imply that he is of his age but only of his age, that he was relevant only to his own era. From our privileged viewpoint here over 175 years on, we can say that he was only partly correct. Wordsworth was certainly the man of his moment, but he speaks to all eras – a poet speaking to mankind.

That Wordsworth was the genius of his age is due also in great part to his very close friendship and collaboration with Samuel Taylor Coleridge. From the occasion of their first momentous acquaintance (they probably met for the first time in Bristol in 1795) they clicked together emotionally and in terms of mutual inspiration, poetic theory and critical support. During their most creative period they gathered around them an exceptionally gifted circle of fellow artists and intimates that was to shape the course of English Romanticism in the nineteenth century.

It would be simplistic to follow Hazlitt's formula and argue, as some have tried, that one man supplied the poetry while the other the theory, yet Hazlitt's distinction does possess the seeds of what the two men were about. At the time of their meeting, Wordsworth was somewhat in awe of Coleridge the published poet and charismatic public speaker (and as a young man Hazlitt himself claims to have walked ten miles to hear one of his sermons). Coleridge was a sparkling bundle of human contradictions: a brilliantly engaging raconteur with a dazzling intellect, variously a newspaper editor and political agitator, woefully unreliable, frustratingly unsystematic yet winningly congenial overall. He was an intensely humanitarian and sensitive man, and a wild dreamer of stunning originality.

By contrast Wordsworth was a steady, forthright individual with a strong conviction in the promise of his own genius as well as in the necessary means of realising it. As a poet he is very much a writer of his own soul, whose eye is resolutely focused on the quotidian reality of the ordinary life and on its potential for transcendental revelation. At the time of *Lyrical Ballads* he was no less a humanitarian or political radical or thinker than his associate but, unlike Coleridge, Wordsworth was not a philosopher and no system builder. He was highly responsive to the spell of words and poetic voices, which made him an inveterate reviser, constantly alert to the dynamics at work in a text.

This cannot do anything like full justice to either man, of course, but it does go some way in describing the diversity of qualities and emphases that converge in the marriage of these two disparate minds. It is the very diversity of their separate geniuses that goes some way to account for their amazing impact on literature through *Lyrical Ballads*.

Why is it important to study *Lyrical Ballads*? One reason for its sustained appeal lies, as Hazlitt hints, in their combination of 'seeming simplicity' and 'real abstruseness'. His paradoxical phrasing draws attention to the fact that the poems are accessible on such a diversity of levels and viewpoints. However, his pointed use of the term 'seeming' also draws attention crucially to their stamina as relentlessly and delightfully elusive productions, their capacity to stimulate and fulfil critical enquiry.

The ballad form is one of the most basic, ancient forms of storytelling, arising from a timeless oral tradition, the need to communicate yarns and to transmit myths and cautionary tales, so that they became a rich store of local wisdom. They were sturdy dramatic narratives, originally sung to a group, enacting extraordinary events in the lives of ordinary people, inspiring wonder in the potential for the strange, the dangerous, and the supernatural within the humdrum.

On one level *Lyrical Ballads* is significant in reviving or extending this tradition – of discovering the mystical in the mundane, sometimes with spine-tingling effect. Over two centuries on from their first appearance, the poems still offer a great read and some of them have become celebrities in their own right (most modern readers are likely to nominate the first and the last in the original collection: *The Rime of the Ancient Mariner* and 'Tintern Abbey').

At the same time, while Wordsworth and Coleridge undoubtedly had one eye on the popular appeal of this form (they did set out to make some money on it, after all), they had at least one other eye on the innovativeness of their project, particularly in terms of their use of language. Their feisty, ambitious enterprise was intended to muscle in on and supplant prevailing modes of writing, to proclaim the arrival of the exciting new vision of 'Romanticism' with its vibrant new poetic experiences. This is made clear by Wordsworth's introductory comments in the Advertisement and Preface that were both a commentary on the poems and a revolutionary manifesto. Indeed many analysts have considered these comments as just as crucial to literary history as the poems themselves, and they are generally regarded as the first documents in modern literary theory.

The following chapters set out to offer interpretations of most of the important poems of *Lyrical Ballads*. However, there is nothing sacrosanct about their arrangement, which centres on five topics, and it is important to bear in mind that my interpretations are just that – mine – and are not intended to be definitive or exclusive. I have referred to the ideas of other critics where it seemed appropriate to challenge or reinforce a point.

The reading list at the end is offered as a route for broadening your responses to the poems and each of the chapters of Part 1 ends with suggestions for further research. As well as being very much a text of our era, *Lyrical Ballads* is, of course, a product of its own time. Part 2 attempts to provide a flavour of the context in which *Lyrical Ballads* was composed and you may find it interesting to begin there.

If, in the end, you find some of the poems perplexing, it is worth remembering Coleridge's famous declaration: 'Poetry gives most pleasure when only generally and not perfectly understood' – though it is also worth remembering that tutors and examiners have seldom accepted this as a valid excuse for under-achievement.

# PART 1

# ANALYSING
# *LYRICAL BALLADS*

# 1

# *Childhood and the Growth of the Mind*

if the child be not constrained too much, and be left sufficiently to her own pursuits, and be not too anxiously tended, and have not her mind planted over by art with likings that do not spring naturally upon it ... she will become modest and diffident.

(Wordsworth, letter to a friend, 1806)

In this chapter I want to begin our discussion of *Lyrical Ballads* by concentrating on one of the major themes of Wordsworth's poetry, that of childhood, and to focus in particular on his special interest in the development of the mind of the child. As well as being a major theme, childhood is also for Wordsworth an important location for a discussion of wider philosophical ideas involving the imagination and nature, which are discussed in subsequent chapters. Accordingly, although I have treated these (and other themes) in separate chapters it is important to be aware of their interrelatedness.

Here, the four poems we will be analysing in detail are:

'Lucy Gray'
'We are seven'
'There was a Boy'
'Nutting'

### 'Lucy Gray'

The ballad 'Lucy Gray' was written in 1799 during Wordsworth's brief and unhappy residence in the Harz mountains of Germany. His isolation and solitude found sympathetic expression through a story suggested by Dorothy in which a girl becomes 'bewildered' by a snow storm, and falls and drowns in a canal lock near Halifax.

The poem is in three main sections. The first (stanzas 1–3) is in the narrative 'present', looking back to her time and place; the middle section (stanzas 4–14) relates to Lucy's fruitless search for her mother in the storm; the final section returns to the 'present' and the memory of her disappearance.

I have chosen to analyse stanzas 1–9:

> Oft I had heard of Lucy Gray,
> And when I crossed the wild,
> I chanced to see at break of day
> The solitary child.
>
> No mate, no comrade Lucy knew;                    5
> She dwelt on a wild moor,
> The sweetest thing that ever grew
> Beside a human door!
>
> You yet may spy the fawn at play,
> The hare upon the green;                          10
> But the sweet face of Lucy Gray
> Will never more be seen.
>
> 'To-night will be a stormy night,
> You to the town must go,
> And take a lantern, Child, to light              15
> Your Mother through the snow.'
>
> 'That, Father! will I gladly do;
> 'Tis scarcely afternoon –
> The Minster-clock has just struck two,
> And yonder is the Moon.'                          20
>
> At this the Father raised his hook
> And snapped a faggot-band;

He plied his work, and Lucy took
The lantern in her hand.

Not blither is the mountain roe –                                    25
With many a wanton stroke
Her feet disperse the powdery snow
That rises up like smoke.

The storm came on before its time,
She wandered up and down,                                           30
And many a hill did Lucy climb
But never reached the town.

The wretched parents all that night
Went shouting far and wide;
But there was neither sound nor sight                               35
To serve them for a guide.

The opening four stanzas make very clear Lucy's isolation but also
anticipate her end by the warning that she will 'Never more be seen',
highlighting the poem's balladic sense of doom. The opening of the
poem is typical of ballad style, with a simple but memorable, mythical anecdote, often handed down by word of mouth concerned with
the life (or death) of a local figure.

Stanza 5 suggests a readily compliant, obedient Lucy who is
respectful of her father with a strong sense of filial duty. The immi-
nence of the storm reveals her trusting innocence, and eagerness to
please ('That, Father! will I gladly do …', l. 17). Her assignment also
reveals her vital function in the family, with a specific role to fulfil
and it is filled with a quite onerous mission.

'Not blither' in line 25 stresses her eagerness as well as her naive,
trusting nature, which helps prepare her role as the victim. The
remainder of stanza 7, with that image of Lucy idly kicking up the
snow, beautifully evokes the heedless complacency of childhood –
while the word 'wanton' points up her utter absorption in this casual
fun. Gradually, and tragically, this abstraction transforms into disori-
entation, she loses her way, and Lucy becomes enveloped in the snow
and consumed into the landscape.

Some of these important elements are hinted at and reinforced
elsewhere in the poem. In line 7 she is described as the 'sweetest

thing' and this charm is taken up again with the girl's 'sweet face' four lines later. As well as her endearing cuteness, these references also endorse the feeling of vulnerability she exudes. The simplicity of the natural setting together with its minimalist details are in naturalistic sympathy with the girl's disposition in the poem. However, these points also have the effect of extending Lucy beyond her actuality as a living girl by implying that she is herself part of nature, or at least in close affinity with it. And this idea is further emphasised by the associations made between Lucy and the local animals: the fawn (9), hare (10) and the mountain roe (25). The fact that these endure after her death reminds us of the sense of her as innocent victim.

Some of these issues are anticipated in the second stanza where she is described as

> The sweetest thing that ever grew
> Beside a human door!                        (7–8)

in which 'Beside a human door' implies a strange metamorphism, not quite human but indigenous and somewhere on the mysterious threshold between the human and the natural.

So while Lucy is intrinsic to the family she also belongs inherently to the natural scene outside the house. Perhaps this accounts for her readiness to obey her father and her 'wanton' absorption into the landscape once outside. But what can we make of her parents? In the above passage the fact that Wordsworth gives us the actual words of Lucy's father presents him directly before us. Yet at the same time the father seems dogmatic and imposing towards Lucy:

> You to the town must go,
> And take a lantern                               (14–15)

After his instruction he turns suddenly, back to his tasks, sharply (and fatally) cutting off his daughter to the storm. His manner is cold, peremptory but, with evident irony, he is redeemed by Lucy's cheerful innocence – at first anyway. He too comes across here as a lonely figure, lost in his work but somehow confident of Lucy's familiarisation with the wilderness. A commanding patriarchal figure, her father seems god-like and the deftness with which he raises his hook and 'snapped a faggot-band' (22), strengthens the impression of a brusque and forthright man.

The symbolic role of the parents in the poem is pointed up by their oddly curt attitude to Lucy. In blunt terms, Lucy is exploited by her father, shirking the job himself, though stanza 6 implies that he is inattentive rather than culpable, taking her for granted. This in turn heightens Lucy's function as the innocent victim, one strand of the poem being the way she is subjected to the will of others (compare two other poems in which children are sent away: 'The Idiot Boy' in which Betty sends her son for a doctor and he gets lost, and *Michael* in which Isabel reluctantly sends her son Luke to his kinsman and he too becomes 'lost', but in a slightly different sense).

In spite of this, line 33 describes the parents as 'wretched', pointing to their own sense of guilt as well as remorseful loss, and Wordsworth is careful not to wag fingers or turn the poem into a lament. Instead the final section of the poem (stanzas 15 and 16) directs attention away from the parents and onto the mysterious aftermath concerning Lucy herself.

This unexpected ending wrong-foots the reader of course. Yet, further, by suddenly raising the tempo towards that enigmatic void at the end, Wordsworth foregrounds the symbolic elements of the poem and of the eponymous heroine herself. She was never found but has, apparently, become elemental, transmuted into the very nature of the landscape itself (a point anticipated in lines 6–8), taken back into and reclaimed by nature. But since she was never found alive again, we too are led back into the poem for clues.

As so often with Wordsworth's lyrical ballads the simple diction makes the lyric seem simple, even banal. It is even so here, that we have more than a sorry tale of a young girl's death in the winter storm. The final two stanzas enigmatically re-route us back into the poem for a re-reading of its signs. Although her father orders Lucy out on a mission, it is ironically the careless parents themselves who embark on the mission, in search of a lost or evasive childhood. It is they who follow *her* tracks, and try to decipher her signs left in the snow: childhood becomes the moral guide to adulthood and ironically Lucy takes over the educational role. Significantly she holds a light before her in the storm, 'to light / Your Mother through the snow' (15; and we recall her name derives from the Latin *lux/lucis* for 'light'). Furthermore, her recognition of the moon in line 20 suggests that she sees in it something of a natural, celestial father. She is the light and this, together with her blithe uncomplicated innocence, discloses her role as moral leader.

In death she becomes teasingly elusive. The poem's final line implies that she endures within the moorland wind, ephemeral, immortal and incorporeal, the *genius loci*. In line 62, she 'never looks behind', colloquially suggesting the clearness of her own conscience. Conversely, though 'lost', she persists as a haunting reality of stoicism, loyalty and release from care as her careworn parents trace the ghostly prints of 'Lucy's feet' and 'footmarks small' (lines 44 and 46): like the reader, they will have to interpret such signs in order to interpret and recover the lost life. The death of Lucy is the loss of childhood in the storm of approaching adult life.

In the end Wordsworth is teasingly silent on Lucy's exact position, her 'message' in the poem. Instead he alerts us to the special character of childhood, its mysteriously transcendent quality and special relationship with nature. At the nub of these is Lucy's solitude, a point which is underlined by the fact that when Wordsworth later revised the poem he extended its title to 'Lucy Gray, or Solitude', making explicit what was simply implied

> No mate, no comrade Lucy knew;
> She dwelt on a wild moor                                            (5–6)

The wild moor (Wordsworth later changed this to 'wide moor') and the absence of friends draw attention to the desolation and loneliness of a lakeland childhood – though Lucy herself does not actually experience loneliness. Yet 'No mate' goes significantly further and even denotes her pre-sexual status.

At the time of her disappearance she is transitional between childhood and adulthood. Literally and figuratively she is moving towards the mother. But her disappearance fixes her at pre-pubescence in the storm of adolescence, and like the 'bride of wood' she represents a sort of linkage, but incomplete. (The storm symbol also appears in

'Three years she grew' and there are echoes of it in 'Nutting' and 'There was a Boy'; see below for a discussion of the 'storm' symbol.)

She can be seen as a pivotal, if incomplete, link in a poem constructed of antitheses: between country and town, father and mother, high and low, calm and storm. Lucy herself, however, is not presented as incomplete though she is departing into a sort of limbo apparently before her time. In fact her most crucial transition – that between mortal and immortal – has the unmistakable air of fulfilment, even if this remains an unhappy conundrum for her parents.

Central to this theme of bridging mortal and immortal states is that of time. The poem has numerous references to the temporal – for instance, each of its main sections opens with a specific reference to time as well as to physical actions. For Lucy the storm represents a matrix of conflicting natural elements and, ironically, it is through these that she will eventually transcend the realm of the human (which is characterised by the pre-eminence of time and the turmoil of human actions). She enters the realm of the immortal, becoming at one with the ghost-like spirit of nature, an elemental being. This has the effect of subverting the typical ballad ending, away from loss, sadness and remorse, and into an affirmation of the heroic spirit of solitude with its echoes of infinity and eternity. This heroic lesson is the parable which little Lucy sets her parents to learn.

Having said this, Wordsworth's poem manifests many of the traditional ballad features: simple, musical rhythm, using deceptively plain diction, focused on an intensely dramatic narrative. The poem is also set in conventional ballad metre: four lines alternating iambic tetrameter and trimeter, rhymed ABAB. 'Lucy Gray' is essentially a species of cautionary tale and one which Wordsworth moulds, extends and elevates, loading with metaphysical themes to breaking point.

This experiment with such a simple poetic form clearly runs the risk of buckling the lyric under its metaphysical cargo. However, Wordsworth successfully manages to avoid this risk. One reason for this success is that he underplays his themes, using the mystery of the narrative (including its surrealistic ending) to provoke the reader into exploring deeper interpretations. His supple and highly imaginative verse, too, with its hints and pointed impressions also suggest a dimension beyond a plain account of a tragic death. For example, in the above extract,

> The storm came on before its time,
> She wandered up and down, (29–30)

the expressions 'storm', 'before its time' and 'wandered' function colloquially but, as we see time and again in Wordsworth's writing, he empowers his diction to work both literally and figuratively often with little discernment between the two.

This sort of semantic economy is evident too in terms of imagery. I have already referred to there being many references to time and action and these help to flag up the poem's underlying themes of mortality and human turmoil. At the same time they help to deepen a sense of urgency in the ballad, thereby intensifying the drama of the tale too. References to light also figure strongly (see lines 15 and 24, for example), suggesting the theme of enlightenment, and have their correlation in the large cluster of words connected with 'seeing' (lines 3, 12, 35, 43, 59 and so on).

Two other points worth noting here are, on the one hand, references to bridges or to crossing (for example in lines 2, 39, 42, 49, 52, 62) and, on the other, images of parts of the body. 'Bridging' endorses Lucy's symbolic and moral role of bonding in addition to the idea of her 'crossing over' to the other realm of elemental immortality. Conversely, references to parts of the body give vitality and vividness to the actions of the poem (such as when Lucy takes up the lantern and her feet 'disperse the powdery snow') – as well as reminding us of her mortal origins.

Consistent with traditional ballad form, the poem exudes a strong air of fatalism. Wordsworth's use of past tense from the very beginning and the starkly forbidding statement in line 12 give the whole poem a mythic tenor, the tragedy doomed to be played out in each retelling. However, the switch to present tense in the final section helps to stress Lucy's immortality, the eternal in her new status as an ever-living child. The supple flexibility of verb tense and the early disclosure of Lucy's fate act to moderate any tendencies to melodrama inherent in the events by distancing them from the reader. They also witness the narrator's firm control over the narrative, at the same time bolstering the plot, while his explicit voice in the first and final sections works as a framing device around the events (and the latter is a recurrent feature in *Lyrical Ballads*).

Wordsworth's deft management is apparent too in his manipulation of the reader's expectations. This occurs frequently in his use of negatives: Lucy 'Will never more be seen' (12), 'never reached' (32), 'nor ever lost' (51), 'further there were none' (54) and now she 'never looks behind' (62).

It is not difficult to see that 'Lucy Gray' is an acutely subtle and expansive treatment of a simple dramatic tale. Many of its themes are the major themes of Wordsworth's poetry as a whole. For example, most of the other 'Lucy' poems involve the image of a lost or doomed young girl, especially in the sense, as here, of one crossing over to merge her human existence with that of nature's extensive soul.

In 'She dwelt among th'untrodden ways' the subject's unnerving solitude is underscored in the images of the half-hidden violet and the solitary star (as well as literally in the absence of companions). In fact Wordsworth's fascination with her, her exceptionality, seems to subsist in this very state of being overlooked or undiscovered, virginal. She is, like Lucy Gray, having no mate, 'And very few to love'.

Lucy Gray is in part defined by the negative words and ideas in which she is couched, a correlative for her incompleteness as a developing adolescent. As such, the poem also stresses her eternal juvenescence, intact and fixed. Making similar use of negative sculpting, 'A slumber did my spirit seal' goes even further as a Lucy poem (if indeed it does feature Lucy) and its complex finale again develops the theme of the child coalescing with nature. In an uncanny atmosphere which is almost supernatural, Lucy is again alive, beyond mortal life, beyond the 'touch of earthly years', fused into and subject to the natural forces, 'Rolled round in earth's diurnal course' (7). The atmosphere here is uncanny because we can imagine the dead girl, with no will of her own, subject to the mysterious forces of nature (and that troubling phrase 'rolled round' clearly points to this nullifying of the will, the 'spirit' sealed). It is uncanny too because the corollary of her death and altered state is to induce in the poet an uncomfortable realisation of the corpse-like slumber of his own spirit.

## 'We are seven'

A different view of childhood and one from a different angle is
offered in 'We are seven', written in the spring of 1798. The poem's
central theme is anticipated with some irony in Coleridge's introductory stanza: 'What should it know of death?' (4). It quickly emerges
however that what she does not understand is simply the adult's peculiar perspective on death. She interrogates it and then invalidates it in
favour of her own alternative. Her perspective is both a major theme
of the poem and the vehicle for presenting it.

'We are seven' is structured into four sections: stanzas 1–3 famil-
iarises us with some of the materialist elements of the girl and her
landscape; stanzas 4–9 outline the facts of her family background
responding to the narrator's puzzling enquiry; stanzas 10–15 fill out
her enigmatic reply, on her own life and the deaths of her siblings; the
final leaves a stand-off between these two polarised and entrenched
positions. For analysis I have decided to focus on stanzas 13–17.

> 'The first that died was little Jane;
> In bed she moaning lay,                                        50
> Till God released her of her pain,
> And then she went away.
>
> 'So in the churchyard she was laid,
> And all the summer dry,
> Together round her grave we played,                            55
> My brother John and I.
>
> 'And when the ground was white with snow,
> And I could run and slide,
> My brother John was forced to go,
> And he lies by her side.                                       60
>
> 'How many are you then, said I,
> If they two are in heaven?'
> The little maiden did reply,
> 'O master! we are seven.'
>
> 'But they are dead; those two are dead!                        65
> Their spirits are in heaven!'

'Twas throwing words away; for still
The little maid would have her will,
And said, 'Nay, we are seven!'

This passage seems to me to be important because in it the girl expands her account of the fates of her sister and brother, but also because it exposes Wordsworth's view of the child's mind, revealed through her attitude to death and mortality.

Beginning with the death of her sister, Jane, the modifier 'little' in line 49 is interesting because, in addition to pointing to Jane's youthful frailty, it takes up a word which the narrator repeatedly uses to demean her. However, the girl's own use of the word has the ironic effect of raising her status in regard to her deceased brother and sister – though it sounds the sort of colloquialism she has picked up from her mother, perhaps. Adult usage is evident too in her account of their deaths,

> God *released* her of her pain                    (51)

and

> My brother John was *forced to go*                    (59) (my italics)

They quit their earthly, mortal existence by 'release' and 'force', but the two descriptions sound like a mother's euphemistic report of the mystery and injustice of premature deaths. In spite of this adult echo, the girl's plain outlook is quite un-adult-like as she continues to sit and somewhat manically sing to them (line 44). And this, of course, is the point of the poem.

Quite often Wordsworth's ballads and shorter lyrics are so simple as to seem (on a first reading at least) deeply obscure or even banal. Often, too, as here, the lyric sets down a situation in a plain, unadorned style as if the point were either simplistically trivial or deviously cryptic. Consequently, Wordsworth's silence and the poem's wide-eyed mystery challenges the reader to go deeper into the poem to discover what he is really about. And when we do this in 'We are seven' we share with the narrator himself some of the mystery concerning this young girl's world view.

What we have, of course, are two distinct ways of seeing and knowing. In addition we have the result of these two ways colliding, plus Wordsworth's silence in between. These ways are clearly evident throughout the poem but are reiterated most bluntly and trenchantly in the final two stanzas – and the exclamation marks there serve to underline the silent gulf set between.

Taking up a theme from 'Anecdote for Fathers', the adult persona tries to impose his bullying and officious logic onto the child's intuitive and spontaneous wisdom. She is just as obstinately loyal to her way of thinking but without the threatening, overbearing intimidation of the adult. In fact the child displays as little emotion concerning the fact of death as she does about the facts of her own view of it,

> My brother John was forced to go
> And he lies by her side.                                  (60)

After rehearsing their opposed positions on this point, they reach an impasse which parallels the antitheses in the poem (life/death, age/youth, movement/stasis) implying that the gulf between youth and age is unbridgeable – at least by the adult.

However, she does not evade nor is ignorant of the reality of death because in line 49 she declares prosaically 'The first that died' whereas the adults have previously weakened the truth with euphemisms. This is enacted in her games around her sister's grave (line 55) and sitting or singing to both her dead siblings in the churchyard (43–4). At the same time the essential point about her logic lies in the significance which death plays in her outlook: the relationship between the living and the ones who were 'released' or 'forced to go'. For her, the dead are not inanimate objects but living spiritual presences: a dead sister is still no less a sister.

Nor can we accuse her of morbidness concerning her brother and sister. The poem witnesses the vitality of her youth from the beginning,

> That lightly draws its breath
> And feels its life in every limb.                          (3–4)

The adult too recalls this later in 'Your limbs they are alive' (34), while the extract presents other reminders of her vigour in playing, running and sliding (55 and 58). Although lines 41 and 42 hint at the shades of adulthood that later may close about her (knitting and hemming, in stanza 11), she has an untroubled sparkle of imagination. This along with her energy and self-assurance readily help her to accommodate the idea of death.

In contrast to Lucy Gray, the girl of 'We are seven' has great strength of will, particularly in the overbearing presence of adult willpower

> The little maid would have her will.　　　　　　　　　　(68)

At the same time she politely defers to the adult enquirer with 'master' in line 60 (and 'Sir' in line 45), making her confrontation less personal, less excitable by contrast. Significantly, where Lucy Gray was *sent* outward to become an elemental, wind-blown spirit, the girl here is steadfastly located in a physical context, namely beside the cottage (the 'cottage girl', l. 5). Her strong sense of self-identity and loyalty to her siblings as well as her obdurate rationale help to generate the poem's strong atmosphere of the uncanny. The adult narrator repeatedly attempts to undermine this resolve with his seven-fold use of the epithet 'little'.

So in the end the 'little cottage girl' outsmarts the stern and mighty philosopher. His encounter with her becomes an educational experience for him and the proof of this is the poem itself, which she has directly inspired. A kind of preacher, he attempts to give a moralising sermon as well as a lecture in arithmetic (compare the rationalist father in 'Anecdote for Fathers'). His attitude is a hangover from eighteenth-century rationalism, while his dogmatic persistence reveals him to be a domineering chauvinist – whom the girl satirises as a comic figure. In the end the poet learns *her* lesson. The poem warns against the stultifying intransigence of some adult reasoning but, like 'Lucy Gray', also reveals the great power of the childhood imagination to deconstruct and liberate adult thinking.

Although the general tone of 'We are seven' is one of simple spontaneity, it is, of course, a finely wrought production. On one level the poem is structured via the antiphonal exchange of speakers; but it is organised around its prepositions, especially those referring

to time: till ... then ... And when ... so ... if ... then. The movement
at times sounds like an old elementary school arithmetic test led by
some dreary pedant,

> 'How many are you then, said I,
> If they two are in heaven?'
> The little maiden did reply,
> 'O master! we are seven.'                                              (61–4)

In fact there are not two but at least three main figures in the poem
and the moral of the piece may depend on this fact. Beside the girl
and the pedant we hear the poet, the man as he is now, modified by
his encounter with this girl. In contrast to the persistently exasperated
voice of the querulous adult, the poet's mood is subdued and acqui-
escent, now distanced by time and change from the original moment.
However, while Wordsworth offers no direct comment on his former
self, by making the girl seem more percipient, he generously satirises
this early version, making himself the ready butt of his mockery.

As well as dictating the form and tone of the poem, the young girl
largely determines its diction too. The language as a whole is
doggedly simple, even austere, a tribute to Wordsworth's skill in
evincing such complex and heroic themes from humble premises.
While it is quite spare, its leanness acts to focus the attention firmly
on its concrete, realistic details. For example, in the extract, *names*:
Jane and John (plus Conway, line 25); *locations*: in the churchyard,
the ground, by her side; and *actions* 'went away' (52), 'played' (55),
'run and slide' (58). Elsewhere in the poem we hear precise details of
the girl's appearance (stanzas 2 and 3), ages, and the distance of the
cottage from the graves (39). In contrast to 'Lucy Gray', *place* here
takes precedence over *time* and important background ideas are con-
noted by some deft switching between action and static-ness, both
rooted in place; for instance, in the extract, stanzas 14 and 15 (lines
53–60) each juxtaposes playing against lying.

The emphasis on the concrete is, of course, all one with the theme
of cold arithmetical logic and it accounts too for the poem's dearth of
figures of speech. This dearth tends to lend eminence to particulars
which thereby assume metaphorical or symbolic significance; thus

'white with snow' (57) conveys suggestions of death and innocence (likewise 'dry' in line 56). On the other hand 'green' (37), in pointing to the freshness of the graves, also manages to embrace the living girl who intuitively 'feels its life in every limb'. This last quotation appears in the opening stanza and represents the chief figurative element in the poem because, as well as being the means by which the poem's moral is to emerge, it also signals to the reader that the girl stands for more than just herself and operates as a symbol of childhood with its uniquely elusive ways of thinking.

I mentioned a moment ago that in general terms the poem has a deceptive simplicity. A major factor in the creation of this effect lies in the sounds of the poem, especially its rhythm. Clearly the regular ballad metre contributes much to this effect as it does in, say, 'Lucy Gray' and 'The Fountain'. Stanza 13 is a regular example of the English ballad metre, with the stressed syllables indicated

'The <u>first</u> that <u>died</u> was <u>little</u> <u>Jane</u>;
In <u>bed</u> she <u>moaning</u> <u>lay</u>,
Till <u>God</u> re<u>leased</u> her <u>of</u> her <u>pain</u>,
And <u>then</u> she <u>went</u> aw<u>ay</u>. (49–52)

In terms of the rhyme, too, simplicity is the key: here ABAB, though a traditional ballad would use ABCB. Obviously such simple and repetitive patterning has affinities appropriately enough with children's nursery rhyme, but also runs a high risk of monotony or of sounding jingly.

I have argued that the very simplicity of the poem is one of the devices by which Wordsworth draws attention to the serious themes of the poem. The repetitive syndrome of the metre also plays a useful function by reiterating the 'When we are seven' refrain which gradually takes on an insistent drone-like effect, undermining the adult speaker in the poem. This quasi-hypnotic rhetorical feature is supported too by the shortfall of the final line of each stanza whose abruptness echoes the young girl's obstinacy. The result is that the staccato effect helps her to discompose her inquisitor's fluency.

On the other hand, and as we might have expected, Wordsworth successfully minimises the risk of monotony and he achieves this through a range of measures. Most of the lines of the poem are end-stopped but the occasional enjambement creates a natural fluency (see lines 23–4 and 27–8). Then there is internal rhyme which the poem uses extensively – and typically in the following lines

> Their graves are green, they may be seen.          (37)

> Twelve steps or more from my mother's door.          (39)

While this contributes to the variety and density of the poem's overall sounds, it perhaps detracts from the natural speech rhythms which Wordsworth explicitly aims for elsewhere in the poem.

Variations in the metre too are a major source of diversity in 'We are seven', working in sympathy with natural speech cadences. For example, in the extract Wordsworth anticipates the closing of the poem by incorporating irregularities in the two final stanzas. Lines 62 and 63 break the regular pattern but the final stanza goes further. As well as sporting an additional line, stanza 17 finishes the poem with two lines containing the 'full' four stresses in each, emphasising the finality of the girl's refrain,

> The little maid would have her will,
> And said, 'Nay, we are seven!'

(and note the resolute, unexpected stress on 'Nay').

Is the poem a success? Given the inherent divisiveness of the two voices and perspectives there is a strong risk here of fragmentation. However, the presence of the 'later' persona, the poet himself acts as a medium for cohesion. The convergence of theme, character and poetic resource injects a strong sense of cohesion as well as much of the poem's interest. The girl's character is a major contributor to this interest and instils the poem with deeper curiosity, along with some comic perverseness and an uncanny, even discomforting quality. In this matter Wordsworth's silence also undoubtedly adds to the strength of her position here, holding back on psychological conjecture. The adult character's persistent questioning, however, does supply structural momentum at the same time drawing attention to the key question of the girl's psychology and her persistent refusal to mourn, which is the poem's crux.

In reviewing this poem late in his life, Coleridge praised Wordsworth's 'wonder rousing' insights here. In referring to the child's mysterious gift of philosophy, he talked of one who has read the 'eternal deep'. Coleridge himself believed that such childhood percipience probably sprang from the eternal spirit of God at work within the young unfettered child. Although he himself was not always positive about such a source, he believed that Wordsworth's silence on the origins of the girl's perspicacity here was a weakness of the poem. On the other hand, in the Preface to *Lyrical Ballads*, Wordsworth insists that his intention in what is, after all, a relatively small-scale composition was quite limited, being simply to portray

> the perplexity and obscurity which in childhood attend our notion of death, or rather our utter inability to admit that notion.

### 'There was a Boy'

'There was a Boy' is another important poem of childhood in which silence again plays a key role. Contemporary with 'Lucy Gray' and 'We are seven', it also has at the heart of its narrative a mysterious untimely death. That Wordsworth thought highly of it as a treatment of the 'growth of the mind' is shown by the fact that he published it again in 1815 (in *Poems*) and included it as an episode in his epic biographical poem *The Prelude, or The Growth of the Mind* (it appears in Book 5, where it is usually referred to as 'Winander Boy'):

> There was a Boy, ye knew him well, ye Cliffs
> And islands of Winander! many a time,
> At evening, when the stars had just begun
> To move along the edges of the hills,
> Rising or setting, would he stand alone,      5
> Beneath the trees, or by the glimmering lake,
> And there, with fingers interwoven, both hands
> Pressed closely palm to palm and to his mouth
> Uplifted, he, as through an instrument,
> Blew mimic hootings to the silent owls      10
> That they might answer him. And they would shout

Across the watery vale and shout again
Responsive to his call, with quivering peals,
And long haloos, and screams, and echoes loud
Redoubled and redoubled, a wild scene                    15
Of mirth and jocund din. And, when it chanced
That pauses of deep silence mocked his skill,
Then, sometimes, in that silence, while he hung
Listening, a gentle shock of mild surprise
Has carried far into his heart the voice                 20
Of mountain torrents, or the visible scene
Would enter unawares into his mind
With all its solemn imagery, its rocks
Its woods, and that uncertain heaven, received
Into the bosom of the steady lake.                       25
      Fair are the woods, and beauteous is the spot,
The vale where he was born: the churchyard hangs
Upon a slope above the village school,
And there along that bank when I have passed
At evening, I believe, that near his grave               30
A full half-hour together I have stood,
Mute – for he died when he was ten years old.

The poem consists of three sections: the first recalls a solitary boy who stands amid the trees, cliffs and islands of 'glimmering' lake Winander and imitates the hootings of owls until their answering calls and echoes crescendo in a riot of sound; in the middle section the sudden silences would startle him with a deeply incisive shock reaching 'far into his heart'; the final part involves a leap in time as Wordsworth stands in silent meditation beside the grave of the boy.

A much brighter poem than 'We are seven', 'There was a Boy', however, begins in a reflective quietness. 'There was a Boy' sets up a chatty, balladic opening to the poem while the past tense 'was' prepares for the elegiac tone to follow (and the phrase 'I believe' in line 30 makes explicit the subjectivity of Wordsworth's recollection). Once more the poem appears to be established on a fairly bare circumstance of an odd fellow calling to the birds, yet its mere 32 lines involve a daring interplay of thought and allusion which sets it apart decisively from the two previous 'childhood' poems. A further important contrast with them is Wordsworth's self-confident use of blank verse here, its longer measure reinforcing the conversational effect while also offering a more substantial vehicle for this poem's sophistications. Again, Wordsworth's voice is the structuring principle but the chief centre of interest lies, at first anyway, in the bizarre chaos of sound kindled by the boy, followed up by the intriguing phrase, that 'gentle shock of mild surprise' (19).

Wordsworth clearly identifies with and has deep sympathies with the boy of Winander. On the other hand, he never quite involves us directly in the emotions experienced – not until the very last line at least. He holds the reader at arm's length to keep his own meditations in the foreground (the sudden switch in time in line 25 is another device to objectify the reader). Like the boy himself (who is in fact the young Wordsworth) the poet ends up in silent meditation over troubling thoughts: the passage of time, the 'death' of his own childhood, and the significance of the role played by childhood in the growth of the adult mind.

We come back again to that important word 'was' in the first line. It is a key pointer accentuating the pivotal factor of time in the poem's memory as well as in the development of the poet's psychology. The following lines seem to me important in keeping these features to the fore:

> many a time,
> At evening, when the stars had just begun
> To move along the edges of the hills,
> Rising or setting, would he stand alone. (2–5)

The timeless stars and the ancient hills frame the boy within the context of eternity as well as within the localised homeland of the lakes. The almost endless spiralling turbulence of birdcalls plus the reference to heaven in line 4 render the scene a dizzying maelstrom of history and terror. The word 'far' in line 20 hints at the depth and intensity of this danger but also the sublime potency of the human heart and mind.

The poem has a profusion of time imagery: as well as the evening and the rising and setting of the stars, there are 'pauses', 'half-hour',

'ten years old', birth and death, memory, plus the many adverbs of
time ('when', 'then', 'sometimes'). The effect of all this is to mould us
to the poem's subtle temporal framework: dealing with two separate
but crucial moments, the whole composition springs from the operation of memory, or 'association'. Most menacingly, time is death, the
graveyard, 'hangs / Upon a slope above the village school'. Time
oppresses childhood with an image which recalls stanza 10 of 'We are
seven': death is ever-present even in the full bloom and pleasure of
youth. Paradoxically, even amid the eternal, mortality exerts a deep
sombre awareness. This moment of silence, in which mind and
nature are no longer in certain coordination, is the prefiguring for
Wordsworth here of his own death.

In the poem 'Lucy Gray', Lucy is described as a 'living child' (58)
even though she was lost in the storm and in 'We are seven' the young
girl imbues her dead siblings with an obdurate immortality. But what
of the boy of Winander who 'died when he was ten years old'? In literal terms, Wordsworth again cannot conceive of the boy as other
than dead and in his grave. In allegorical terms, however, the situation is more complicated. The 'cliffs / And islands of Winander'
knew him well and probably still do. The poem itself gives life to the
boy so long as men or women have eyes to read it. But if we think of
Wordsworth here as meditating on his own childhood, symbolised by
the Winander boy, then the boy lives on as the changes that the poet
himself has undergone and which are also represented in the middle
sections of the poem.

Although we know that the boy dies at age ten (Wordsworth later
altered this to twelve) it is not clear how old he is when the main
events of the poem take place. While the cause of his death remains
a mystery (and is something of a loose end in the poem) his untimely
decease comes before the onset of self-consciousness. We observe him
as a familiar figure of the local natural landscape – again the *genius
loci* – a Puckish fellow with an impish vigour, fully in tune with
nature, figured in his rascally power to deceive the birds in 'mirth and
jocund' (16). By virtue of this skill he takes on the very nature of the
owl, adding a sort of natural animalism to his boyish cunning and
playful vitality. Until line 17 it is the delight of boyhood that we
witness, but then the murmur of a more solemn music intervenes.

In a preface to the poem in 1815, Wordsworth drew more attention to the power of internal events, set off by the deep silence after the birds' failure to return the boy's calls,

> The Boy, there introduced, is listening, with something of a feverish and restless anxiety, for the recurrence of the riotous sounds which he had previously excited; and, at the moment when the intenseness of his mind is beginning to remit, he is surprised into a perception of the solemn and tranquillising images which the Poem describes.

It is easy to imagine the lad delighting in his hubristic knack of inflicting madness on the landscape. Line 15 describes it as a 'wild scene', pointing both to the natural environment but also to the chaos of sound that fills it so rapidly and completely ('Winander' is Lake Windermere in Cumbria if you fancy visiting the spot and flexing your own hooting muscles).

Wordsworth's fine linguistic economy selects just sufficient pastoral detail for the reader to grasp an impression of the 'visible scene' (21): the cliffs, islands, hills, glimmering lake, watery vale, evening and the stars, rising setting, rocks, woods. Hootings speedily become the 'riotous sounds', and riot speedily, mysteriously becomes an awesome silence, a void. The poem begins with an almost palpable evocation of scene and sound, yet the middle section (lines 17–25) points to a much deeper pact with nature and a knowledge of its psychological influence on the young person. We can now move on to trace its process and effects.

As in so many of Wordsworth's 'nature' poems, solitude is an essential element in communion with the spirit of nature. When alive, the boy 'stands alone' and his grave also seems lonely, while Wordsworth too, companionless, mirrors him. As corollary to the absence of human mates, the boy enjoys a close intimacy with nature, so much so that a strange reciprocity coheres between them. Surprisingly, although Wordsworth briefly dematerialises the cliffs and islands, the bosom of the lake, he does the reverse with the boy, identifying him with material nature.

All the same, while the boy stands outside of nature, stirring and disrupting its complacent serenity, he becomes deeply affected when

nature suddenly replies to his tormenting art with her equally
troubling silence,

> Listening, a gentle shock of mild surprise
> Has carried far into his heart the voice
> Of mountain torrents, or the visible scene.                    (19–21)

Her power to shock entails him being receptive to her penetrating
images and torrents (compare the moralising effect of the 'silent trees'
on the boy in 'Nutting').

At this point, the boy's hooting calls connects him spiritually with
Lucy Gray. He momentarily transcends into purely natural, elemental being, recalling the way that Lucy transmuted into the mountain
winds. The silence mocks his art, carrying into his innermost core the
voice of nature together with a vision of her landscape: this generates
a new profound type of silence, now internalised as an inner serenity
and expressed metaphorically in the 'bosom of the steady lake' (25).

It is, of course, a defining moment for the child. It is also an
awesome, frightening moment originating in his idly hubristic 'mirth
and jocund'. The joke turns cold, worse than cold, shadowing forth
his death only five lines later. Solemn music converts the boy's fun
and games into a prescience of disaster.

Wordsworth's poetry has many such unnerving premonitions of
human transience. For example, from *Lyrical Ballads*, the movement
of the moon in 'Strange fits of passion' and the chilling 'murmurs'
which perturb many of the poems ('Nutting', 'Three years she grew',
'Tintern Abbey', for example). And in *The Prelude* there are the well-
known examples of the flood in Books V and XIII and of the decay-
ing Alpine trees in Book VI. In 'There was a Boy' the boy himself is
too young to interpret the full burden of the 'solemn imagery' here
but the many references to time point to a dawning sense of mortality, the approaching shades of what Wordsworth describes elsewhere
as the 'Shades of the prison house' growing about the child ('Ode:
Intimations of Immortality', l. 67).

Nature and her icy lore bring the joke to a sober end. They strike
deep within the boy's 'heart' (20), even if but dimly understood by

him. A sort of hint, a shadowy forewarning, it is unformulated except on the level of an occult amorphous idea, but nevertheless intelligible on those terms. And even nature's material delights – fair words and beauteous spots – are ultimately unconsoling. By the same token, that 'uncertain heaven' in line 24 even undermines the promise of a Christian afterlife (compare the heaven promised in 'We are seven' and the diurnal fate at the close of 'A slumber did my spirit seal' – which perhaps emulates the fate of the Winander boy).

What then does happen to this boy after he has incited this madness on the landscape? What does *it* do to *him*? The complexity in lines 20–5 is important here and their meanings are entwined with Wordsworth's elegant and surrealistic vision. The middle section of the poem is a kind of literal whirlpool within whose knotty currents the drama is enacted. It is a twisting arc of sounds which reverberate against each other until the eerie silence slashes through it all,

> carried far into his heart the voice
> Of mountain torrents, or the visible scene
> Would enter unawares into his mind
> With all its solemn imagery, its rocks
> Its woods, and that uncertain heaven, received
> Into the bosom of the steady lake.                    (20–5)

The widening coil of sound mirrors the widening circle of chaos he has provoked. 'Heart' (20) and 'bosom' (25) both imply the emotions, of course, but at the same time suggest a central point of refuge within it, calm within or beneath the confusion. While this lad is utterly engrossed in his mischievous prank, nature furtively ('unawares', l. 22) steals 'into his mind'.

The external landscape also finds its inner, mental, landscape. What Wordsworth engages with here is one of his foremost poetic themes: the effect of the natural landscape on the sensitive, especially the youthful, imagination. The first part of the poem reveals that the boy is already attuned to the natural wavelengths of the landscape whereas lines 20–5 speak to the precise moment when nature fastens on the receptive imagination, so that its 'solemn imagery' – rocks, woods, etc. – becomes imprinted acutely on the consciousness.

Wordsworth referred explicitly to the process in his 1815 Preface to the poems

> I have begun with one of the earliest processes of Nature in the development of this faculty. Guided by one of my own primary consciousnesses, I have represented a commutation and transfer of internal feelings, cooperating with external accidents to plant, for immortality, images of sound and sight, in the celestial soil of the Imagination.

The power of nature (both in its turbulent elements and in its power to penetrate the mind) is matched by and mixes with the tremendous power of the human imagination.

Like the girl in 'We are seven' and the Lucy of 'Three years she grew', this boy of Winander has a highly charged imagination, playful, spontaneous, by turns innocent and fiendish. Lucy's mind too is amorphous, and receptive, highly attuned to the call and influence of nature. Here, in 'There was a boy' the crucial moment in the centre of the poem brings to a climax those first gropings of the boy's ripening imagination, stimulated by nature's shaping hand.

But then, again like Lucy, the boy dies. The poem, like the boy, is snatched from us. 'There was a Boy' is one of the most important of Wordsworth's early poems on the interaction between nature and the child's mind, especially the faculty of the imagination. It is a vital theme in many of the poems of this early phase in Wordsworth's verse, but here its treatment is less explicit and not quite fully realised, largely because meaning defers to the brilliant feast of imagery. The occasion described is undoubtedly a prelude but exactly to what remains elusive. The moment is indeed gnomic – highly suggestive but ultimately indefinite.

In talking about the theme of the imagination it is of course salutary to distinguish between that of the boy (who experiences its thrill) and that of the poet (who attempts the describing, having been the boy himself). The imagination of the boy is manifested both in his impersonation of the owls as well as in his incipient responsiveness to the natural setting. Wordsworth's imagination is evident here, too, in his artistic choices – the selection and arrangement of narrative, images, sounds, metre, voice and discourse and so on. The two personas are linked by two key momentary silences (the 'deep silence' of the boy in line 18 and the 'Mute' Wordsworth in line 32) which further encourages us to see that the young child is indeed the 'father' of the mature poet himself. Seen in this way, the present silence (of Wordsworth's in line 32, that is) taps into the lineage of silence trailing back to that key formative moment in his youth.

Man and boy are re-united in a curiously artistic manner. Like the boy's hootings, the poem itself is addressed to 'ye cliffs / And islands of Winander!' (lines 1–2) and this is in order to make us aware of yet another symbolic role of the boy's hootings. He holds his own sort of mirror up to nature and his mimetic skill successfully deceives the birds. These hootings are perfect onomatopoeia – and the poem itself actually begins to hoot in onomatopoeic sympathy (between lines 8 and 10: 'too', 'to', 'through', 'blew', 'hootings', 'to'). The boy and the man are both poets in sound effects and the poem as a whole is the artistic outcome of Wordsworth's mute meditation on the boy's communion with nature, the growth of his own artistic imagination.

Furthermore, there is present in the poem a third strand of the imagination theme: the reader himself. I have already referred to Wordsworth's Preface to his collected poems of 1815 and in it he comments on the highly important influence which may be exerted on the reader's own imagination by the key words of a poem. Such words ought to (and do) reach into our minds to trigger off the imagination as a prelude to our own constructions of the poem. In this respect, it seems to me that the word 'wild' in line 15 is just such a key item. In 1798 the word 'wild' carried a much stronger impression than it perhaps does today, with slightly shocking resonances, and for us it acts to connect raw and primitive nature with the riot of crazed noise which fills it, together too with the torrents of emotion that are borne into the boy's imagination.

The poem as a piece is, of course, superbly effective in evoking the pictorial scene and the sounds of a quite intensely critical moment, the fusing together of the audible and the 'visible scene'. Its language, like its ideas, is clearly that of an adult while adopting the uncomplicated *parole* of the child (using it to convey quite complex concepts). However, the diction is also among the poem's weaknesses, at least on a simple level, with over-dependence on the conjunction 'and' – though we might generously forgive its twelve incidences in thirty-two lines as the recreation of childlike excitement.

In contrast to the two previous poems under discussion 'There was a Boy' is mercifully spare of Wordsworth's pieties. As a statement of nature's power to enthral the mind and as an evocation of a momentous episode it is beautifully successful – even if the lyrical beauty subordinates the poem's metaphysics. In our next poem, 'Nutting', Wordsworth focuses on familiar themes but produces a gem of both metaphysics and descriptive effect.

## *'Nutting'*

With the poem 'Nutting' we reach a different order of childhood – and an altogether different order of poetic quality. It is a beautiful, brilliant piece of writing and it is one of the highlights of *Lyrical Ballads* – though strictly speaking it is not a ballad but a more elegiac, conversational poem. In a later memoir of the poem, Wordsworth explained that the poem had been intended for his autobiographic *The Prelude*, and it shares some of that work's magnificent condensation of feeling and artistry (it also anticipates themes richly articulated in his *Immortality Ode* and *The Excursion*). Unlike the poems discussed so far 'Nutting' focuses on an older youth, one on the hesitant threshold of adulthood, and its main event deals with first steps towards the world of the adult. I have chosen to concentrate on the following extract (lines 20–55) for discussion:

<br>

| | |
|---|---:|
| A little while I stood, | 20 |
| Breathing with such suppression of the heart | |
| As joy delights in; and with wise restraint | |
| Voluptuous, fearless of a rival, eyed | |
| The banquet, or beneath the trees I sate | |
| Among the flowers, and with the flowers I played; | 25 |
| A temper known to those, who, after long | |
| And weary expectation, have been blessed | |
| With sudden happiness beyond all hope. | |
| Perhaps it was a bower beneath whose leaves | |
| The violets of five seasons re-appear | 30 |
| And fade, unseen by any human eye, | |
| Where fairy water-breaks do murmur on | |
| For ever; and I saw the sparkling foam, | |
| And with my cheek on one of those green stones | |
| That, fleeced with moss, beneath the shady trees, | 35 |

Lay round me scattered like a flock of sheep,
I heard the murmur and the murmuring sound,
In that sweet mood when pleasure loves to pay
Tribute to ease; and, of its joy secure,
The heart luxuriates with indifferent things,                40
Wasting its kindliness on stocks and stones,
And on the vacant air. Then up I rose,
And dragged to earth both branch and bough, with crash
And merciless ravage; and the shady nook
Of hazels, and the green and mossy bower                     45
Deformed and sullied, patiently gave up
Their quiet being: and unless I now
Confound my present feelings with the past,
Even then, when from the bower I turned away,
Exulting, rich beyond the wealth of kings,                   50
I felt a sense of pain when I beheld
The silent trees and the intruding sky. –

Then, dearest Maiden! move along these shades
In gentleness of heart; with gentle hand
Touch, – for there is a Spirit in the woods.                 55

Again the surface narrative is fairly straightforward: the poet recalls a day when, as a youth, he was decked out by his landlady ('my frugal Dame') for a solitary excursion to collect hazelnuts; resting in unspoilt seclusion, he relishes the deep natural joys of this place until in a sudden frenzy he sets about the savage plunder of the trees; eventually he comes to regret his destructive outburst, and in the final lines the older man delivers a penitential prayer to the deity in nature.

Once more our theme is time. Unlike the poem as a whole, the extract opens with a reference to time, 'A little while I stood' and there are many such references throughout (for example, lines 26, 30 and 47–8). As line 48 makes apparent, the poem deals chiefly with two important moments: the 'past' of the central episode, framed by the 'now' of the adult's memory and conscience, convened through lines 48–9. There is also a third important element of time in the poem, as we shall come to below.

The early mention of the Dame's advice on clothing helps to establish his youthfulness and inexperience and then the novelty of the experience, his freedom and independence. 'Breathing with such suppression of the heart' (21) recalls the awe of the boy on entering the mysterious copse while at the same time emphasising the breath-catching effect on the older narrator as he recalls it. Such sharp psychological touches are distinctly redolent of the mature Wordsworth.

Rolled round in this psychology (and shared with the reader too) is his awful realisation in line 51 that youth and its acute sensitivity has now passed away even at the moment of its rich indulgence ('I felt a sense of pain'). This sadness is hinted at too in the highly significant word 'shades' in line 53 and the characteristic Wordsworthian 'murmur' in lines 32 and 37.

Conversely, the narrator comforts himself with the reflection that such moments 'cannot die' (3), they are 'heavenly', immortalised in the memory. The sensitivity of youth – so highly alert to the effects of nature – is also extended in another way; it is transmuted into the adult's recognition of nature's power but also into the poet's creative sensibility, the fact that he has converted his private experiences into poetry. This and other moments (or 'spots of time' as Wordsworth called them) became immortalised through their deep moral effects, as here, working on the young man's conscience and emotions to bring about those feelings of shame and discomfort referred to in the conclusion of the poem and implicit in its diction (for example, 'ravaged' in line 44, and 'Deformed and sullied' in 46). The spirit in the woods has entered and slyly transformed his soul.

After the opening to the poem, whose main task is to lead us into the bowery dell, the verse undergoes a clearly noticeable change (at line 20) in mood and tone. As the boy enters the romantic dell, the poetry itself becomes enchanted in a rich sinewy diction, synthesising image and music in studied rapture. He presses his cheek against one of the mossy stones at the water's edge, and

> I heard the murmur and the murmuring sound,
> In that sweet mood when pleasure loves to pay
> Tribute to ease; and, of its joy secure,
> The heart luxuriates with indifferent things. . . .        (37–40)

Notice the effect here of the word 'that', revealing Wordsworth's confidence in a shared feeling, with a reader young once and partnering in these effects and those to follow. The sense of happiness is so exultant and profound that the boy begins to commune with indifferent, non-human things in nature. It luxuriates too in the simple joy of words.

It is a poem focusing on a rite of passage, of youth in transition, beginning and ending in experience, though two very different experiences it has to be said. At the core of the extract, the excursion by the boy falls into two parts: the discovery and delight in the nature of the dell and then his despoilment of it. And as we would expect, the two contrasting moods and activities are reflected in the style of the verse. In the first (lines 20–42) combining joy and tranquillity, with imagery of happy sensual pleasure and discovery, Wordsworth deploys longer vowels together with soft 's' and 'f' sounds and the murmuring 'r'. At this point, the blank verse is characterised by regularity with loose sentence structure, the calmness underpinned by the use of run-over lines (the longest utterance of the poem appears at this moment, extending over lines 33–42).

Such freedom in the verse not only sympathises with the calmness of the original occasion but also collaborates with the tenor expected in a conversational poem, recollected in tranquillity. At the same time, the words 'suppression of the heart' (21) and 'restraint' (22) hint that the happy calm confines the burgeoning youthful energy so that it wells up below. This is likewise echoed in the muscular music of the verse: for instance, note the richly palpable blend of consonant and vowel in line 38,

> In that sweet mood when pleasure loves to play

(try reading it aloud, or whisper it to a close friend, and mark the voluptuous sensuality of those lip and tongue syllables).

What image, though, does this create of youth itself? Above all, there is freedom of course. After the patronage and tutelage of adults, the boy is set free to roam, to explore, discover, feel and express himself, first in joy and then in destructiveness as emotion overtakes him. And this is another way in which this poem differs from the two previous: freedom as the inspiration of the whole experience. It is, as I have already noted, Wordsworth focusing on a stage in life that is highly responsive to nature's allure, with a deep capacity to be moved (by nature but also by what nature provokes inside). All of experience lies before the boy in a time of discovery and imagination, and he finds a new type of awareness, a new type of joy, one symbolised by the romantic bower.

Nevertheless, in Wordsworth experience is never a neutral occurrence and the important point here is, of course, the element of learning: both about nature and about oneself. When the boy hears the 'murmur' in line 32, he hears a figurative premonition of the voice of nature and of something urgent within himself (as well as a foreboding of the 'pain' and 'shades' of much later).

The poem presents the boy with two teachers, two women: the 'frugal Dame' at the start, advising him to wear rough beggar's clothing for the expedition, and the 'dearest Maiden' (53), realised and acknowledged by the adult poet. The maiden is clearly the personification of the spirit of nature, and in a Rousseauesque impulse the boy breaks away from school learning (signified by the Dame) in favour of experiential learning, experience at first hand in nature. Dressed in beggar's weeds and in tremulous solitude he becomes immersed in the music and the lore of nature.

A virgin himself, the boy steps into an archetypal maidenly landscape ('green' and 'unseen', lines 31 and 34). The reference to fairy (32) and later to the 'Spirit in the woods' (55), signals to the reader the prospect of strange, even supernatural phenomena, of transformation and transcendence. And Wordsworth does not disappoint us. The virgin boy discovers the bower and in doing so also finds a new awareness of self and his sexuality. Wordsworth explores all three as destinations for the changes which the poem explores.

The poem essentiality symbolises a first sexual encounter for the pubescent boy. It abounds in sexual and quasi-sexual imagery: the 'dear nook' is the 'virgin scene' (20; and 'unvisited', 16) which he forces his way into (14). Overwhelmed by his emotion at the discovery and then his penetration, he 'luxuriates' in its 'voluptuous' sensuality until in the 'merciless' act of robbing its fruit he reaches a climax of orgiastic riot and ravishes it, leaving it 'sullied' (46). The final lines of the middle section rehearse a sort of post-coital tristesse, a cadence of silence and pain.

Underpinning the spontaneous arousal and joy is Wordsworth's marvellously subtle shading of emotion. In fact it is the heart that governs the centre of this poem. Wordsworth brilliantly draws together atmosphere, setting and action along with the delicate, almost imperceptible modulations of the boy's feelings. The latter are mirrored in the soft nuances of alliteration, building up by degrees to the climactic violence and rapine in line 43 with its strongly pulsating, monosyllabic measure,

> And dragged to earth both branch and bough, with crash
> And merciless ravage.                  (43–4)

Now set free, the boy determines his journey ahead and forces the way in, blindly as it happens, too. He is at this moment unaware of the tenacious effects of nature's grasp on him as he blunders into the secret, trap-like bower, until at last he reaches the admonitory silence in line 52.

Like Blake before him, Wordsworth poignantly draws out the full sense of anguish and post-coital melancholy in the lost innocence of childhood. The onset of sexuality, of carnality, is the irreversible moment of loss, too, of that very childhood, sensibility and freedom which led to the experience in the first place. Wordsworth foregrounds this not as joyous fulfilment in the consummated moment but as the melancholy of deflation, 'when from the bower I turned away' (49). Although superficially exultant, 'rich beyond the wealth of kings' (50) it has brought no lasting recompense, but instead a 'sense of pain' and 'shades' of morose nostalgia, and a tension between the two.

Departure from the magic bower is also departure from childhood. It is Wordsworth's departure of course, written by the mature man so the metaphors of lust and rapine issue from him not the young 'nutter', a point that further underlines the latter's innocence – he is not at that moment aware of the real significance of his actions, nor of the critical power of nature's nurture and moral influence.

Nature here functions of course as both the setting or landscape of the poem and also as the interacting spirit of that landscape (with the power to 'kindle or restrain', as Wordsworth emphasises in 'Three years she grew'). What more precisely he intends by 'nature' will be the ongoing question of our whole discussion (and especially Chapter 5), but here we can take a few important steps towards a preliminary understanding of his ideas concerning nature. A good starting point is – ironically – the final line of the poem:

for there is a Spirit in the woods                                    (55)

After he has been kitted-out in protective clothing the boy sets off to discover the 'unseen' virgin bower and when he does he is overwhelmed and transfixed by its beauty, the 'sudden happiness', in line 28. A moment of stillness ushers in the primordial setting and he delights in its sensual charms. It is an almost sacred religious instant (a 'suppression of the heart') as he kneels to savour the caress of the mossy stone on his cheek. Falling beneath the enchantment of the 'Spirit in the woods', he has become seduced by the delicate pleasure of leaves, flower and stream.

At length, however, this gentle repose is spontaneously put to flight by the intervention of his frenzied passion. Wordsworth clearly posits a strong potential for wanton destructiveness in the human (or at least the male) psychology, which is latent and released in the process of seduction and arousal. As I have already pointed out above, his use of the word 'that' in line 38 proposes that these impulses are commonly shared – a radical psychological idea for Wordsworth's day. After a holy communion with nature the boy breaks violently away from it in a blind tumult of devastation.

Consistent with this idea of a shared human fallibility Wordsworth abstains from judgemental comment on the youth, his own younger self. The implication is that youth is not culpable, acting from human nature, and in any case, his excursion is approved by his 'frugal Dame' ('frugal' identifying her with nature). Such discordant acts are not unfamiliar in Wordsworth (see *The Prelude*, 1805, I.461–4, for instance) and are usually proffered as a significant element in the process of nature learning.

The moral formula of the poem admits of a further allegorical facet. The boy is graced with a glimpse into spiritual bliss attended by overtones of eternity and immortality (the third thematic element of time, which I mentioned above). Here destructiveness too links into this allegorical strand: the bower as Edenic garden permits the boy a vision of paradise and eternity, existing outside of time, with its fruit and maiden, and his nature draws him blindly on to re-enact the fall of man, into 'pain' and 'shades' of lost innocence. He is 'turned away' not by God but by his own sense of shame.

This is a lapse on the personal level, of course, yet Wordsworth seeks to draw a more universal psychology of mankind in nature, or indeed nature's effect on mankind. In this we are necessarily mindful of the important role played by the imagination. Beginning at the beginning, the boy sets off physically resistant to nature's effects, inured within his protective rags. Yet the very object of the trip is to exploit nature by collecting hazel nuts. He is completely unprepared for nature's devious moral and spiritual sway on himself, which has begun by the moment he enters the grove – if not before.

The chief indication of this translation appears in line 40 where he 'luxuriates' in nature's objects, its stores, trees, flowers and so forth, as 'indifferent things'. Yet the boy's imagination has already succumbed to its spell, exampled in his childlike simile in line 36, which compares a group of stones to a 'flock of sheep'. So marked is its transfiguring effect on the youth that the adult is now unable to fix exactly when the change began (lines 51–2; compare 'Three years she grew' in which Lucy becomes a changeling, a nymph of the river and mountains, and as such transcends the human world to the natural, existing eerily on the margins between the two).

The boy discovers that nature is not only active but virulently so, and yet it is not as a man that he recognises the educational effects of this encounter, (the child is father to the man). The poem sets out, implicitly at least, the processes by which the child learns to see nature in this new light. The condition of solitude is again recognisably important since, in this condition, nature can work directly without diversion on the young receptive senses. Through the senses nature works first on the emotions (while subduing the reason and logic) and eventually transfiguring the mind in rapture. Nature, a highly mercurial if cryptic agent is personified in the coda of the poem as a goddess 'a maiden' with the power to induce calm and joy and, eventually, after some destructive frenzy, a kind of mental rebirth. The whole process is signified in the conventional symbol of the spiritual journey undergone by the boy, concurrent with his actual physical journey (a journey which naturally inspires ready comparisons with that of *The Rime of the Ancient Mariner* not least because both main characters come to penitential sadness and wisdom by way of guilt and shame at their offences against the natural world: see Chapter 5).

It is not difficult to recognise how central to the process is the boy's imagination. Nature is enabled to act on the predisposed senses and emotions by triggering off his imagination. It succeeds as a species of teacher since his imagination is such an actively responsive faculty – so responsive in fact that it gives rise to the violent overflow of emotion in the latter part of the poem (it is this element of the *active* imagination that differentiates the boy from the younger children in 'Lucy Gray' and 'We are seven'). Through the imagination he learns directly from the 'dearest Maiden' the goddess of nature, 'Spirit in the woods' (contrasting with the Dame, the other female 'teacher' in the poem, who as his school house matron is associated with more formal pedagogic learning). Through his encounter with natural, physical objects the child's inward eye is permitted a momentous vision of eternity and this, together with some equally potent hormonal forces, impels him beyond the threshold on his transition into adulthood.

## Conclusions

This chapter has examined in detail two important areas in Wordsworth's poetry: the poet's attitude to childhood, and the role of nature in the development of the young mind. Childhood is a time of vulnerability, innocence, discovery, a distinctive form of inner space and a unique vision entailing a special relationship to time and mortality.

We have seen that for Wordsworth childhood is a vitally important period in life because the child's mind is particularly sensitive to the highly formative influences of nature or, as the critic Nicola Trott has described it, 'an immaculate openness to natural influence'.

This is not to say, of course, that Wordsworth adopts a simplistic attitude to childhood as merely a sort of idyllic golden age untroubled by care or mortal need. It seems to me to be quite the opposite and the complexities for Wordsworth are encapsulated in two paradoxes which have emerged from our discussion of childhood.

In the first, childhood is characterised as a period of both physical and spiritual freedom, but these freedoms are threatened by the pressures of maturation and adulthood intervention. At the same time a more poignant dilemma for Wordsworth is that while childhood is literally a beautiful period of innocence and intimacy with the spirit of nature, its significance for adults is, resignedly, only a metaphorical one. In other words, we discover too late the great power and moral joy of childhood and it exists as a constant reminder of our unwelcome fall from this condition.

We cannot reach childhood again, much less recover it and this syndrome is most forcefully brought home here by the symbol of premature death. On a bleakly historical level, this reflects a very real threat of illness and death for children in eighteenth-century England, while thematically it serves as a constant reminder of human mortality.

In Wordsworth children frequently die before consciousness and individuation can reach full fruition. Such processes are arrested in their tracks and opened up for closer scrutiny. The same is true for Wordsworth's theory of the process by which nature acts on the young mind as a *tabula rasa*, and he is more explicit: typically, nature works on the child's senses, speaking directly to the child's highly receptive imagination. The exact process of interaction remains a mysterious, evasive one even for Wordsworth himself, but he is firmly convinced of its results, which are both moral and creative. In the post-Freudian era it is easy to forget just how revolutionary was Wordsworth's view of childhood seen as the crucial formative stage in the process of the adult, 'the child as father to the man'.

## Further Research

To consolidate and broaden your understanding of Wordsworth's treatment of this theme, take a look at some of the many other poems in *Lyrical Ballads* touching on childhood: in particular, see 'Three years she grew', 'The Idiot Boy' and 'The Idle Shepherd Boys'.

Read each poem and try to establish Wordsworth's attitude to the childhood portrayed in it and especially the relationship between, on the one hand, children and adults and, on the other, between children and nature.

# 2

# *Imagination*

> I shall now proceed to the nature and *genesis* of the Imagination; but
> I must first take leave to notice, that after a more accurate perusal
> of Mr Wordsworth's remarks on the Imagination, in his preface to
> the new edition of his poems, I find that my conclusions are not so
> consentient with his as, I confess, I had taken for granted.
>
> (Coleridge, *Biographia Literaria*, Chapter XII)

Chapter 1 touched briefly on Wordsworth's conception of the role played
by the imagination in childhood development. We can extend that
discussion now by analysing the concept of imagination itself in the
work of both Wordsworth and Coleridge. The imagination is highly
important for both poets, and critics have traditionally regarded the
special significance accorded the imagination by Romantic verse and
thought as one of its major defining characteristics.

In order to explore this subject I have chosen to analyse
Wordsworth's 'Lines written a few miles above Tintern Abbey', and
Coleridge's 'The Nightingale' and 'Love'.

## *'Lines written a few miles above Tintern Abbey'*

'Lines written a few miles above Tintern Abbey' was written in July
1798 at the close of a momentous twelve months for Wordsworth –
he had at last established his friendship with Coleridge on a creative
footing and their partnership now inspired Wordsworth to consider

ambitious plans, including the collaborative *Lyrical Ballads* itself. In July 1797 he had set up home with his sister in Somerset (it was rumoured that they and Coleridge were French spies) and, after surviving a series of aesthetic and political crises, he had become very convinced of his vocation as a poet, now strengthened by the support of Coleridge. Wordsworth threw himself into *Lyrical Ballads* as much out of poverty as of artistic commitment and the volume was already at the printers when in the summer of 1798, as he was becoming increasingly fascinated by profound issues of imagination, truth and nature, he set off with his sister on an extended tour of the Welsh–English border. Reflecting later on the composition of 'Tintern Abbey', he told his biographer Isabella Fenwick

> No poem of mine was composed under circumstances more pleasant for me to remember than this. I began it upon leaving Tintern, after crossing the Wye, and concluded it just as I was entering Bristol in the evening … Not a line of it was altered, and not any part of it written down until I reached Bristol. It was published almost immediately after.

Outwardly at least and in general terms 'Tintern Abbey' celebrates a happy return visit to the Wye valley and Wordsworth's discovery of his new vision of nature, its sublime spiritual presence, and the role of imagination in this new vision. Wordsworth announces loud and clear his own spiritual regeneration together with a renewed commitment to humanity, figured most vividly here in his love of Dorothy and in his hope of sustained joy.

It is a highly crafted poem, of finely modulating moods and deceptive perspectives, presented in a more accomplished verse style than anything else by Wordsworth in *Lyrical Ballads*. It is also a production of dexterous paradoxes: for instance, it sets out Wordsworth's impassioned confidence but also undermines it, its opening promises topographical specifics yet the substance of the poem yields metaphysical abstraction.

Wordsworth signalled the poem's importance both to himself and to the *Lyrical Ballads* as a whole by placing it as the final valedictory item in the original 1798 collection. By doing this and fixing the specific date of the poem in its masthead he announces its pivotal significance – in looking back to the personal and political struggles of the 1790s as well as on the themes and conventions of the eighteenth-century topographical verse that Wordsworth here challenges. It looks forward (for us at least) with great artistic maturity and fervour to the achievement of *The Prelude* of 1805.

The poem is divided into five sections. The opening fanfare announces the poem's theme of time, then settles to establish the dominant mood of tranquil repose in a secluded, 'inland' river landscape. It sets out the key symbolic markers of cliffs and river, and the sensations of eye and ear that will reverberate throughout the thoughts and feelings of the text. Its tricksy diction (lofty, wild, connect, green, uncertain) draws the reader out of any easy expectations of Neo-classical picturesque and mildly hints at the metaphysical discourse to follow. The second and third sections advance this movement by extolling nature in its manifold effects for humanity, its many references to the feelings, and its sublime capacity to work on the imagination and the memory. This follows Wordsworth's recollection of nature's healing influence experienced during his unpleasant urban interlude when reflections on his early Wye visit helped to sustain him through anguished periods of fever and fret.

The aesthetic and metaphysical climaxes of the poem appear in the fourth section just as Wordsworth's memories of the previous visit begin to revive, fusing them into his present consciousness with new responses; and out of this fusion of old and new sensations, of feelings and ideas, a new poetic consciousness springs forth. The poem ends with a renewed tone of joy and mature love, and a highly personal plea that, in the future, his sister Dorothy may experience this same deep spiritual exhilaration: the unity of the poet's mind and soul with the objects and spirit of nature.

One of many important points about this fascinating poem is that Wordsworth uses it to set out the presiding metaphysical aim of his life (and of *Lyrical Ballads*) at this time: the union of the poetic mind and soul with the objects and spirit in nature. We need now to discuss the implications of this union by examining in turn the themes of nature, the imagination and, finally, the poet himself. The extract I have chosen for analysis is lines 59–112.

And now, with gleams of half-extinguish'd thought,
With many recognitions dim and faint,                                60
And somewhat of a sad perplexity,
The picture of the mind revives again:
While here I stand, not only with the sense
Of present pleasure, but with pleasing thoughts
That in this moment there is life and food                           65
For future years. And so I dare to hope
Though changed, no doubt, from what I was, when first
I came among these hills; when like a roe
I bounded o'er the mountains, by the sides
Of the deep rivers, and the lonely streams,                          70
Wherever nature led; more like a man
Flying from something that he dreads, than one
Who sought the thing he loved. For nature then
(The coarser pleasures of my boyish days,
And their glad animal movements all gone by)                         75
To me was all in all. – I cannot paint
What then I was. The sounding cataract
Haunted me like a passion: the tall rock,
The mountain, and the deep and gloomy wood,
Their colours and their forms, were then to me                       80
An appetite: a feeling and a love,
That had no need of a remoter charm,
By thought supplied, or any interest
Unborrowed from the eye. – That time is past,
And all its aching joys are now no more,                             85
And all its dizzy raptures. Not for this
Faint I, nor mourn nor murmur: other gifts
Have followed, for such loss, I would believe,
Abundant recompence. For I have learned
To look on nature, not as in the hour                                90
Of thoughtless youth, but hearing oftentimes
The still, sad music of humanity,
Not harsh nor grating, though of ample power
To chasten and subdue. And I have felt
A presence that disturbs me with the joy                             95
Of elevated thoughts; a sense sublime
Of something far more deeply interfused,
Whose dwelling is the light of setting suns,

And the round ocean, and the living air,
And the blue sky, and in the mind of man,                    100
A motion and a spirit, that impels
All thinking things, all objects of all thought,
And rolls through all things. Therefore am I still
A lover of the meadows and the woods,
And mountains; and of all that we behold                     105
From this green earth; of all the mighty world
Of eye and ear, both what they half-create,
And what perceive; well pleased to recognize
In nature and the language of the sense,
The anchor of my purest thoughts, the nurse,                 110
The guide, the guardian of my heart, and soul
Of all my moral being.

The poem's opening section offers us some familiar Wordsworthian imagery helping to set the local matter of time and place: after five years the poet returns in summer 'season' to these secluded woods and steep and lofty cliffs (lines 5 and 158), the river Wye. We could be back in the copse of 'Nutting' or the cliffs of 'There was a boy'. Then in this wilderness a human presence is betrayed by the cottage-ground, orchard and pastoral forms (though the hedgerows have now run wild) and by the smoke wreathing silently above the trees, suggesting vagrants, gypsies or a Romantic hermit. This static image of the present moment is contrasted, in the passage, with the moment five years before when

> like a roe
> I bounded o'er the mountains. . . .                    (68–9)

The 'deep rivers, and the lonely streams' (70) suggest that nature is still for him a vital and interactive force and he is still 'A lover of the meadows ...' (103–4). This force is symbolised in the opening section by the word 'green', repeated in lines 14–18 and here at 159. Early on it refers to the unripeness of the farm fruits – and of Wordsworth's own poetic unripeness – but 'this green earth' (106) also indicates the regenerative possibility that he feels on this visit and which he prays for in the final section.

As in 'Nutting', the magic natural landscape, involving seclusion and silence, induces sensual tranquillity and repose, leading to reflection. This section is similarly prepared so that 'recognitions dim and faint' (60) begin to stir and nature 'revives again' the mind. But change is manifestly evident too, brought on by contrast between the sameness of the setting and the turmoil that has occurred in Wordsworth's life between these two moments in the poem. In fact the complexity at work is hinted at by the word 'perplexity' in line 61 since the apparently realistic landscape of the opening has already become internalised by the continuous workings of Wordsworth's imagination in the intervening period.

The opening lines of the poem (especially lines 5–7) suggest that the landscape has already been internalised as both a memory of the previous visit and as a symbolic or poeticised landscape. The symbolic is suggested in the archetypal Wordsworthian elements such as cliff, stream, trees that are here presented in abstracted form rather than given a fully naturalistic treatment/exposure. For us the poem has little to do with the Wye valley *per se* and what has become more important is the relationship between the original physical setting transposed inside the poet's mind and the setting revisited by the older man, so that

The picture of the mind revives again.                            (62)

It is this fluctuating relationship that prompts Wordsworth to identify all the benefits that nature offers to mankind, benefits that individually co-relate with the many moments or spots of time that co-exist within the poem as a whole. Nature represents: a source of pleasure and joy (lines 68–9); a source of relief from the stress and tedium of urban life (26–31); a moral guide (111); a force for tranquillity, adjusting/manipulating the mind to permit the imagination to function well (44–7); yet as 'A presence that disturbs me' (95) nature can act as a check, an interrogation; nature's simple pleasures often present healing from 'the heavy and the weary weight' (40) of intellectual wrangling; and, in a poem of many divisions, nature significantly as a unifying force working through all things (101–2).

Wordsworth here also takes up his earlier idea of a vigorous inter-active nature and carries it further. Many words imply that nature not only affects us but goes further and actually drives us, causally or 'naturalistically'. For example, in the above passage 'impels' (101) and 'led' (71) plus 'lead us on' (43) and 'made quiet' (48) all point to a deterministic view of nature's influence. Nature is so active and potent, that the receptive human soul and imagination are suscepti-ble to its heady influence. Nature is still a 'guide' or 'guardian' but it is much more, more than the gentle 'Maiden' in 'Nutting'. Yet while Wordsworth does envisage nature now as a force that can exert con-trol through our feelings and senses, he also regards it as force unde-niably for human good, 'we are laid asleep / In body, and become a living soul' (46–7).

However, as in 'Nutting', time is an important and integral ele-ment in the discussion of nature. It lies at the heart of the regenera-tion theme, introduced above and manifested in the imagery of the colour 'green'. Time itself is manifested in the numerous prepositions, phrases, adjectives and adverbs of time: (now, again, present, still, future, first, when, then, boyish, now no more) as well as in more explicit discussions of time itself

> That in this moment there is life and food
> For future years.                                                      (65–6)

> That time is past
> And all its aching joys are now no more.                 (84–5)

Time (and its effects) is one of the key markers by which the character/ poet measures the altering/fluxing relationship between his imagina-tion and the spirit of nature.

'Tintern Abbey' presents to us an array of different moments, or 'spots in time' as Wordsworth later termed them: his original visit of five years 'ago', alongside the present visit, the intervening moments spent in 'towns and cities' (27), and a projected future moment which, in the figure of his sister Dorothy, draws together past and present moments too (138–46). There is also the period of Wordsworth's writing the poem, the 'now' that looks back on both visits and also the occasions of his revisions. There is for us, too, the different moments of our reading and re-reading.

Memory is of course an important concomitant of the theme of time and perhaps its most important human issue. Both Wordsworth and Coleridge were interested in the theory of 'Association' especially as developed by the psychologist David Hartley (1705–57) and this has important implications for the themes of memory and imagination in both poets (though Coleridge eventually rejected Hartley's version). The theory was given systematic description by Aristotle and in simple terms it seeks to explain the process by which an individual stores up (or learns) and recalls received impressions by linking or associating one impression with another. Coleridge explained the process:

> Ideas by having been together acquire a power of recalling each other; or every partial representation awakes the total representation of which it had been a part.  (*Biographia Literaria*, Chapter V)

In other words, where two impressions have been stored together in the memory, the repeated appearance of one will act to trigger off the recall of the other.

In 'Tintern Abbey' Wordsworth exploits association to account for how natural objects visited after five years invoke recollections of the earlier scene, its atmosphere and his state of mind. Some early impressions have become so ingrained in Wordsworth that their origins have become obscure and 'unremembered' but others are vividly revealed in Wordsworth's use of the deictic 'these' (line 68), which thereby attributes continuity to the external objects in nature (if not also to his response to them, as we shall see). Nevertheless the natural landscape revisited is a highly active stimulus to Wordsworth's sensitised imagination. So much so that this extremely resonant setting appears to function in a way similar to the 'Method' system of medieval mnemonics, each part of the integrative setting triggers off in the imagination different elements of (internalised) mental imagery. Although in 'Tintern Abbey' the operation of imaginative memory or association is a highly charged process, Coleridge himself, on the other hand, became disenchanted with the theory because its stimulus/response operation suggested a too mechanistic and passive role for the creative imagination. However, Wordsworth himself was introducing his own variation on the theory and these are explored below.

Here Wordsworth is clearly insistent on both feeling *and* reason, the meeting of both in the matrix of the imagination both the gateway/portal of the mind/reality and matrix of poetic creativity. The imagination is the vital means of creating the world both in seeing (i.e. interpreting) the natural world and in recreating that perception in art/literature.

> And I have felt
> A presence that disturbs me with the joy
> Of elevated thoughts: a sense sublime
> Of something far more deeply interfused. (94–7)

Vision is not only a matter of 'recognise' (108), it is also creative, as in 'half-create' (107). The physical senses as a group 'behold' (5 and 105) while the imagination perceives with an inner eye that interprets and understands and thus Wordsworth's mature joy in his revisited setting is now enriched and elevated by recognising the new facet of nature. Further, where previously his joy was characterised by ecstasy as confusion ('For nature then ... was all in all', 73 and 76) now it is characterised by order in repose ('To chasten and subdue', 94). (This preface, added to the 1800 edition of *Lyrical Ballads*, also points to this exercise of the imagination when Wordsworth asserts that all good poetry 'takes its origin from emotion recollected in tranquillity.)'

Unlike the early eighteenth-century scientific concept of seeing as a sort of objective photographic record of reality, the Romantic attitude acknowledges the subjective role of the imagination – seeing is now a matter of part-behold and 'half-create', imposing on sense data the stamp of personal psychology, memory and experience (William Blake described this as 'seeing through the eye' rather than 'with the eye'). We can see examples of this in 'Tintern Abbey' itself: for example in lines 20–3 Wordsworth sees only smoke wreathing above the trees but his subjective imagination projects his thoughts beyond the facts to think about unseen vagrants or a hermit. The abstracted passage points up that Wordsworth envisages at least three strands to the imagination. There is what we might call an 'affective imagination' (line 81) relating to a chiefly emotional interreaction. Wordsworth adds to this a rational imagination, a cognitive faculty actively interpreting and making connections, 'Of elevated thoughts; a sense sublime' (96). While these refer primarily to responses in the world, the third element, the 'artistic imagination' seeks to give artistic expression to the emotions, understanding, sensations, recollections that are received and modified in the consciousness. As he explains in the 1802 Preface to *Lyrical Ballads* his aim was 'to choose incidents and situations from common life' and to adorn and elaborate them through a 'certain colouring of imagination'.

Coleridge called this actively creative operation the secondary imagination and claimed that it possessed the power to dissolve, to idealise and to unify perceptions. In doing this the Romantic creative imagination now takes on religious significance because every work of art or perception is an act of creation, imitating the primal act of Creation in the mind of God. Where Neo-Classicists regarded Reason as the most God-like of human faculties, for the Romantic poets the imagination is the most divine and therefore the most mysterious (note the many religious references in 'Tintern Abbey', such as 'blessed' in lines 38 and 42, 'holier' in l. 156, and 'worshipper', l. 153).

Going further, the Romantic imagination makes it possible to perceive a deeper, richer reality:

> While with an eye made quiet by the power
> Of harmony, and the deep power of joy,
> We see into the life of things.                 (48–50)

Wordsworth explains that this imaginative, subjective perception permits us with 'a sense sublime' to see 'something far more deeply interfused' (96–7). In other words, the artist in particular is empowered to transcend the physical world of the senses, the appearance of the Wye valley for instance and to penetrate to the qualia, the life of things. Here this visionary dimension has enabled the poet to see beyond the beauties of the pastoral scene of the Wye, to understand the spiritual and moral forces in nature, but, further, to understand the relationship between these forces, the objects in nature and his own powerful imagination.

As we might expect, his perception of the essence as lying beneath the surface reality of nature is found elsewhere in Wordsworth – and usually with the eye/vision metaphor. In 'I wandered lonely as a cloud' he sees, glances and gazes but does not discover the deeper reality of the daffodils until:

> In vacant or in pensive mood,
> They flash upon that inward eye
> Which is the bliss of solitude. (20–2)

That inward eye is of course in the visionary imagination again, acting in tranquillity and bringing him into close harmony with the natural scene as recollected and offering a fuller, more enlightened engagement with the found world.

'Tintern Abbey' as a whole is, of course, a celebration of the subjective Romantic imagination – in its philosophical discussion and an illustration of this, in its narrative and imagery. It also celebrates Wordsworth's new, fuller vision – with its cognitive or nature-as-thought element – a vision that the imagination has made possible. Wordsworth's voice has an unmistakable tone of spontaneous assertiveness about this new way of seeing, as though he were breaking this discovery to us at the very moment of its happening.

All the same, it is not hard to detect here a deeper trace of uncertainty that rolls through that voice. In line 76 he modestly admits 'I cannot paint / What then I was', which suggests that either he lacks the skill to do this or words are not really adequate to capture the profound or esoteric truths of life (for example religion, mind, imagination, nature). Or perhaps that the imagination cannot comprehend or fully recreate true states of living. All of these constitute the complex challenges that Wordsworth's poem sets out to meet and overcome. This murmuring uncertainty is most noticeable in the details of the language, hesitant, occasionally unfixed, wavering, even fluid in its signification; for example, the line

> With <u>some uncertain</u> notice, as <u>might seem</u> (20)

is clearly straining under its hesitation. Elsewhere, things can be half-created (107) and 'half-extinguished' (59), as well as 'dim and faint' (60). The oxymorons in lines 85 ('aching joys') and 95 (disturbs me with joy) and the anacoluthon in 89–94 are semantic obstructions that point to the same deep cognitive hesitancy. And how is it possible to speak meaningfully of 'unremembered pleasure' (32)?

In the above extract, the poem strives to find independence and resolution, seeking an 'anchor of my purest thoughts' (110), but because this does not quite come off there, Wordsworth turns to his sister Dorothy. As well as a sister, she functions as a complex metaphor in the poem: of nature, female muse, lover and even of Wordsworth himself as he had been five years previously (see line 118). Significantly she is also an 'anchor' of stability in his uncertainty: dependable and loyal, his *fidus Achates*, supporter, artist-wife, nourisher. And in her he prays for and recognises the same resilient presence as the Wye landscape, the 'steep woods and lofty cliffs' (158 and 5). She is his 'mansion … a dwelling place' (141–2).

Although the poem ends by turning attention towards Dorothy to express his great love for her, and closing with the words 'for thy sake' (160), the poem is really all about Wordsworth himself. This is clearly so in spite of his efforts throughout the poem to moderate the prominence of his ego; for instance, his modesty in line 76, self-effacement in 66, shame in 74, and the figuring of his callowness in the recurrence of the colour green.

In a poem in which division and connection are important themes (see 7, 49, 152), the presence of Dorothy as a synthesising medium offers Wordsworth the chance to present a chastened more humane image of his own self. And in any case, the foregrounding of this egoistic consciousness is not unreasonable in a poem that unashamedly foregrounds the subjective imagination and seeks to acclaim and share a new relationship with the world. Significantly 'Tintern Abbey' is not about rolling waters, hedgerows and wreaths of smoke but how Wordsworth sees, hears, feels and interprets those waters, hedgerows and smoke. As a result the poem's fears and joy are Wordsworth's own: his joy that he has survived to overcome both his fear of separation from the sources of regeneration and his fear of that apocalyptic end that had threatened him in, for instance, 'There was a boy' and 'Nutting'.

The conversational tone and apparent spontaneity of the style also help to reduce the visibility of the egoistic personality by seeming adventitious, uncaused, without palpable design upon us. Crucially, however, this effect is highly crafted. The point of view and structuring principle of the poem are both determined organically by Wordsworth's observing consciousness. It is an elegiac response to nature and the structure is intrinsic and organic rather than imposed from without as it might be, say, in conventional Neo-classical art forms.

Modulations in mood and subject are clear to follow. After the exuberant opening of rediscovery, with the scene revived with new eyes, the mood settles to pleasant thoughts, love and even memories of urban gloom until, at line 84, a false cadence briefly dips the mood. The tempo is not restored until line 89 when Wordsworth turns to the rich 'recompense' of his maturer vision (lines 86–94). After a brief uncertainty, a reflux of his feelings with a 'presence that disturbs me with the joy' (95), the poem ends, fusing the new complexity of understanding with a rededication of love and hope, an affirmation of humanity.

And yet, given the organic nature of the poem's structure, is there any sense of intensity of pitch, of climax even, in this poem of measured resonances? The critic Geoffrey Hartman thinks not and the poem the weaker for this. But while he does believe that there is, here and there, an acceleration of feeling, the overall effect is of oscillation between hope and doubt, a 'wavering' effect. There is certainly an intensity of discourse and the poem proceeds by a series of philosophical propositions whose gloss provides a carefully plotted set of reference points: 'Though' (23), 'And now' (59), 'And so' (66), 'For' (73 and 89), 'Therefore' (103 and 135).

The randomness is meticulously plotted. Beneath the surface, the poem's substructure belies Wordsworth's brilliant skill in marshalling a range of resources: lingering run-over sentences extended to surprising lengths; reiterative phrases that gather up and deepen the poem's thought (for instant, compare lines 89 and 94); the shrewdness of his positive 'denials' (lines 86, 90 and 93); the strange murmuring sound working through the poem created by the recurring phonemes /g/, /n/, /r/ and /en/ – all of which emanate from the words 'again' and 'green' in the opening section.

In fact 'Tintern Abbey' is an astonishingly supple production, in which Wordsworth compels the reader to experience directly both continuity and development, the same anew. Change is manifested in every level of the text – and the critics Frances Austin and Roger N. Murray have each demonstrated how important Wordsworth's use of verb clauses contribute to this impression.

It is a text vitally concerned with the theme of 'becoming'. It is also absorbed with the dialectic between, on the one hand, the awareness of this theme and, on the other, the emotional and imaginative evocation of nature as landscape. In terms of the theme of becoming, the poem is also very much an allegory of the transition from childhood to adulthood, the trajectory of change. It is a poem rich in the nuances and scales of time, and it is these that give the poem its two main climaxes: of 'think' in lines 89–112 and of 'feel' in the final section.

## 'The Nightingale'

Having discussed some of Wordsworth's ideas about the imagination, we can now turn to examine Coleridge's views on the same topic. As in Wordsworth, 'imagination' is both a psychological theory and a literary method. We can consider this theme again, both in terms of his theory about imagination and also in terms of how this is manifested in the poems, the imaginative expression itself. 'The Nightingale' was written in April 1798 and was included in *Lyrical Ballads* chiefly as a replacement for 'Lewti', which, because it had already been published, undermined the anonymity of the new collection. Like 'Tintern Abbey' it is an apparently rambling, conversation poem provoked by direct experience of a natural setting which becomes the starting point for deeper thematic investigation.

Because 'The Nightingale' is a relatively long poem I have decided to extract a passage for detailed discussion, which will also serve as a way into the poem as a whole. The passage selected consists of lines 1–49:

> No cloud, no relique of the sunken day
> Distinguishes the West, no long thin slip
> Of sullen light, no obscure trembling hues.
> Come, we will rest on this mossy old bridge!

You see the glimmer of the stream beneath,                          5
But hear no murmuring: it flows silently
O'er its soft bed of verdure. All is still,
A balmy night! and though the stars be dim,
Yet let us think upon the vernal showers
That gladden the green earth, and we shall find          10
A pleasure in the dimness of the stars.
And hark! the nightingale begins its song,
'Most musical, most melancholy' bird!
A melancholy bird? O idle thought!
In nature there is nothing melancholy.                          15
– But some night-wandering man whose heart was pierced
With the remembrance of a grievous wrong,
Or slow distemper or neglected love,
(And so, poor wretch! filled all things with himself
And made all gentle sounds tell back the tale          20
Of his own sorrows) he and such as he
First named these notes a melancholy strain;
And many a poet echoes the conceit,
Poet, who hath been building up the rhyme
When he had better far have stretched his limbs          25
Beside a brook in mossy forest-dell
By sun or moonlight, to the influxes
Of shapes and sounds and shifting elements
Surrendering his whole spirit, of his song
And of his fame forgetful! so his fame                          30
Should share in nature's immortality,
A venerable thing! and so his song
Should make all nature lovelier, and itself
Be loved, like nature! – But twill not be so;
And youths and maidens most poetical                          35
Who lose the deepening twilights of the spring
In ball-rooms and hot theatres, they still
Full of meek sympathy must heave their sighs
O'er Philomela's pity-pleading strains.

My friend and my friend's sister! we have learnt          40
A different lore: we may not thus profane
Nature's sweet voices always full of love
And joyaunce! 'Tis the merry Nightingale

That crowds, and hurries, and precipitates
With fast thick warble his delicious notes,                               45
As he were fearful, that an April night
Would be too short for him to utter forth
His love-chant, and disburthen his full soul
Of all its music!

'The Nightingale' begins with a surprise sequence: six negatives
arranged symmetrically around the main verb establish and act to
control the opening characterised by absence, an appropriate prelude
to the poem's oddities and differences. The mildly imperative 'Come'
in line 4 buttonholes and invites us intimately into the company of
Coleridge, Wordsworth and his sister, and, throughout the poem, the
point of view of remains distinctly conscious of the reader too. With
little or no light from the dim stars and 'no murmuring' (6) Coleridge
directs his attention onto the glimmering stream and its 'mossy old
bridge', the balmy aura of the night and its prospect of vernal showers
on the green earth.

Having set the mood of enchantment with some hint of his
direction Coleridge suddenly arrests this dreamy idyll with another
dramatic imperative 'And hark!' (12). He now hears the awaited song
of the nightingale, real and vivid to him in the stilly dark. Yet, in spite
of this natural reality, his imagination immediately diverts him into
literary associations of the bird, quoting Milton's 'Most musical, most
melancholy' ('Il Penseroso', line 62). Then, in line 14, as if he
becomes aware of his literariness and of clichéd poeticism, Coleridge
abruptly halts the flow with 'O idle thought!'

What follows is a deconstruction of the literary convention of the
nightingale and he dismisses his first impulse as a naturalistic *faux
pas*, or a pathetic fallacy (as Ruskin would later dub it). However, his
own poetic reactions to the bird (for example the reference to
Philomela in line 39) do have the effect of setting up the poem's principal thematic interest: the literary response of the imagination in
direct contact with nature.

Accordingly, in the second section of the poem (lines 12–49)
literature, poetry and the imagination are foregrounded ahead of the
nightingale itself. For Coleridge the nightingale is specifically

associated with 'passion' and 'joyaunce' in place of the 'melancholy strain' (22), while his revisionary perspective insists on a 'different lore' (41), one which he shares with Wordsworth, here standing beside him.

After rejoicing briefly in the present music of the bird (45–9) we get a typical Coleridgean digression into the misty realms of a Gothic supernatural landscape: a wild rambling grove by a great deserted castle, in which nature is subverted through a sort of deception (by which the bird's song translates night into seeming day; 64). Then this idea too is dissolved in the uncanny image of bright bird eyes and glow worms glistening in the shadowy grove.

Evident too are resonances of Coleridge's unfinished gothic, *Christabel*, as a 'gentle' virgin glides spectrally along the broken pathways. All at once the moon re-appears from a cloud to stir again the riot of song in the dense thicket as together girl, bird and moon giddily coalesce in a 'dizzy rapture' (82–5).

In the closing section, the poet bids farewell to the nightingale and his attention digresses for a third instance: into a homely memory of his son. As a baby, Hartley demonstrates an exemplary response to nature, a spontaneous and pre-verbal affinity with nature represented here in the moon and nightingale. The episode ends with Coleridge's supplication that he might raise his son within his new ethos, that 'different lore', and the promise of contingent joy which this proposes.

A first reading reveals that 'The Nightingale' can be regarded in some ways as a nocturnal complement to 'Tintern Abbey' with a similar conversational tone, apparently accidental in focus and form, and also employing direct experience in nature as a starting point to explore the metaphysics of imagination plus the moral and educational roles of nature. We can now examine the relationship of all these elements and consider too some of Coleridge's attitudes to the theme of poetry itself.

Coleridge's eminent theory of the imagination is very much all one with his extensive ideas on human psychology – which became an abiding pre-occupation for most of his adult life. Some of these are hinted at in lines 12–23 in vigorously dismissing the clichéd poetic notion of the nightingale's song as melancholy and a 'grievous wrong'. He cites Milton's description of the 'most melancholy' bird, though both poets have in mind the classical myth of Philomela (line 39). In this Greek legend (taken up by numerous poets, including famously John Keats and T. S. Eliot), after the princess Philomela is raped and her tongue ripped out to prevent her revealing the rapist's identity, she is metamorphosed into a nightingale and her mournful lament is continually transliterated as 'jug jug' (see line 60 earlier; the Latin poet Ovid gives a detailed version of the legend in Book VI of *Metamorphoses*):

> And many a poet echoes the conceit (23)

Coleridge's point is clearly that it is only by human association that the nightingale (and nature as a whole) comes to signify a particular emotion, since nature is emotionally neutral:

> In nature there is nothing melancholy. (15)

This parallels Wordsworth's meditation in 'Tintern Abbey' of 'By thought supplied' (line 83) – in other words, it is human beings who interpret and impose on nature their own feelings, thoughts and ideas. In absolute terms nature is emotionally impersonal. Feelings are attached to phenomenon by the process of associationism – as the early poets attached melancholy to the nightingale, and as Coleridge's son will too (hopefully):

> that with the night
> He may associate Joy! (108–9)

The process of 'associationism' is already in evidence in the poet's son, Hartley (see lines 101–2) and is a key element in Coleridge's concepts of the imagination and of nature as educator (much of which is shared with Wordsworth, that 'different lore' referred to in line 41).

The poem raises crucial issues concerning theories of the imagination and to explore them we will need to digress a little. To understand more fully Coleridge's own highly influential views on the imagination, we can refer to his *Biographia Literaria*, which was first published in 1817 but worked on for many years either side of this date. In chapter X of the *Biographia*, Coleridge coins the expression '*esemplastic* imagination' (from the Greek, 'to mould into one') in order to establish his idea of the imagination as an active, modifying and shaping power, and to distinguish it from what he termed the 'market place' view of the imagination as a relatively passive process. Coleridge called this latter, looser process the 'fancy' – and later claimed that what Wordsworth himself called the imagination was actually only the fancy (for more on this see Chapter 8).

*Biographia*'s rambling philosophical cum psychological thesis reaches a climax on the final page of its chapter XIII where Coleridge at last crystallises his distinction between the imagination and the fancy:

> The Imagination then I consider either as primary, or secondary. The primary Imagination I hold to be the living power and prime agent of all perception, and as a repetition in the finite mind of the eternal act of creation in the infinite I AM. The secondary Imagination I consider as an echo of the former, co-existing with the conscious will, yet still as identical with the primary in the *kind* of its agency, and differing only in *degree*, and in the *mode* of its operation. It dissolves, diffuses, dissipates, in order to recreate: or where this process is rendered impossible, yet still at all events it struggles to idealise and to unify. It is essentially *vital*, even as all objects (*as* objects) are essentially fixed and dead.
>
> FANCY, on the contrary, has no other counters to play with, but fixities and definites. The fancy is indeed no other than a mode of memory emancipated from the order of time and space.

The detail provides the devil of Coleridge's theory. Decisively, he refers 'living power and prime agent', and 'the eternal act of Creation'. Critically, and most of all, the imagination for Coleridge is both active and vital, an echo of the conscious will-power.

'The Nightingale' neatly demonstrates the poet's view of both the fancy and the imagination. For instance, when he idly and conventionally depicts the nightingale as the 'melancholy' bird (line 13) he immediately rebukes himself for his inattentive response as though now rousing himself from sleep,

O idle thought! (14)

The fancy is associative, a 'mode of memory' which simply draws thoughts and ideas from storage.

Akin to the fancy but less actively controlled is dream (or 'reverie' as Coleridge called it). In 'The Nightingale' a reference to this state is 'that strange thing' or nightmare which awoke his son (line 100). Both fancy and dream (or hypnagogic imaging) contrast with the vital imagination in both of its modes.

As does Wordsworth in 'Tintern Abbey', Coleridge asserts the view that thinking, or cognition, must be *actively* applied in the direct, sensuous encounter with nature as an act of the imagination, the 'prime agent of all human perception'. It is in this process that the poet 'filled all things with himself' (19) or could 'make all nature lovelier' (33). Here 'filled' and 'make' stress the view that the poet can and must deconstruct the stale and clichéd view of nature and replace it with his own genuine originality.

This view of the imagination, as actively creating original concepts, is also what lies behind Wordsworth's phrase 'By thought supplied' in 'Tintern Abbey' (line 83). Or as Hamlet has it 'There is nothing either good or bad, but thinking makes it so'. Coleridge articulates the view more explicitly in his brilliant 'Dejection: An Ode' (begun in 1802) where he talks of

> we receive but what we give,
> And in our life alone does Nature live.                    (47–8)

There again he defines the key element in the process as his 'shaping spirit of Imagination' (86), the source of intense joy as well as of creativity and understanding.

But there is a strong sense in which Coleridge actually goes further than Wordsworth in this 'different lore' (though not altogether more lucidly). In 'Tintern Abbey' Wordsworth talks first of beholding with the subjective eye and then of employing the imagination to *see* into the nature or essence of things. Coleridge, taking his cue from the idealist philosophies of Kant and the Schlegels, emphasises the role of the imagination as actively informing reality, filling his world 'with himself', in effect a subjective reality. In other words, for Coleridge we do not so much see into as *construct* our truth through the imagination (and 'The Nightingale' has key references to active processing such as filling, making and building: see lines 24 and 33).

This is reality as created (the 'eternal act of creation') instead of reality as observed objectively or scientifically, devoid of the reflective observer. By creating poetry from the encounter with nature, the poet, for Coleridge, makes reality, literally realises in his work the subjective and esoteric process undertaken by the imagination (and 'The Nightingale' implicitly sees the poet as the influential architect of our responses to the world; see lines 35–9). As far as the poet is concerned the initial act of perception, or experience in the world, corresponds to what Coleridge calls the 'primary Imagination'; the literary composition corresponds to what he refers to as the 'secondary Imagination'.

Furthermore, Coleridge believed that this dichotomy created two cardinal points in poetic communication: one excites the reader's empathy by reference to the actuality of experience, and the other stimulates his or her total engagement by modifying the experience through the poet's (and hence the reader's) subjective imagination.

Undoubtedly, this stress on the imagination as projecting rather than seeing into truth raises important epistemological questions: what exactly is truth and what constitutes knowledge? The fundamental principal of Romantic knowledge is clearly the subjective imagination. Coleridge's subjectivist theory of imagination implies that truth does not exist independently of the subjective observer – the nightingale has no intrinsic, independent mood (see line 19 again) and all physical nature, relationships, emotions, art itself, are reflections of oneself, as the experiencer of them.

The danger now, however, is the slippery slide into the cul-de-sac of solipsism even as the tensions generated between the realms of the physical and the mental worlds in 'The Nightingale' contribute much of its vital interest. Coleridge's solution (not altogether convincing) is to repeatedly anchor internal states to external physical points; so in the poem the attention returns to the material setting: the old bridge, vernal showers, birdsong, castle and so on.

However, and significantly, knowledge does include accumulated learning in the form of memory, in addition to direct experiences. And this accumulated learning is what Coleridge means by the 'fancy', which lies at the heart of his view on associationism.

Although Coleridge later modified his views on learning and associationism, in 'The Nightingale' he presents two useful examples of
the theory. In line 74 the maid who *'knows* all their notes' has learned
by association to link 'tipsy Joy' with the nightingales' 'choral min-
strelsy' (80–6). Then, in the final section, young Hartley Coleridge's
intuitive response to nature's curative influence (represented by the
moon) is regarded as a part of this extended process of association
which his father prays will continue throughout his life:

> But if that Heaven
> Should give me life, his childhood shall grow up
> Familiar with these songs, that with the night
> He may associate Joy!                    (106–9)

It is indicative that in both instances Coleridge chooses the word
'knows' to reveal the persistence of the effects of this process (lines 74
and 97). Associationism also enables Coleridge to resolve the issue –
raised in 'Tintern Abbey' too – of how the internal and abstract
(mind) can interact with the external and physical (nature) – in other
words two contrary substances commingling. However, where
Wordsworth looks to the pantheistic spirit of nature to unite observer
and observed, Coleridge adopts a less theological stance by looking to
the psychology of perception and interpretation. But, in spite of 'The
Nightingale's abundant imagery of cognition (see again lines 74–86,
but also 14, 40, 49 and so on), Coleridge rejects out of hand the Neo-
classical rationalism that is characteristic of early eighteenth-century
literature. The poem exhibits abundant evidence of his subversive
stance in, for example, the non-rational (lines 29, 52, 83, 100) and
the ardent emotions (lines 11, 16, 38–9, 109), as well as the lyric and
orphic elements. As always in Coleridge, there is the strong tempta-
tion to become rapt in the non-rational, to escape completely into the
imagination and into the mind, away from the pains of waking,

> Surrendering his whole spirit, of his song
> And of his fame forgetful!                    (30)

Vitally, though, 'associationism' also offers the writer a highly
effective structuring principle and is adopted by Coleridge in

'The Nightingale' – or so it would seem, anyway. By describing the poem as a 'Conversation Poem' Coleridge – like Wordsworth in 'Tintern' – implies that the poem's content is recorded in the unsorted, amorphous manner of the unfocused mind, one element or strand linked to the next by association or the fancy ('a mode of memory'). He uses this same approach in other poems, notably 'A Frost at Midnight' and 'This Lime Tree Bower my Prison'. The impression of accidental shapelessness is reinforced by the lazy loose syntax and the repeated use of 'and' as a continuer in the extended reflections (see lines 7–12, 19–23 and 49–61).

Other speech devices support this impression: non-fluency effects such as the repeated interruptions (as by the nightingale itself, in line 90), the use of fillers (such as 'Well', in line 105) and the repetition of redundant subject pronouns (in the extract, 'he' in line 1 and 'they' in line 37) to purport an absent mind or rambling conversationalist (Coleridge was notoriously an inveterate buttonholer and a charismatic if meandering raconteur).

As well as the style, the structure seeks to reflect the random unimposed texture of the poem. The poem's structure is apparently determined by the observer's roaming, adventitious viewpoint: beginning in the 'present', a night setting by the bridge, and moving backwards to the historic poets (line 16), then to imagined 'youths and maidens' in dances and theatres (35), back to the present (40), visiting a castle and a grove of the past (49 and 69), to the present (87), the past (98) and finishing in the future (107).

This drifting complexity of moments, places and feelings enriches the poem with its supple imaginative variety, and Coleridge is successful in producing an impression of a spontaneous stream of consciousness. Some critics have dismissed this structure as a ragbag of disjointed fragments, sometimes finding it formless, disjointed, perplexing even. But the 'ragbag', if it is one, is given coherence by the interaction of its simple elements (nightingale, moonlight, landscape and so on) especially through the unifying mind of the poet. And it is worth remembering that the poem's random 'associative' effect is precisely engineered, and not by the fancy (as it might seem) but by the 'esemplastic' imaginative, which has consciously dissolved, recreated and reshaped the materials in the 'eternal act of creation'.

As with Wordsworth, Coleridge also acclaims the deep therapeutic influence of nature. This is exemplified most explicitly in the ameliorative effect on the mood of his frightened child who:

> Suspends his sobs, and laughs most silently          (103)

The nightingale itself has a mollifying influence because it is specifically associated with happiness (43) and harmony (62). At the same time, as one of 'Nature's sweet voices', it intones a message 'always full of love / And joyaunce' (42–3). Although these days 'jug jug' (60) is likely to bring to mind T. S. Eliot and echoes of violence or Elizabethan bawdy, Coleridge's bird is much less sensual. In fact, as part of his revisionary project, Coleridge actually hypothesizes a masculine nightingale (45–8), but one less sexualised, except perhaps as a shadowy nuance of desiring.

The nightingale is realised more interestingly as a trope, a representation of art itself. In its associations of 'wild' and 'tangling' (52), 'tipsy' (86) and 'capricious' (59) it points forcefully to Coleridge's characteristic fascination with complexities of the mind, the imagination and of art itself. In this function it also attests to his well-known appetite for complexity as well as for the mystification of life and perception.

From the outset, however, Coleridge is strident in his view that nature is devoid of intrinsic emotional content: 'In nature there is nothing melancholy' (15). By the same token he is still eager to stress (as also in *The Rime of the Ancient Mariner*) a view of nature as blessed Creation, sacred, and entailing veneration,

> we may not thus profane
> Nature's sweet voices          (41–2)

As a hallowed (and hallowing) entity, nature is unequivocally due this respect, and is to be reverenced accordingly (in 'The Eolian Harp', for instance, nature is defined as 'the one Life within us', and the idea of the 'one Life' is a central motif in Coleridge's thought).

As Wordsworth in 'Tintern Abbey', Coleridge valorises the pre-eminent causal link between nature and the action of the imagination. In 'The Nightingale', the moon – symbolising the imagination – triggers the birdsong symbol of art and of literary creation (lines 77–82). Equally as much as Wordsworth, Coleridge affirms that direct encounters with nature are the ideal life- and art-enhancing experiences. For the poet, instead of accepting and retailing the tired old notions of a plangent nightingale, he 'had better far have stretched his limbs / Beside a brook' (25–6). By thus surrendering himself to the warm inspirational loam of nature, his imagination may achieve a fresh and timeless attitude, birdsong and poetsong united in empirical realism

> so his fame
> Should share in nature's immortality (30–1)

Conversely, in Coleridge's poem there is a less-clear sense of the working process involved between the imagination and nature. Typically he is formulaic, more recondite than Wordsworth about the mechanism. Three convergent elements – at least – are seen here to be propitious for Coleridge in the operations of the imagination: silence (6), tranquillity (7) and, usually, solitude (the 'I' in 55). And frequently the action of some external ministry or motivating force is essential – here the moon, while in 'The Eolian Harp' it is the breeze.

The events recounted in the poem come across as a convincing evocation of an actual evening or evenings. Yet the natural settings of a mossy old bridge over the silent glimmering stream, a balm starry night, plus the castle and the wild grove, eventually merge into a tremulously idealised dreaminess. The superbly evocative atmosphere of the opening combines with oddly minimalist elements to translate the poem beyond the realism of the specific moment into the realm of the supernatural. Wordsworth denounced any drift towards the supernatural in *Lyrical Ballads* (though many of his own poems at least approach it; for example, 'Lucy Gray' and 'The Idiot Boy'). However, in *Biographia Literaria* Coleridge claims that they had agreed that he should develop the supernatural material while Wordsworth was to concentrate on those subjects 'chosen from ordinary life'.

The effect of Coleridge's supernatural tendencies here is to translate us beyond appearances of course, beyond im-mediating reality.

But where Wordsworth might see into this surface reality or nature to reach its essential *truth*, Coleridge sees through it with the imagination as an escape into an ideal realm of universal harmony – an *ideal*, uniting with all of nature, or the 'one Life'. In this respect, it is indicative that Coleridge's setting is nocturnal, against Wordsworth's 'daily life'. Where 'Tintern Abbey' is much concerned with seeing, 'The Nightingale' is a poem of hearing. Like the nightingale, Coleridge himself is a *philo-mela*, a lover of the dark and of song.

Akin to Wordsworth, however, Coleridge is of course a worshipper of nature. In 'The Nightingale' the grove carries with it nuances of Eden's innocence (compare 'Nutting') as well as hints of 'Kubla Khan's sexuality, the 'deep romantic chasm'. And here the romance is eroticised by the lambent hint of danger encircling this 'most gentle maid' (69). Characteristically, Coleridge flirts with hints and nudges, provoking deeper, 'half-disclosed' possibilities, as in the lines:

> Even like a Lady vowed and dedicate
> To something more than nature in the grove                    (72–3)

But what is this 'something more than nature'? Nun-like chastity? the super-natural? neo-Platonist idealism? or perhaps something enticingly unnatural? It is not easy to say, and it could well be all of them.

Yet, equally characteristic of Coleridge is his evident commitment to human society. A solitary worshipper of nature here, he adduces the essential communalism of the nightingales. The poem's imagery too is much concerned with friendship (lines 40 and 110), harmony (62), sharing (31) and social gathering (35–7), all of which projects the poet's interest in people, their society and welfare. But even in his poems of solitude (for example, 'A Frost at Midnight' and 'This Lime Tree Bower') Coleridge's metropolitan principle comes through. His advocacy of human society is undeniable and is all one with his philosophy of pantheism, the Pantisocratic enterprises of his youth, his joy in convivial engagement with fellow humans and with the whole of God's creation.

This positive outlook is vitally revealed in 'The Nightingale' in his insistence on loving and fellowship rather than on the rape of Philomela as the central imaginative root of the poem and the source of the deconstructive project in the poem, the overthrow of the traditional connotations of subject matter (or 'conceit', line 23) and he is not afraid to challenge literary tradition as a whole.

Too many critics have dismissed 'The Nightingale' as formless or disjointed and, because of its last-minute inclusion in *Lyrical Ballads*, have cavilled at it as outside the overall design of the volume. Yet it has many affinities with 'Tintern Abbey': both poems are in blank verse, employing an associative or biomorphic form, ending on a prayer for future happiness; both focus on and apostrophise the spirit of a particular place for insight on the imagination and the physical correlative of its power; and both adopt a potent lyrical language, deeply interfused with a strongly authentic voice of commitment.

While Coleridge's poem does not attain the subtle interiority or metaphysical finesse of 'Tintern Abbey', 'The Nightingale' is an heroic production, a fertile corpus of rich and complex intensities that arise, through difference as well as its range of antitheses, including subjective mind and objective physicality, nature and supernatural, solitude and fellowship – all held in an uneasy (but nevertheless vibrant) tension of mystical and esthetic drama.

### 'Love'

Coleridge's 'Love' shares some of the same concerns as 'The Nightingale': a first person lyrical composition in which poetry itself and the imagination play a central role and across which, again, a mysterious woman wanders, and who while exerting a pervasive presence in the poem remains (slightly) out of reach to us, not fully focused, liminal.

'Love' too opens with a series of absolutes, this time positives, 'All thoughts, all passions, all delights'. Love lies at the heart of everything we do and think; but we are all in its thrall. The opening stanza announces the issues of seduction and sexual politics which lie at the heart of the poem. After Coleridge's proem, the narrator, or Singer, recalls an episode in which he meets and serenades the mystery woman, rehearsing a plangent ballad of a knight (the 'armed man') who had sacrificed his life in wooing and rescuing his 'Lady of the

Land'. His singular loyalty to her has finally 'crazed his brain' (60), broken him, driven mad by deception and illusion, and he dies in her caring embrace. The Singer himself, by cunningly overplaying the feelings of the ballad, confidently overwhelms his blushing 'Genevieve' and sees her reduced to a weeping, bosom-heaving, 'bright and beauteous Bride' (96).

It is significant that Coleridge wrote the poem while he himself was deeply embroiled in romantic turmoil (one of many in his life). On a visit to Sockburn-on-Tees in October 1799 he fell intensely in love with Sara Hutchinson (sister of Mary, Wordsworth's future wife) at a time when his relations with his wife, Sara, were often under considerable strain. For the rest of his life Sara Hutchinson (referred to as 'ASRA' in his writings) remained a hauntingly elusive love-obsession, his yearnings an open and uncomfortable secret to all in his circle. The poem is inspired by his introduction to her and by the enchanting setting of Sockburn (which possesses the effigy of a local knight said to have slain a monstrous wyvern).

'Love', which has many affinities of theme and atmosphere with its contemporary 'Christabel', is written in a variation on the ballad metre while its rhythms, tensions and melodic cadences also antici-pate the supernatural of *The Rime of the Ancient Mariner*. Significantly, its form also resembles the French roundelay of the thir-teenth century, the mainstay of the troubadours with which there are important correspondences in Coleridge's poem.

We have here one poem that is actually about and comments on another poem. In fact, there are no less than three narratives at work: the poem as a whole contains a lyric in which the Singer narrates to 'Genevieve' the ballad of a knight who falls for the Lady of the Land. The Singer (I will label him thus to distinguish him from the Coleridge of stanza 1) begins with a conventional balladeer's opening of 'Oft' and 'I / Live o'er again that happy hour' (5–6) and he refers explicitly throughout to his literary role as narrator/Singer (see lines 19, 22, 29, 33, 67 and so on). And as the Singer implies with that highly significant word 'interpreted', he presents his own love through the love of another, the allegory

> With which I sang another's love
> Interpreted my own.                                        (35–6)

These complex perspectives control and intensify the experiences of
the poem, and to see how they work we will need to examine the text
in detail. Because this is a long poem, I have again extracted a passage
(lines 49–96) for analysis:

> There came, and looked him in the face,
> An angel beautiful and bright;
> And that he knew it was a Fiend,
>    This miserable Knight!      52
>
> And that, unknowing what he did,
> He leapt amid a murderous band,
> And saved from outrage worse than death
>    The Lady of the Land;      56
>
> And how she wept and clasped his knees
> And how she tended him in vain –
> And ever strove to expiate
>    The scorn, that crazed his brain.      60
>
> And that she nursed him in a cave;
> And how his madness went away
> When on the yellow forest leaves
>    A dying man he lay;      64
>
> His dying words – but when I reached
> That tenderest strain of all the ditty,
> My faltering voice and pausing harp
>    Disturbed her soul with pity!      68
>
> All impulses of soul and sense
> Had thrilled my guileless Genevieve,
> The music, and the doleful tale,
>    The rich and balmy eve;      72
>
> And hopes, and fears that kindle hope,
> An undistinguishable throng!
> And gentle wishes long subdued,
>    Subdued and cherished long!      76
>
> She wept with pity and delight,
> She blushed with love and maiden shame;
> And, like the murmur of a dream,
>    I heard her breathe my name.      80

Her bosom heaved – she stepped aside;
As conscious of my look, she stepped –
Then suddenly with timorous eye
    She fled to me and wept.           84

She half inclosed me with her arms,
She pressed me with a meek embrace;
And bending back her head looked up,
    And gazed upon my face.         88

'Twas partly love, and partly fear,
And partly 'twas a bashful art
That I might rather feel than see
    The swelling of her heart.        92

I calmed her fears; and she was calm,
And told her love with virgin pride.
And so I won my Genevieve,
    My bright and beauteous Bride!      96

One of the important tasks we need to perform in analysing the complex interplay of love, art and imagination in this poem is to distinguish what *appears* to happen to the Singer from what probably does happen to him. The title together with the prologue to the poem announce the poem's love themes, but what are the characteristics of love here? In the story of the Knight (starting at line 29) we find the conventional chivalric or courtly traits of literary lovemaking. Here love is innocent and passion is constrained by conventions; it is a 'sacred flame', implying a certain reverence or even preciousness about physical love. The Knight courts his lady and suffers ten years for his troubles, eventually becoming mad through celibate fidelity (his 'outrage worse than death', l. 55).

His ordeal or trial also involves the harrowing wasteland where he is scorned and tormented by a 'Fiend' in the guise of an 'angel beautiful and bright' (50). He heroically and selflessly rescues his 'Lady of the Land' from the rapine clutches of a 'murderous band' (54) and eventually, becoming 'crazed', he dies, nursed by the Lady in her hospitable cave. The Knight's tale advances by a series of stylised and highly affective tableaux and yet their emotions are to some extent curbed by the allegorical framework (a point underscored by the name 'Genevieve', which also acts as a bridge between the two narratives).

Alongside the tender pieties of 'amour courtois' Coleridge presents us with more realistic, earthy aspects of love. The poem as a whole attests to the poet's ideal of 'love' as human companionship and his own susceptibility to impulsive and intensely passionate infatuations (69). The 'sacred flame' refers as much to the intensity and impulsiveness of love as to its carnality. But where 'Nightingale', for instance, was involved with parental and spiritual affectation, 'Love' centres on the physical and sexual, as well as the politics of seduction.

Alongside the seduction theme Coleridge insists on the role played in it by deception and the conscious reason (the strange item 'scorn' in line 60 connects all three elements). In addition to thrilling emotions and sensual pleasure, cunning too ('All thoughts') lies at the heart of the game. The poem is driven forward by the almost palpable energy of desire which strives to remain objective but becomes overwhelmed and subverted by subjectivity (as the Knight too eventually loses rationality and self-control). Seduction is characterised by deception, invention, false surfaces, feints and exaggerations (all corollaries of the creative imagination).

Desire is predicated on difference and both are strongly evident here. Coleridge was greatly motivated by the theory of opposites in the philosophy of Giordano Bruno and by the view that meaning was generated by tension in the fertile interplay of contrast. So, in the extract, we have the tensions of angel and Fiend (50–1), 'soul and sense' (69), outrage and 'maiden shame' as well as 'knew' and 'unknowing' (51 and 53). Such polarities also divulge the poem's own deceptions – of which more soon.

Among these important contrasts is that between the Knight's chivalric courtship of the Lady and the lusty strategies of the more worldly Singer. The reader could be forgiven for seeing the ballad of the Knight as simply the moral standard by which to assess the other lover, a warning by which to judge the Singer's siege on Genevieve. But it does not quite work out like that: while we are made continually aware of the presence of this Other and the vibrant tensions generated by it, the Knight's tale actually sets out to charm *us*, its readers. It does so less by a strategy of probity and faint heart than by flagging up the dangers of such probity, namely, the 'scorn that crazed his brain' (60) from 'wishes long subdued' (75). The poem thus charts the journey of desire which connects Genevieve as 'My hope' in line 18 to 'And so I won' in line 95.

The tender art of seduction is one of the leading expressions of the creative imagination in the poem (though not the sole one) and it therefore invites closer, careful scrutiny. The Singer's potential success here depends (as he himself warns) upon his conscious reasoning – but also on his accurate estimate of the woman (whose real name may or may not be Genevieve, of course). Significantly his diction betrays his devious subtext: he talks of 'stealing' (9), of 'lingering' (16) and in the extracted passage, of 'expiate' (59), 'inclosed' (85) and 'art' (90). These references blend together predatory desire and guilt, at the prize already gained.

Our impressions of Genevieve are, of course, those received via the fallible Singer. As Coleridge himself often did, he pedestals the woman while remaining convinced that he has the true, objective measure of her. He insists on her virgin frailties and 'modest grace' (26) and idealises her emotionalism, the self-fiction of her easy charm. She seems to egg him on,

> She loves me best, whene'er I sing
>    The songs, that make her grieve.                    (19–20)

She weeps with 'pity and delight' and blushes compliantly with 'love and maiden shame' (77–8). Already in his imagination he rules her with a sort of overpowering indulgence which teeters on the mawkish.

In his seduction of Genevieve, the Singer is already well ahead of the knight – and he has safely avoided the pains too of that strange 'scorn' (line 60). He reads the sure signs of her submission, that heaving bosom (81) and then she flees to him in tears. The crazed knight had to wait 'ten long years' at least, for this with his chivalric reverence, where a good song might have knocked her out in one. The dreamy moonlit setting helps, of course, mingling with the undoubtedly hypnotic rhythms of his voice and the harp, and the confusion of her feelings. She is by turns thrilled, delighted, fearful and at last charmed into a trance. From line 77 she seems to swoon into something like an orgasm, moans his name and, barely managing a meek embrace, gazes upward into his face.

Understanding the woman as a slave of feeling, quite passive, he overwhelms and subdues her conscious self with the brute power of his will and he becomes triumphant (and cocky with it), 'And so I won my Genevieve' (95). This emphasises the extent to which control is the key – control and a good song. He is apparently taller than she (87) which probably helps. But he portrays himself as the active figure while she dutifully succumbs to his artful devices. It is an old song that 'fitted well' (22 and 23), so it has probably done the trick before, while even his 'faltering voice' looks like a cunning ploy. And that highly significant word 'interpreted' in line 36 also functions in the seduction since he seeks her to draw the parallel or allegory between himself and the poor desolate knight:

> The low, the deep, the pleading tone,
> With which I sang another's love,
> Interpreted my own. (34–6)

The sly old dog! While he controls 'All thoughts, all Passions, all Delights' his 'guileless Genevieve' (70) falls victim to his irresistible charm and to her own undeniable pity. But is this really what happened?

There are enough counterfactuals to question the version with which the Singer/Coleridge tries to seduce us, the reader, too. Taken at face value, the poem begins to look like the old but plain fantasy of easy male seduction of a simple 'timorous' maid. Genevieve's blushing responses and palpitating bosom 'told her love' (94), giving outward suggestions of her frail emotionality and compliance, whereas the Singer presents an image of himself as the winner, which along with the roles of narrator and serenader give him a strong presence of mind. But the word 'interpreted' is important because it is aimed as much at us as at Genevieve; we too are warned of the allegory, of the possibility of parallels between the two apparently distinct narratives (i.e. of the knight and of the Singer).

There are other clues as to the truth (or at least to the deception) of what is actually going on here. The key question is, who seduces whom? Genevieve seems a very biddable, cooperative conquest and far from being exclusively the 'feeler', she may actually be the manipulator.

Line 27 offers a possible, if ironic, clue: 'For well she knew'. The question is further complicated (or disrupted) by the fact that the Singer himself concedes early on that the whole thing is one of his 'waking dreams' (5), a fantasy about seducing his idolised lady. He fantasises his own prowess, as well as her guileless compliance and her flattery of his charisma. However, even if the whole thing is not a fantasy but a real seduction, he is probably not the active seducer but the victim. And another clue is in the final lines,

> And so I won my Genevieve,
> My bright and beauteous Bride! (95–6)

As we have noted already, the word 'interpreted' invites us (like Genevieve) to see allegorical parallels with the tale of the knight and the Lady of the Land. As the knight crosses the wasteland,

> There came, and looked him in the face,
> An angel beautiful and bright;
> And that he knew it was a Fiend. (49–51)

The fiend or witch or succubus torments him in the guise of an angel and the words used to describe her are ironically almost identical to those used at the end to describe Genevieve. And one further clue is presented in that troubling phrase in line 90

> And partly 'twas a bashful art.

In the light of the other hints and nudges (like the Singer) we are faced with the realisation that *she* is the calculator, the controller, the knower preying on the Singer's feelings. As he admits in line 27 he is at least as susceptible to 'feel' as she is,

> For well she knew, I could not choose.

So all that blushing, bosom heaving, pitying and weeping was to entrap this poor, erring and errant male. In the early version of the poem, published in the *Morning Post*, Coleridge originally had a coda which loosely pointed to a sequel, 'The Ballad of the Dark Lady' (never completed). However, Coleridge judged it exactly right in finishing the poem on that sardonic exclamation mark, with the equivocal silence hovering enticingly after it. Lines 36 and 96 of this poem work in collusion with that silence, which is also the silence between two parallel narratives. Line 53 – 'unknowing what he did' – applies to the 'miserable Knight' but by extension relates equally to the Singer (and to Coleridge himself) who thus, by a satire on himself, effectively acknowledges his own ingenuousness.

The effect of this final twist is, at the very least, to cast the poem into uncertainty with a seismic, deconstructing shift in the meaning, while the idea of a demon witch preying on an honest knight has its precursors of course. The Arthurian romances of Spenser and Malory spring readily to mind and 'Love' itself has direct successors in John Keats's brilliant ballad of 'La Belle Dame sans Merci' (and *Lamia*) and in Tennyson's *The Lady of Shallott*.

Like these pieces, 'Love' raises interesting questions about Coleridge's attitude to woman. In the highly charged atmosphere of *Christabel*, he splits the central female character of 'Love' into two roles: the angelic Christabel herself and the 'fiend', Geraldine, while *The Rime of the Ancient Mariner* recreates the fiend as the nightmare woman, Life-in-Death ('Who thicks man's blood with cold'). The phrase 'Interpreted my own' (36) casts some light on Coleridge's personal plight and in particular his divided affections for his wife, Sara, and his new passion, Sara Hutchinson. Thomas De Quincey – who knew both Lake poets intimately – claimed that Coleridge's melancholy at this time was due to loving his wife over much, but it could equally be attributed to the complexities in his divided passions. And 'Genevieve' as tormentor may refer to either or both of the Saras.

As well as dealing with the deception of the knight and the Singer, the poem concerns the deception of the reader. The desired effect of the Singer's ballad is to emphasise the similarities in the fates of the knight and the Singer himself. However, Coleridge's own deception of the reader depends on maintaining the differences between them, thus setting up a fine tension between the two strategies. As we also find in 'The Nightingale', the dreamy moonlit scene hopes for a mildly soporific effect on the reader as the poem's stylistic effects set to work. The mazy hypnotic rhythms of repeated words and phrases create musicalities that mimic song, uniting the poet with the Singer, evading and dislocating meaning (for example, see the phrases in lines 45–7, 57–9, 81–2 and the 'flitting blush' of lines 25 and 37).

The simplicity of the ballad metre too is complicit in our seduction by focusing attention on the distant past as the key matter, while the repeated short fourth line of each quartet produces a strangely chiming refrain, a curious dissonance, hinting at the poem's silences. It is disingenuous of the Singer, of course, to use present tense for 'loves' in line 19 (and stanza 2 also seeks to send us in one particular direction). But Coleridge's master touch comes in lines 65–8 when, as the rondelay reaches its climax and the doomed knight is about to warn us of his fate, the Singer's voice falters in a confusion of welling emotion. We become stranded in the ironic silence of Coleridge's own 'bashful art'.

Both Coleridge and Wordsworth share a conception of imagination that is at the same time visionary yet close to the earth and ordinary humanity. However, in 'Love' Coleridge presents us with a view of art or poetry in the service of secondary or instrumental purposes – namely poetry as manipulation and deception, in other words, seduction. We too are the victims of this con-man and the key words in this context are, of course, 'I won' (95) and 'bashful art' (90), both of which encapsulate the politics of love and encompass its tensions (though both are finally ironic within the broader context of deceit).

The poem is very much concerned with the power and effect of poetry itself, a poem about a poem (or song). This is evidenced in the fact of Coleridge giving us a running commentary on the effects of the song or poem on 'Genevieve'. For her responses to his music see lines 67–8, 70 and 77–80 in the extract and the Singer too gives many explicit references to his recital: 'I played' (21), 'I sang' (22), 'I told her' (29, 33, 47), continually drawing attention to the art and to performance of it. This indulgence is part of our deception too, like the mazy hypnotic music of his cunning repetitions referred to above, conflating mood and desire:

> The music, and the doleful tale,
>    The rich and balmy eve ...                    (71–2)

Consonant with the Singer's commentary are the numerous references to Genevieve's activities: leaned, stood, listened, grieve, blushed, stepped, inclosed, gazed, told.

The distance and control implicit in the Singer's commentary are created by Coleridge's use throughout of reported speech. This helps to control the flow of information from the omniscient poet (that is, Coleridge, manipulating a first person Singer) which in turn collaborates in the deception of the reader too. This control is very much in terms of the poem's silences, particularly the subtle silence of Genevieve's knowledge and intentions, brilliantly handled by Coleridge, and culminating in that final uncertain silence after the exclamation mark in line 96 – and which is only partly resolved by Coleridge. It is also most significantly evident in the fact that the Singer's narrative collapses just at the point where we might have heard the knight's revelations, the 'tenderest strain of all the ditty' (66): the Singer's voice falters, his harp pauses, and Genevieve starts blubbing.

One other important factor that contributes to the cognitive uncertainties of the poem (while enhancing its heroic atmosphere) is the fact that the poem recounts a waking dream. Typically Coleridge is not especially clear about the nature of the dream, chiefly as it relates to either the imagination or the fancy. Dream and other similar states exercised a lifelong fascination for Coleridge and from early childhood he had been afflicted by the most awful and vivid nightmares. As his Notebooks make clear, these in later life were aggravated by opium addiction and dreams are the recurrent subject matter or pretexts of his most popular verse (for example, 'Kubla Khan', 'The Nightingale', 'The Pains of Sleep', 'Dejection: An Ode' and *The Rime of the Ancient Mariner*).

Coleridge held the radical view that our dreams, even the most disorganised, were in fact highly logical experiences. A letter of July 1820 to his son Derwent confirms Coleridge's conviction that dreams are rational accounts, when he writes of 'the exceeding order and wild ... rationality of the Images in my Dreams', a comment which naturally accords with his early views on Associationism. He makes no distinction between sleep-dreams and daydreams and he cherished daydreams as the matrix of his poetry (the critic Jennifer Ford has pointed out too the importance that Coleridge attached to dreams as a means of exploring bodily health and the diagnosis of disease).

Applying Coleridgean 'definitions' to 'Love', Imagination is the esemplastic creative faculty in which the broad text is created, by which the Singer devises the ballad of the knight. Fancy, the process of memory, is employed by the Singer at the outset of the poem to recall the 'happy hour' of his meeting with Genevieve. Dream is a sort of reverie which is part active imagination and part fancy, a condition of the mind in which poetry comes forth through pleasant smotherings, or 'a richy and balmy eve' (72); what Keats called:

> The silence when some rhymes are coming out.
>
> (*Sleep and Poetry*, l. 321)

But fanatics have their dreams too and Coleridge also held the view that dreaming could be a process of fantasising or idealising reality. Thus in 'Love' he evokes a pliant and accommodating maiden, framed within a platonic fantasy of chivalric love which eventually becomes his own undoing (for other good examples of this view see 'A Day-Dream' or 'Fears in Solitude'). In this regard dreams offer Coleridge a superb liberating form by which to explore psychology, metaphysics and the supernatural through the interplay of symbolism as here, in 'Love'.

Poem as dream lends itself admirably to classical psychoanalytical interpretation. Anticipating twentieth-century theorists, 'Love' opens with a frank inscription of the enormous potency of sex in the moulding and fulfilment of human lives:

> All thoughts, all passions, all delights
> Whatever stirs this mortal frame,
> All are but ministers of love,
>     And feed his sacred flame.                    (1–4)

Coleridge himself fosters a psychoanalytical account of the poem through his fondness for symbolism and allegory, minimalist detail, and (as his prose makes plain) through his deep enthusiasm for psychologising.

As an alternative to drugs, dream-symbolism and poetry are also royal roads to the deep unconscious and particularly to the realms of sexuality and desire through what Coleridge calls 'fixed', that is public, symbolism. Sexuality is signalled quite clearly through allusions to sex and the body; for example, 'outrage' and 'blush'. The 'burning brand' (30) suggests displaced desire in the face of that male impotence implied in the 'ruined tower' and the petrified knight. Genevieve, archetypal Arthurian adulteress, is clearly linked with blushing (lines 25 and 37 – indicating sexual arousal as well as guilt) and she is eroticised as a binary figure of both virgin angel and vamp. The dying knight has rescued his maiden from gang-rape and his reward is to be nursed in her cave in an ecstasy of madness before dying away – prelude to Genevieve's own orgasm in stanza 22.

Clearly Coleridge is exploring taboo elements, 'interpreted' through the cypher of symbolism. As we have seen, the 'other', or opposite and the desire for it are recurrently vital sources of energy in the poem and the dream symbolism here is part of the same vigorous fluxes of the imagination. In contrast to 'The Nightingale', Coleridge successfully works out a highly satisfying and integrated landscape of symbolic imagery. 'The Nightingale' spawns its own internal world but one which is firmly anchored in worldly reality through the looming presence of the Wordsworths. ('Tintern Abbey' too has been interpreted by some critics as espousing a relatively simple code by which to explore the taboo of William's supposed sexual feelings for his sister and this could also be extended to the 'Lucy' poems.)

## Conclusions

In this chapter I have tried to draw out the essential features of Wordsworth's and Coleridge's views on the imagination. For both poets, 'imagination' is crucially a theme, a psychological or theoretical concept, and also a poetic method. For Wordsworth, the imagination is a part-active, part-passive mechanism for retrieving materials from the memory. In 'Tintern Abbey' we noted the role played by the theory of association in this mechanism, in particular that the poet's later visit to the Wye valley triggers off memories of his previous tour and enables him to discover the regenerative benefits of nature, both then and now, that have helped him through adversity. This process has worked for Wordsworth as a dialectic, the later visit taking up and reshaping in the imagination impressions from five years before and then projected forward. The imagination (an 'eye made quiet') has also powered his insights on nature and on himself, revealing essential spiritual truths, the 'life of things'.

Where Wordsworth takes his understanding into the religious realms of seeing and discovering, Coleridge's theory of the imagination is rooted in his wider metaphysical and psychological interests. More particularly, he distinguishes imagination from dream and fancy. Later in his life Coleridge downgraded Wordsworth's view of imagination as simply what he would call the 'fancy', that is a passive mechanism of memory that works along the lines laid down by Hartley's theory associationism. Dream is a more active form of 'fancy', though he is at pains to specify how. For Coleridge the 'imagination' holds the supreme place in this triumvirate because it is the truly creative instrument of the mind, calling up but also reshaping impressions to produce new materials in the form of art. He describes this process as 'esemplastic' or moulding, and coadunating, that is, seeking to draw impressions into unity and harmony (these ideas are explored further in Chapter 8).

## Further Research

Read (or re-read) Wordsworth's 'Lines written near Richmond' and compare its modulation of mood and tone with that in 'Tintern Abbey'. In particular examine the roles played by memory and imagination in the former poem. What do the wave and the river represent in terms of Wordsworth's treatment of the theme of the imagination there?

# 3

# *Old Age: a 'vital anxiousness'*

> As we came up the White Moss we met an old man, who I saw was
> a beggar by his two bags hanging over his shoulder ... He was
> 75 years of age, had a freshesh colour in his cheeks, grey hair, a
> decent hat with a binding round the edge, the hat worn brown and
> glossy, his shoes were small thin shoes low in the quarters, pretty
> good. They had belonged to a gentleman.
>
> (Dorothy Wordsworth, *Journal*, 22 December 1801)

Following the moderate commercial success of the first edition of
*Lyrical Ballads*, an expanded, two-volume edition was published in
1800. Volume I retained almost all of the poems in the 1798 edition
and volume II contained the additional material that included a
number of new poems whose subjects referred explicitly to and illustrated the theme of old age.

With a distinct note of heroic reverence for his Cumberland countrymen Wordsworth's Preface asserted that no poetry can hope to
match 'the freedom and power of real and substantial action and suffering'. However, perhaps more than any other verse in the collection,
his poetry of 'old age' encapsulates the suffering and endurance that
so vigorously exercised Wordsworth's interest.

In this chapter I would like to examine in detail Wordsworth's
discussion of the theme of old age by focusing principally on three
poems, all of which are taken from volume II of the new edition.
These are *Michael*, 'The Old Cumberland Beggar' and 'The Fountain'.

## Michael: A Pastoral Poem

*Michael* seems to have developed from the same didactic impulse as 'The Ruined Cottage' and 'Pedlar' sections in Book I of Wordsworth's long poem *The Excursion*. All three are concerned with silent suffering and a homely faith in a sort of 'wise passiveness'. Wordsworth himself had observed the dire impact of expanding capitalist industrialism, both in terms of the collapse of the rural economy and the increasing migration of the poor to England's cities. His great fear was of the disastrous disappearance of traditional small-holdings, driving families out of the rural uplands.

Michael himself represents this poorer class of independent landowner ('The Female Vagrant' vividly portrays the disastrous career of another example; see Chapter 4). His realistic depiction of this social issue incorporates the conservative moral and political values that he understands as integral to the upland subsistence.

The basic outline of the narrative is straightforward enough. If, among the wild, desolate lakes and mountains we turn our steps 'from the public way' we may chance upon a deep secluded valley by whose 'boisterous brook' there stands a 'straggling heap of unhewn stones'. These are all that remain of Michael's project to construct a sheepfold with the help of Luke his only son. Wordsworth continually reminds us of Michael's exceptional nature: his extraordinary age, remarkable strength and resourcefulness, as well as his exceptional rapport with the land and its weather. Remarkable too is Luke's late appearance in the lives of Michael and Isabel. The poem pays close attention to the bonding of father and son as Michael grooms him to take over the small-holding. However, before Luke can succeed to his inheritance, hopes are wrecked by news of the failure of a kinsman's enterprise in which Michael was guarantor. Torn by conflicts of loyalty he tearfully despatches his son to work off the debt, a decision that leads eventually to Luke's ignominious perdition in the 'dissolute city' and exile abroad. After the death of the parents their house and land are sold and ploughed up.

Even from this cursory synopsis, it is easy to extrapolate the poem's dominant interests: old age and time in general, the role of love in families and communities, and the relationships between people and their context, a wild rural context in which they form deep and lasting bonds. We can take each of these in turn, focusing foremost on the first of these, the theme of old age.

*Michael* is inspired by and predicated upon the lives of real people. Equally important is the fact that it is rooted in actual physical locations (the sheepfold, Michael's house, the ghyll and so on), as Wordsworth's letters and his sister's journal attest. They help to generate the poem's great sense of material place, but above all to establish the dominating presence of the eponymous shepherd himself. Writing of the poem to his old Somerset friend, Tom Poole (in part the model for Michael) Wordsworth explained

> I have attempted to give a picture of a man, of strong mind and lively sensibility, agitated by two of the most powerful affections of the human heart; the parental affection, and love of property, *landed* property, including the feelings of inheritance, home, and personal and family independence.    (9 April 1801)

Michael is indeed clearly and deeply motivated by these powerful and highly complex affections that help to direct the poem towards the figure of Luke, while the tragedy in the story arises from the mutual destruction wrought by them.

The narrative is simply told, as a ballad, in an uncomplicated blank verse. Yet its apparent ease of statement does not diminish the profound thoughts or 'powerful affections' brilliantly forged within it.

The passage I have chosen as the starting point for analysis of the poem is lines 332–92, which follows Isabel's reluctant acquiescence in Michael's decision to send Luke away to work.

> Near the tumultuous brook of Green-head Ghyll,
> In that deep valley, Michael had designed
> To build a Sheep-fold, and, before he heard
> The tidings of his melancholy loss,                                335
> For this same purpose he had gathered up
> A heap of stones, which close to the brook side
> Lay thrown together, ready for the work.
> With Luke that evening thitherward he walked;
> And soon as they had reached the place he stopped,                340

And thus the Old Man spake to him. 'My Son,
To-morrow thou wilt leave me; with full heart
I look upon thee, for thou art the same
That wert a promise to me ere thy birth,
And all thy life hast been my daily joy.                              345
I will relate to thee some little part
Of our two histories; 'twill do thee good
When thou art from me, even if I should speak
Of things thou canst not know of. – After thou
First cam'st into the world, as it befalls                            350
To new-born infants, thou didst sleep away
Two days, and blessings from thy Father's tongue
Then fell upon thee. Day by day passed on,
And still I loved thee with increasing love.
Never to living ear came sweeter sounds                               355
Than when I heard thee by our own fire-side
First uttering without words a natural tune,
When thou, a feeding babe, didst in thy joy
Sing at thy Mother's breast. Month followed month,
And in the open fields my life was passed                             360
And in the mountains, else I think that thou
Hadst been brought up upon thy father's knees.
– But we were playmates, Luke; among these hills,
As well thou know'st, in us the old and young
Have played together, nor with me didst thou                         365
Lack any pleasure which a boy can know.'

Luke had a manly heart; but at these words
He sobbed aloud; the Old Man grasped his hand,
And said, 'Nay do not take it so – I see
That these are things of which I need not speak.                      370
– Even to the utmost I have been to thee
A kind and a good Father: and herein
I but repay a gift which I myself
Received at others' hands, for, though now old
Beyond the common life of man, I still                                375
Remember them who loved me in my youth.
Both of them sleep together: here they lived
As all their Forefathers had done, and when
At length their time was come, they were not loth
To give their bodies to the family mould.                            380

> I wished that thou should'st live the life they lived.
> But 'tis a long time to look back, my Son,
> And see so little gain from sixty years.
> These fields were burthened when they came to me;
> 'Till I was forty years of age, not more          385
> Than half of my inheritance was mine.
> I toiled and toiled; God blessed me in my work,
> And till these three weeks past the land was free.
> – It looks as if it never could endure
> Another Master. Heaven forgive me, Luke,          390
> If I judge ill for thee, but it seems good
> That thou should'st go.' At this the Old Man paused ...

I chose this section because it focuses so closely on the old man's relationship to his son, forming a nexus of age and youth ('our two histories', l. 347), or as Michael himself says, 'in us the old and young / Have played together' (364–5). As such, this moment also forms the major climax to the narrative, drawing together some of the poem's other key themes, including those of love, nature and the land itself.

The crucial reference to 'together' in line 365 is taken up again in 377 when Michael recalls his own parents and that they 'were not loth / To give their bodies to the family mould' (379–80). In other words he reminds Luke of how the family is rooted, literally and figuratively in the landscape of these mountains, implying generations of kinship and 'Being' with the ancient earth. (Michael expresses the rootedness that Wordsworth yearned for at this stage in his own life.) However, in doing this, Michael also seeks to impress on Luke the burden of obligation to the past and its life, chained to his ancestors:

> I wished that thou should'st live the life they lived.          (381)

Their time-honoured life of obligation and moral rectitude with its fierce consciousness of the past is all one with the puritanism of their bleak lives. The conventional virtues of endurance, fortitude and stoicism are clearly hinted at in the start of the poem analogous to the obdurate terrain and its associations: 'rocks and stones', 'struggle', 'tumultuous', 'boisterous', 'struggle', 'bold ascent', 'courage'. It is a hard scene emotionally as well as topographically, in which the despair suggested coldly and abruptly in line 13 is an ever-present reality:

> It is in truth an utter solitude                                          (13)

Theirs is a life of hard physical labour and isolation as well as of a strong awareness of history and their obligation to it. As Michael trenchantly but cogently expresses it, 'Our lot is a hard lot' (243). In addition to tradition and routine the lives of Michael and Isabel also involve a vague, instinctive belief in God (for example, see line 387 above) as well as a strong moral probity, both of which elements come under threat from later events in the poem. They are connected ineluctably with the past, of course, but connected specifically in a localised sense of the 'land', with its work having a sort of quasi-sacred dimension.

Yet even while they display this commitment to the past and its ghosts it is important to see the tale as concerned with the enterprise or adventure of the new and the future, despite the resulting catastrophe. For instance, in materials terms, Michael's beginning to invest in the sheepfold is a projection into the future, while Luke represents the spiritual promise and involvement in posterity,

> a child, more than all other gifts,
> Brings hope with it, and forward-looking thoughts.        (154–5)

Further, both parents are, if only tentatively, prepared to send their child into the future. In their three figures, the old and young, past, present and future 'play together': the past acts on them through the working of the kinsman's debt and impels them forward into a personal and political future in the distant city.

Michael is described explicitly (and frequently) as 'the Old Man' (see, in the passage, lines 341, 368 and 392), symbolically the ancient past, almost time itself, like the primordial mountains and the ghyll of his particular context. At the time of Luke's birth he refers to himself as having 'one foot in the grave' (92), but this seems the mere piety of an old man. He seems conscious not only of his own great age but also of its connection with the time of Luke's arrival, with the period of his own labour on the land (383) and the period of his inheritance of it, while the passage has numerous references to time in general: tomorrow, daily, histories, two days, 'Month followed month' and so on. This should not strike anyone with great surprise, of course, but the effect of this accretion of references is to direct us onto the time-bound mind of the central character.

In addition to his exceptional age, Michael stands out in other aspects too: he is of 'unusual strength' (44), 'watchful more than ordinary men' (47) and he responds acutely to the local weather when 'others heeded not' (50). The keenness of his mind appears to match the strength of his body and, moreover, his CV includes among his merits, 'Intense and frugal, apt for all affairs' – which is what we would naturally seek in any prospective shepherd.

Michael is exceptional, a point that is repeatedly stressed. Perhaps because of this he seems to have lived the whole of his adult life in a near-constant state of anxiety, about the land being lost, of sexual sterility, of debt, his own death and the loss of Luke. These are part and parcel of the continuous flux of his life: nothing ever stays the same (except his presence in it, of course). But, unlike Luke, who coexists and copes with it, Michael appears to live in struggle against this flux. Time, endurance, change, decline make up the essence of his life blood:

> It looks as if it never could endure. (389)

Our understanding of Michael is naturally and inextricably bound up with our understanding of his relationship with his surroundings. Indeed, at times the two strands vie for primacy in our attention, each framing the other,

> these fields, these hills
> Which were his living Being. (74–5)

We see again, in this intimate cohabitation of human and natural setting Wordsworth's awe in the 'life of things'.

Lines 46–61 seek to strike Michael's congruence/fittedness with nature, this whole 'living Being'. So, at line 18, we hear 'to that place a story appertains' as if to underline the close connection of Michael to the *genius loci*. The story could not be relevant anywhere else, just as the ancient oak, the Clipping Tree (179) is too, while the house-light, the 'Evening Star', speaks of a local habitation with a name.

Also like the ancient Clipping Oak, Michael has endured as a quasi-permanent presence on the landscape (though he is of course outlived by it). The farmhouse, the unfinished sheepfold and the mountains too, are meant to be seen as colossuses, the reference points of time. The word 'blind' in 'A pleasurable feeling of blind love' (78) seems highly apt in describing old Michael's whole covenant with the land and his powerful feelings for it become subli-mated to the forceful outburst of love for Luke expressed in the extract above (compare, too, lines 1–3 of 'Old Man Travelling').

Michael's life is in large part defined by a set of self-imposed bonds and contracts intended to ease the anxieties that beset it. He is bound to the land, and to his wife, he is contracted as surety for a kinsman, and then seeks a verbal covenant with Luke via the sheepfold project ('a covenant / 'Twill be between us', l. 424) and through teaching him traditional rural trades. However, Michael has come to accept the failure of the latter:

> I knew that thou couldst never have a wish
> To leave me, Luke, thou hast been bound to me
> Only by links of love ...                                    (410–12)

The extract above hints at Michael's strong expectations of Luke's filial obligations, but these are outweighed by heavy forebodings.

Eventually, of course, two of Michael's deeper dreads come to fruition: the estate is lost (241 and 483) after Luke is alienated from his family, from his community and from the 'land' (416 and 453). Although he lives to witness only the latter, he anticipates both things through the deep pessimism that dwells at the core of his being:

> I have lived to be a fool at last
> To my own family.                                            (245–6)

This is a harsh judgement of course. But it is one that flows logically from his severe patriarchalism and it is exposed by a combination of bad luck and historical determinism as the farm and Luke's life become caught up in the broader social scale. If we see the outcome simply in terms of Michael's courageous if folksy stoicism then the narrative is mere sentimentality (that is ever-present in the poem); but if we see it in terms of blind love plus a fortitude, that is rooted in land values, then we may be more inclined to see his disaster as a tragic one. At the heart of the latter lies the family's isolation and ignorance of the alternatives, the 'Other' beyond the 'tumultuous brook'.

Michael has worked the land for seventy-odd years (238) slogging away for a mere subsistence. With Isabel, 'they were as a proverb in the vale / For endless industry (96–7) and in the extract above Michael declares

> I toiled and toiled; God blessed me in my work                     (387)

This blessing is the crowning sanction of his life, which has been defined in terms of his enduring labour. And endurance, as well as being a keyword for the community, also lies at the centre of the time–nature–ethics triad that is at the centre of the narrative. Allusions in the poem to the theme of endurance are numerous (in lines 120, 147 and 418, and in the extract see line 389). This theme is also cognate with the puritanical work ethic and Old Testament notion of the intrinsic moral value of work, which in turn is fundamental to Michael's formal relationships with his son. But, further, Wordsworth uses this aspect of personification to arrange and heighten Michael's symbolic functions in the poem.

One of these functions lies in the hints that lead us to see Michael as something of an everyman. He is both a father and a son: in the extract he talks to Luke of his own time as a son (375–6). He turns his hand to all manner of labour: in addition to his many shepherding duties, he is a builder, he cards wool (108), repairs household as well as agricultural equipment (111) and, in a curiously Shakespearean phrase, he is described as 'apt for all affairs' (45). Not bad for an old man in his eighties. He is a 'mother' too, of sorts, having done 'female service' for baby Luke with 'dalliance and delight' (164).

Above all, it is his great age that dominates our attention. In fact the first thing we learn after his name is that he was 'An old man', and throughout the latter part of the narrative he is most often referred to simply as *the* 'Old Man' (for example, at lines 283, 341, 368 and 431). One effect of this persistence is to make his age proverbial, while another is to depersonalise him, rendering him an anonymously ancient figure like the mountainous landscape around him. It is tempting to see him as one of Wordsworth's familiar tree-like fixtures in the terrain, except that his own mortality seems perpetually imminent.

Although there are references to community (such as at lines 270 and 323) Michael's tenacious single-mindedness serves to stress his isolation. A solitary by nature, there is more than a hint of the Old Testament prophet about his aloofness. Literally, his name means 'one who is like God' and, in lines 243–4, he compares himself to the sun. Michael represents an older order or pattern of control but a form that cannot prevail in the face of newer outside forces.

Michael's aged figure sits square on a texture of religiosity in the poem with its many Biblical as well as generalised religious references. There are numerous allusions to evil, thrift, duty or service, determination. In addition the verse has an unmistakable Biblical cadence as well as rhetoric. In line 102, the 'mess of potage' they sit down to echoes Genesis XXV: 29–34, and thus sets up the parallel between Michael and Luke, and Esau who sells his birthright for minor material gain. There are, of course, hints of the prodigal son parable, while the fact that Luke fails to return underlines the extent of his apparent profligacy. The birth of Luke so late in his parents' lives suggests an ironic correspondence with St John the Baptist too.

In the extracted passage, we hear yet another reminder of Michael's extraordinariness in the oblique suggestion that his life has exceeded the Biblical span of three score years and ten,

now old<br>
Beyond the common life of man           (375)

(compare Psalms 90:10). But where Michael insists on and depicts distinctly Old Testament views of discipline, industry, sedulous individualism and moral probity, the 'apostolic' Luke emphasises the New Testament virtue of love, and the corruption of this is almost certainly the root of his ignominious disaster in the city.

Michael fulfils expectations of the autocratic patriarch when he determines on Luke's assignment, 'He shall depart tomorrow' (327).

His dogmatism recalls that of Lucy Gray's father (line 14) and at first Isabel withholds her consent (305) but then relents, probably as a result of her memory of the Richard Batemen myth (268). In line 83 she is described as 'a woman of a stirring life' and she shares her husband's compulsion for hard work.

Having said this, however, she is normally referred to in some depersonalised form, usually as the housewife (for example, lines 109, 116, 128, 294), and as a 'comely matron' (81) or 'his Helpmate' (149). She has less of a life of her own in the poem than Michael and their austere relationship seems dismally pragmatic. In addition, the fact that what is at hazard are the 'patrimonial fields' (234) – inherited through the male line – presents her as merely a useful adjunct, subsidiary to the male question.

At the time of Luke's departure Michael is aged 84 (line 100) and Isabel twenty years his junior (82). Yet while she is lumped in with him in terms of the theme of age, this wide difference in age is not laboured on by the narrator. She is indelibly associated with her old spinning wheels, equally 'Of antique form' (85) and with her famous night light, 'An aged utensil' (85; an epithet that could easily, if cruelly, be transferred to Isabel herself). When the kinsman problem arises she is deeply uncertain of the proposed solution and her resort lies in history, 'looking back into past times' (267). This, naturally, is solacing but also sets her apart in a strange sort of 'madness' (for example, at 321–2).

As well as the objects, scenery and people all exuding this strong tenor of great age, Wordsworth's language too couches the poem in an antique patina. I have referred already to the biblical cadences and rhetoric, but there are other literary echoes too. In spite of Wordsworth's explicit insistence on modern language some of the lines carry a Shakespearean ring (beside parallels with *The Merchant of Venice*, there are additional Shakespearean cadences and resonances: see lines 355, 364–5 and 384). There are even Chaucerian moments in 'Michael' (see lines 40–1, 80–2 and 180–1) – small lives enlivened by the pervasive sense of allegory and telling irony.

There seems little in the way of rustic or dialectal language (but see 296) though, perhaps surprisingly, the linguist Frances Austen discovers an abundance of legal diction here. On the other hand, Wordsworth's deliberate choice of words of Old English origin is quite marked; from the extracted passage these include 'tiding' (335), 'thitherward' (339), 'befalls' (350), 'else' (361), 'manly' (367), 'utmost' (371), 'herein' (372), 'Forefathers' (378), 'mould' (380), 'burthened' (384). The diction itself, in vocal sympathy with Isabel, harks back to recapture the past, a mythical pre-Norman era of Albion, declaring its allegiance with the old ways. By deploying Old English words Wordsworth taps into history, not only local and personal but of England as a whole, back even to the Roman occupation (in his *Guide to the Lakes* Wordsworth claims that some of the upland families could trace their tenantries back to feudal and even Roman times, but whose small parcels of land were being absorbed by larger estates).

Perhaps because it hints at these larger moments as well as at the metaphoricity of the characters' ages, the poem seems less clear on the detailed passing of time. Imagery of time is ubiquitous but particular moments are often vague, made distant too by both the attentive narrator and the dislocation of the normal chronological time sequence. However, heightened moments of intensity or urgency – such as the crisis of the kinsman's debt or Luke's emotional leave-taking – do attract a more precise focus on time: 'tomorrow' (327), 'that evening' (339), 'two weeks' (408).

As elsewhere in Wordsworth we get the idea of something having its own time, or ascribed moment ('their time was come', l. 379). These occasions include Luke's rite of passage (such as receiving his first shepherd's staff, l. 193) and habitual or routine actions (Isabel's nightly hanging up of the lamp, is a typical example). Thus the premature moments, of timeliness disrupted, are exploited by the narrator to signal the 'untoward' or to anticipate larger threats of change. So young Luke is 'prematurely called' to watch the gate (197), and prematurely sent from the family home, while Michael himself has survived beyond the customary span. Such ominous exceptions bring to mind other ironic prematurities in Wordsworth's ballads: for example in 'Lucy Gray' ('The storm came on before its time', l. 29) and in 'Three years she grew' ('How soon my Lucy's race was run', l. 38).

Michael's anguish at Luke's ominously premature departure is summed up in the interrupted project of the sheepfold and the dread of discontinuity in the family, 'I wish that thou shouldst live the life they lived' (381). In this line the themes of time, duty, inheritance and mortality all converge in a desperate anagnorisis for the old man. In this light the proposed sheepfold is a forlorn attempt to disarm the closing future and the discontinuity of his family. The joint task is to be both an 'emblem of the life' of their ancestors, the past (420), and a thrust into the future (as well as a containment of it): 'a covenant / 'Twill be between us' (424–5). Yet this attempt to make the future obedient to his will is naturally doomed and leads to Luke's disaster. It is left to Isabel to recognise and articulate the integrity, the inter-connectedness between their domestic lives and the naturalistic order:

> do not go away,
> For if thou leave thy Father he will die                    (308)

Luke himself has 'many hopes' (409). And, to be sure, Luke does represent the uncertain future – both in terms of the local domestic situation and in the broader political terms of rural depopulation. To his father he is 'his daily hope' (216), making the old man feel 'born again' (213). He is the 'new', the coming thing and the next generation. Yet his prospects founder, according to Wordsworth, in sterility, the sterility of a heap of abandoned stones beside that boisterous brook.

On the other hand, Luke is not the villain of the piece. His upbringing, such as it is, has been on the grounds of hard physical labour and severe moral rectitude (lines 169–216), not of warm human contact with other children and adults – as far as we can tell anyway. Solitariness, self-sufficiency and steadfastness are its values. In fact, compared to the lives of those boys in 'Nutting' and 'There was a Boy', Luke's quality of life looks utterly dire, worse even than that of the fiky female of 'We are seven'.

While Michael stands for tradition, stability, holding, Luke sym-bolises change, chance, release. He steps out from the world of rou-tine and safety of rural life, completely unprepared for the urban jungle, one giant leap for rural man, a move that is anticipated with unsuspecting irony in the opening line of the poem,

> If from the public way you turn your steps                    (1)

His diversion from the path reverses this opening, the path much trod, and is punished with a sort of lapsarian ruin that swiftly brings down the family house, the 'Evening Star' and all its moral and historical implications.

Luke himself does not seek escape and so we cannot readily attribute any motives to him. In fact, in the text he does not act freely at all nor does he speak. This makes him appear a passive, compliant casualty, victim of his father's reluctant will, mirroring the old man's faithful dog, in line 477. So, when Michael talks of Luke's 'fate' (405), he too expects his son to suffer. Twice more the young man's doom is prefigured, in the overt irony of lines 190–1, in which the father cuts down a young sapling, 'With his own hand', and more obliquely in the fateful 'unforeseen misfortune' of Luke's cousin (223).

Although Luke is, in a strong sense, sacrificed by Michael to save the land, we have arm in arm with this outcome the very real impression of his paternal love for Luke. It is through this that love becomes one of the poem's major themes, instilling the narrative with a complexity of intention and a fine sharpening of its felt humanity. Both of these important elements are heightened by the increasingly ominous departure of the young man for the 'dissolute city'.

With the birth of Luke, Michael's 'blind love' (78) of his land and its nature lays a strong hand on him as a wholly new spiritual sensation and at that point (from line 147 on) the reality of love suddenly bursts 'tumultuous' into the poem – though it does not find full or forceful expression until the crisis over the 'loss' of his son. The narrative implications of the theme of love become considerable, overwhelming the set old man and his fixities, driving a wedge between his obligations to the land and those to his kinsman. His deep love of Luke matures into a powerful hostage to the old man's very 'living Being'.

All the same, love originates in slight, prosaic beginnings, all one with the Puritanical naturalism of these hill people. The language itself austerely obeys:

> He had not passed his days in singleness.
> He had a wife, a comely matron, old                                   (80–1)

The definition of the couple (in reality only Michael) has all the charm of a government census return,

> The pair had but one inmate in their house                            (88)

The narrator here ventriloquises Michael's utilitarianism.

Yet even at this early point there are hints of kinds of love: of the other shepherds for instance, 'men / Whom I already loved' (23–4), while the 'power of Nature' taught the poet the feelings of others, taught him to think 'On man; the heart of man and human life' (28–33). But Wordsworth's love here is in essence egoistic, expressing a relationship with nature. Michael and his family dwell 'in the open sun-shine of God's love' (239). Which is still quite conventional, comfortable, re-assuring again like the dutiful 'faithful dog' (47) and of 'inestimable worth' (94).

We feel that mutual 'inestimable worth' is also the basis of Michael and Isabel's partnership, a shared living. Hence the importance of that other keyword 'common' in line 66, that controls the way we see the relationship, as a sort of fact of life that we come across only *in media res*. It is a sort of life that the couple share in common with the community of shepherds and others on the hard land.

> There is a comfort in the strength of love;
> 'Twill make a thing endurable, which else
> Would break the heart (457–9)

Comfort, companionship, duty, another sort of covenant, making life endurable as they grow old together for their days. These, we imagine, are the significant parameters, the important considerations in their life together 'living a life of eager industry' (124). We have recorded how Michael and the narrator collude to depersonalise Isabel as 'helpmate' (149), 'comely Matron' (81) and 'Housewife' (294). She is also a 'woman of stirring life' (83) 'whose heart was in her house' (84) and yet this seems to get channelled into an obsessive pre-occupation with spinning (yarn, that is, though a certain madness should not be ruled out). This gives no hint of that night of passionate carnality between Isabel and her near 70-year-old herdsman, twenty years her senior, that produces Luke.

Where Michael's dealings with his son are at first related to the practicalities of the kinsman's debt, Isabel's are on a more personal, direct basis, caring for Luke's welfare (see lines 282, 297 and 306). Because of this deeply felt care for Luke and her submission to

Michael's decision, her anxieties do seem eventually to drive her to the brink of insanity (295).

The narrator tells us that while Michael loved his 'Helpmate', Luke was to him 'yet more dear' (149–50). At line 342 he tells his son in slightly surprising terms, 'My son / Tomorrow thou wilt leave me' – 'me' instead of 'us' implying this special place in his world that Luke has filled. As the day of departure educes a crisis in their relationship, both Michael and Luke express their affections each for the other:

> Luke had a manly heart; but at these words
> He sobbed aloud                                                    (367–8)
>
> The old man's grief broke from him, to his heart
> He pressed his son, he kissed him and wept            (431–2)

Over the tightly wrought way of the poem we witness Michael's 'blind love' for his fields and mountains become translated and re-directed towards his son. Subsequently this deep love-light from the natural objects nourishes a new form of perception for the old man, so 'objects which the shepherd loved before / Were dearer now' (209–10) and 'the Old Man's heart seemed born again' (213). We sense that the love of objects and spirit in nature is for him a portal or a precedent to releasing a deep reservoir of cramped emotions (restraint and constraint are two of his governing traits). But a further consequence of the late flowering of love is that Michael even relents in his smouldering scorn of the kinsman, finally forgiving him for his 'evil' or his 'falsehood'.

On the eve of his son's departure Michael acknowledges too the love he had received from his own parents (see lines 374–6 in the extract). Love is his mediator with the past but, as if unable to trust his emotions without the intervention of natural objects, he seeks the covenant from his son in the physical externalisation of the stone sheepfold (it is interesting to record that Dorothy Wordsworth's journal describes the actual original of this sheepfold poignantly as 'nearly built in the form of a heart unequally divided', 11 October 1800).

Michael hopes to impose this as a sort of pledge, a bond of emotion, yet another expression of his domineering solicitude. In the extract, he explains that there are 'things of which I need not speak' (370). Muteness is a recurring motif in the poem (as throughout Wordsworth), but here we are more likely to feel that it is an inability to say, rather than the ineffability of the matter. A gulf lies between them formed by Michael's apocalyptic dread.

In spite of this and in spite of Wordsworth's blast against the supposed wickedness of the city (how would Michael know of it except by hearsay?) the strong suspicion remains that Luke does find some form of love in the purlieus of London or Bristol (in the 1800 Preface to *Lyrical Ballads* Wordsworth warned of what he feared as the stultifying effects on the mind of the 'encreasing accumulation of men in the city').

In *The Prelude* Wordsworth himself often rails against the town, where love cannot 'easily thrive':

> In cities, where the human heart is sick  (*The Prelude* [1805] XII.202)

For he himself had been nurtured:

> Not with the mean and vulgar works of man,
> But with high objects, with enduring things,
> With life and Nature.                    (*The Prelude* [1805] I.435–7)

But though Wordsworth here aligns himself with the conservative Michael and those 'enduring things', he too found love among the chaos of revolutionary Paris and fathered a child there. Luke may thus represent a vision of what Wordsworth himself may have become if his circumstances had been less favourable.

Without doubt the expanding British cities of the late eighteenth century were becoming awful traps of human despair and degradation. On the other hand, the real cause of Luke's ruin lies not exclusively beneath a distopia of the satanic urban smog. In fact the poem itself foregrounds the father's sterilising character while the dissolute city lies pullulating somewhere distantly off-screen.

A failure of love lies at the heart of Luke's tragedy, but the true responsibility for this rests with his father. Consequently, whatever

Michael's intentions, the unfinished sheepfold unequivocally comes to stand for the unripened relationship between father and son, a reminder of the unfulfilled moment.

In the extract Michael confides 'these are things of which I need not speak' (370). But there are things too whereof we must not remain silent. And love is be one of these. We get a strong impression then that the calamity is as a result of and is a comment upon Michael's own failure of love (or at the very least a failure to speak its name, until too late – and at line 412 he appears to undervalue this 'strength of love'). At that point (i.e. from line 341 on) Michael's copious protestations of paternal love look like a belated loosening of his severity, interfused with frustration and regret, though Wordsworth stops short of making this explicit. This is the true emotional climax to the poem since Luke's fate is really only a working through of the narrative factors.

Nature's objects and spirit have been a great educator of Michael's mind, wisdom and feelings, but he learns too late the need and power of human love, something that nature cannot readily effect (though in *The Prelude* Wordsworth talks of love of nature leading to love of man). The 'tumultuous' brook that opens and closes the poem (and resurfaces in the extract above) acts as a vague apocalyptic warning of this and its boisterous course seems eventually to swallow up and consume all human presence.

## 'The Old Cumberland Beggar'

The eponymous drifter of 'The Old Cumberland Beggar' is one of a series of Wordsworthian portraits of the old and impoverished that includes *Michael*, 'The Last of the Flock', 'The Leech Gatherer' and, from *The Prelude*, 'The Discharged Soldier' (Book IV), and 'The Blind Beggar' (Book VII) episodes. Almost all of them are old, exhausted figures, victims of the time, and all of them exert a haunting persistence on the mind.

'The Old Cumberland Beggar', completed in spring 1798, stems from a gathering campaign – both in literature and in Parliament – to deal with a surge in the numbers of destitute people roaming

Britain's streets and lanes. The war with France combined with the weak/feeble harvests of the mid-1790s had deepened the desperate circumstances of the poor. This was made even worse by rising rural unemployment following increased enclosure and technological developments. Dorothy Wordsworth's journals record with compassion the permanent stream of wayfarers that passed along the roads of the Lake District: pedlars, gypsies, chapmen, discharged soldiers and sailors, beggars and 'crazy folk'. In 1797 a bill was proposed 'for the better Support and Maintenance of the Poor' but it was nowhere near as generous as this may imply.

The gathering debate about the nation's poor was given an extra urgency among the well-off by memories of the recent French Revolution raising the spectre of anarchy. One result was that by the end of the decade a number of hasty stop-gap measures were seized at in a desperate attempt to contain the problem. Among them was the project to expand the provision of the dreaded workhouse. Under this regime any person not able to support him- or herself would be lodged in a communal house and put to largely meaningless (but arduous) physical labour in return for a subsistence living. Worse though was the humiliation attached to this 'remedy', which meant that the system generally acted as a deterrent rather than as a humane solution to the problem of dire poverty.

It is against this perspective that we need to consider Wordsworth's crusading ballad. I have chosen a key extract for close analysis and to use this as a means for discussing the poem as a whole. The passage I have selected consists of the third and fourth sections, focusing first on the itinerant routine of the old man and then on Wordsworth's plea that we recognise the full value of the old man to the community.

> He travels on, a solitary man,
> His age has no companion. On the ground           45
> His eyes are turned, and, as he moves along,
> *They* move along the ground; and evermore,
> Instead of common and habitual sight
> Of fields with rural works, of hill and dale,
> And the blue sky, one little span of earth           50
> Is all his prospect. Thus, from day to day,
> Bowbent, his eyes for ever on the ground,

He plies his weary journey, seeing still,
And never knowing that he sees, some straw,
Some scattered leaf, or marks which, in one track,          55
The nails of cart or chariot wheel have left
Impressed on the white road, in the same line,
At distance still the same. Poor Traveller!
His staff trails with him, scarcely do his feet
Disturb the summer dust, he is so still          60
In look and motion that the cottage curs,
Ere he have passed the door, will turn away
Weary of barking at him. Boys and girls,
The vacant and the busy, maids and youths,
And urchins newly breeched all pass him by:          65
Him even the slow-paced waggon leaves behind.

But deem not this man useless. – Statesmen! ye
Who are so restless in your wisdom, ye
Who have a broom still ready in your hands
To rid the world of nuisances; ye proud,          70
Heart-swoln, while in your pride ye contemplate
Your talents, power, and wisdom, deem him not
A burthen of the earth. 'Tis Nature's law
That none, the meanest of created things,
Of forms created the most vile and brute,          75
The dullest or most noxious, should exist
Divorced from good, a spirit and pulse of good,
A life and soul to every mode of being
Inseparably linked. While thus he creeps
From door to door, the villagers in him          80
Behold a record which together binds
Past deeds and offices of charity
Else unremembered, and so keeps alive
The kindly mood in hearts which lapse of years,
And that half-wisdom half-experience gives          85
Make slow to feel, and by sure steps resign
To selfishness and cold oblivious cares.
Among the farms and solitary huts
Hamlets, and thinly-scattered villages,
Where'er the aged Beggar takes his rounds,          90
The mild necessity of use compels
To acts of love; and habit does the work

Of reason, yet prepares that after joy
Which reason cherishes. And thus the soul,
By that sweet taste of pleasure unpursued                              95
Doth find itself insensibly disposed
To virtue and true goodness. Some there are,
By their good works exalted, lofty minds
And meditative, authors of delight
And happiness, which to the end of time                               100
Will live, and spread, and kindle; minds like these,
In childhood, from this solitary being,
This helpless wanderer, have perchance received,
(A thing more precious far than all that books
Or the solicitudes of love can do!)                                   105
That first mild touch of sympathy and thought,
In which they found their kindred with a world
Where want and sorrow were.

The opening section of the poem is unusual in its close observation of the 'aged beggar' at rest in an actual present moment, scrutinised as he fumbles at scraps and fragments of food. The second section steps back from this particular instant to typify the local's attitude to him, their careful attention to him as he shuffles about on his neighbourhood rounds. By the time we reach the above passage he is a familiar figure, especially in the sense of his almost constant travelling, he 'travels on … moves along … plies his weary journey' (44–53).

In common with other old and impoverished characters Wordsworth emphasises his solitude. He is the archetypal wanderer, doomed for a certain time to roam the wide, wide terrain of Romantic poetry. His fellows are the Ancient Mariner, the Old Man Travelling, the lover/knight in 'Love', the Female Vagrant, Michael and so on. In other Romantic verse there are Keats's Endymion and the knight of 'La Belle Dame san Merci', Byron's Childe Harold and Shelley's Prometheus. Typically the Romantic solitary wanderer highlights the persistence of mortal anguish and indignity, suffers a prolonged nightmare of death-in-life, often as a sinner or as a warning.

Here, though, the old beggar connects with other, specifically Wordsworthian themes: the ordeals and endurance of rural man, his independence and resolution, the persistence of the past, and a sort of alienation, 'a solitary man … no companion' (44–5). But he is

alienated less by social or economic causes than simply by choice and
his ailing faculties, locked within himself,

> seeing still,
> And never knowing that he sees                                    (53–4)

This is the curse of age, the 'landscape to a blind man's eye', just as he
feeds yet cannot hear the 'pleasant melody of birds' (19 and 177).
Among other things, the poem is a plea for the dignity and intrinsic
value of old age.

The old Cumberland beggar is the convergence or personification
of a number of issues. Besides old age and solitude he emblematises
poverty, man in nature, as well as a particular sort of freedom too,
freedom as randomness, or wandering. The above extract stresses
some of the crippling infirmities of age; as well as his weak eyesight,
he is 'Bowbent' (52), and painfully slow (65–6), while his stoop
acquaints his eyes with the ever-present prospect of his grave in the
earth (50–1). Elsewhere he is a clumsy feeder (17), helpless (25), with
'palsied hand' (16), and practically always alone.

In these descriptions Wordsworth's approach is, of course, by way
of the reader's feelings (as in 'Poor Traveller!', l. 58). The realism of
the central figure, the physical context and the political issues are all
sustained by the poem's interest in materialistic data (as well as the
sheer weight of it used to bolster the argument). The poem is pref-
aced by a statement of history and then advances (like *Michael*) in a
quite flat, prosaic style detailing the physicality of the setting: a highway, a structure of rude masonry, huge hill, horses, staff, stone, bag
and so on.

This stratagem continues into the extracted passage and fields
'with rural workers', straw, leaf, nail, wheel, staff, dogs. Even his slow
weary movement has a painful palpability about it. Further, imagery
of scrupulous exactitude is evident: the nail marks from the cart's
wheels (56), the studied descriptions of the old man's dining habits
and the irascible post-boy's efforts to avoid knocking him down.
These are all aspects of a deeper interest with, on the one hand, social
concern (see lines 27, 121 and 148) and, on the other, with constraint
or control (such as 'binds' and 'pent-up', in lines 81 and 173).

These may seem like odd-bedfellows, linking together two such interests, yet on further reflection it is possible to recognise that care and constraint both impact at a deeper level in the narrative on the theme of freedom, but also on the theme of care, the two ideas converging in the important phrase 'to husband up' in line 122 (and note too the many references to the law).

The critic Frances Austin has shown that alternating with this preoccupation with concrete realism is what she sees as Wordsworth's weakness for periphrasis, a tendency to blur the focus (examples are at lines 113 and 183; a similar sort of tension between these two effects also occurs in 'Nutting' and 'Tintern Abbey'). At the same time, and more significantly, this antithesis of effect bears crucially on Wordsworth's attitudes in this poem to 'feel' and 'know', as we shall see.

More of this later. But for now, the opposition of minutely focused realism and periphrasis has another important thematic point. From the perspective of his didactic essay on the beggars of Cumberland (and elsewhere) Wordsworth needs to individualise this particular beggar. To validate his predicament, the reader must be convinced of his existence and to some extent Wordsworth succeeds via the physical detailing and the vivid lyricism of the poem. Equally, though, his lecture relies on generalising from the particular, this old man, to beggars as a class, the target of the proposed legislation. The beggar is both this beggar and all-beggars.

In his 'Advertisement' to the 1798 edition of *Lyrical Ballads* Wordsworth proposed that the test of his poetry was whether or not it contained a 'natural delineation of human passions, human characters, and human incidents', rather than merely conforming to stock figures, or 'pre-established codes of decision' (the conventions of eighteenth-century verse). His portrait of the beggar does indeed achieve a 'natural delineation' chiefly through the convincing physical details of his circumstances and the exceptional responses of the community around him. Although these refer principally to his context they persuade us of his authenticity, along with some incidental impressions such as his 'grey locks' and 'withered face' (169) and his 'palsied hand' (16).

This portrait of a man of the hills, wretched and unaccommodated, harks back over the centuries to Shakespeare's old men, and in his 'one bare circumstance' he looks forward too to Hardy's drifters of the heath such as Diggory Venn of *The Return of the Native*. Like these natural figures, Wordsworth's beggar is an integral element of the natural landscape, seeming to grow out of its very peats and furze.

In spite of this, the old Cumberland beggar appears shadowy, turned away from the reader, just as he is also 'Bowbent'. His face is hidden and we do not hear him speak. He has no name and is generally a passive figure:

> scarcely do his feet
> Disturb the summer dust, he is so still                    (59–60)

He makes so little impact on the scene and merely passes through it, while everything around him, even slow waggons and 'newly breeched urchins' leave him behind, subject 'to the tide of things'. Yet he is real enough, a stubborn persistent presence like a shadow or the stone mounting block serving as his dinner table.

He seems bereft of will power and his life is governed by routine. Wordsworth's impersonal narrative mode holds him off from us, at arm's length, which has the added advantage of stressing his 'vast solitude' (159). This anonymity helps to make him as the old beggar an emblem for all beggars, meeting Wordsworth's other social purpose in the poem: an invective against the folly of the workhouse system. Even though the poem highlights the errant freedom of the beggar, its preamble draws attention to this routine, with its 'stated round' and timetable of 'certain fixed days' for his visits. The many repetitions in the poem are expressive of the monotony and restricted outlook of the beggar's life; for example the recurrence of 'ground' and 'along' in lines 45–7 and the exact repetitions in lines 24 and 44, and 155 and 164.

This narrative of fixed days also serves to underline the rhythm of the tramp's time cycle, somewhere between man's and nature's rounds, not quite either, and a kind of isolation. The extract above is important in drawing attention to the theme of time and the old beggar's equivocal position within it. From his first appearance, time itself is stressed as an important theme – 'an aged beggar' (1) – and he is seldom referred to without the modifier 'aged'. He is surrounded too by metonymic associations of time; from the extract: 'one little span of earth' (50), 'summer dust' (60), while he himself is a 'record' of past deeds (81–2). The poem as a whole is a sort of treatise on the relativity of time with the central image of the 'slow-paced beggar' in orbit through his own diurnal course. He is constantly passing people and being passed by them at different rates or paces in a calculus of changes.

Wordsworth points directly to this relativity of time in the conundrum within lines 22–3:

> Him from childhood have I known, and then
> He was so old, he seems not older now                    (22–3)

A similar tension is set up in the oxymoronic phrase 'he is still / In look and motion' (60–1), and in the high incidence of references to both movement and motionlessness. The tension between change and the fixed order reveals Wordsworth's deeper conservatism and his own 'vital anxiousness' (170), an apocalyptic fear of losing the old order.

Lines 22–3, of course, suggest that although a record of the past, the beggar is old past time, outside of history itself. His orbit passes through all of the seasons (see 33, 50, 55, 167) and yet he appears to defy time. Like the River Wye in 'Tintern Abbey' ('Thou wanderer through the woods', l. 57) he is timeless, left behind and disowned by everything, both the 'vacant and the busy'. But he remains ahead of them all and somehow 'At distance still the same' (58). He is so slow-paced himself, infirm of sight, hearing and health and leaving so slight an impression on the landscape that he might be beyond life already.

Certainly it is Wordsworth's express purpose to present an image of such beggars as an intrinsic, deeply ingrained feature of the rural scene. The switch in voice and tone in line 67 from pastoral lyricism to pulpit pragmatism announces the homily in Wordsworth's historicist reading. His tone, previously honeyed and indulgent, even esteeming towards the beggar, is smartly blunted by the brusque injunction in line 67:

> But deem not this man useless – Statesmen! ye
> Who are so restless in your wisdom

That confrontational 'ye' in the marked final position is repeated, thumped in, over the next four lines, a rhetorical flourish that becomes the distinguishing colophon of this the pulpit section (running from lines 67 to 154). This satire, mounting with each repeated 'ye' – through wisdom, pride, power and wisdom – though clearly impassioned, tends to be undermined by the naive soapbox devices.

At first declamatory and hectoring, this didactic passage soon subsides under the weight of its emotional vigour (round about line 79), becoming a more reasoned essay – though one still based on an over-grandiose image of the heroic tramp. At the core of Wordsworth's reasoning is a distinctly liberal humanistic tone of petition, founded on a belief in a unified mind of nature and mankind, 'That we all of us have one human heart' (146).

John Keats, who famously vilified Wordsworth as the 'egotistical sublime', and repudiated poetry that has 'a palpable design on us', nevertheless had a particular fondness for Wordsworth's humanism in this poem, often quoting one of its key affirmations:

> a spirit and pulse of good,
> A life and soul to every mode of being
> Inseparably linked. (77–9)

Thus 'man is dear to man' (140). The pulpit section is the thematic climax to the poem, piling argument on argument in favour of nature's noble beggars. As well as a treatise on liberty, the poem is a statement of Wordsworth's own politics, hoisting his own early communitarian thesis. Yet it remains paradoxical that he does this by focusing closely on a figure who is himself a solitary, stubbornly impervious to the crusading impulse (and possibly of everything else beyond his 'little span of earth'). Indeed, this amiable roadman might be regarded by everyone else as an idle, selfish parasite – as Wordsworth himself acknowledges, and the rest of the passage sets out to answer these charges as well as the impression that his life is futile or paralysed, hinted at in line 58 and the circularity of his county beat.

We can take a moment to examine here the details of Wordsworth's case for the old beggar. In this regard, the eye is drawn inescapably to line 142 as a clue to Wordsworth's approach here – and in his other verse – in the crucial reference to 'know and feel'. This has cropped up previously, most notably in 'Tintern Abbey' where nature arouses 'joy' but also unites it with 'elevated thoughts' (95–6), nature as 'know and feel'. Having appealed to our feelings, the pity and the endearments in the early part of the poem, he now signals a new tack, using reasoned argument when he refers to the statesmen's 'wisdom' ('statesmen' may refer to politicians or to north country landowners, estate men). In the ensuing lines he sets out to disabuse politicians of the notion that this class of beggar is either a nuisance (70) or a social 'burthen' (73).

After the poem's opening image of a helpless beggar fumbling at his food, Wordsworth's strategy switches to show the toleration of the rural community towards their ancient wanderer as he shuffles along. Their benevolence delineates the limits of his circuit, another sort of 'span', but in doing so also binds the whole community both literally and figuratively (88–90). At the same time we discover another Wordsworthian ideal of this time stemming from within the old man, the unity of being (78). This unifying principle is extended in temporal terms too since, as a living record of the land, he binds 'Past deeds' with the present (81–2). He is both picturesque and useful.

The poem's necessary sense of verisimilitude is bolstered too by its balance of know and feel. However, in the extracted passage, Wordsworth's line of approach becomes more linguistic and rationalistic in its purpose. After hoping to subdue the pride of the 'statesmen' he appeals to 'Nature's law', that all creatures, even the most repellent (75) have some trace of good in them and all creatures are 'inseparably linked' in nature's cosmic unity.

Although line 58 hints at the supposed futility of the beggar's career Wordsworth implores that we 'deem not this man useless' (67). Then he points to his utility. At line 67 the poet's voice and tone modulates, and correspondingly the sound too intensifies the voice: plosive sounds (especially /d/ ) become more conspicuous, replacing the murmuring /s/ and /c/ sounds of the preceding sections. An increase in the frequency of terse monosyllables; for example,

> Of forms created the most vile and brute,
> The dullest or most noxious, should exist
> Divorced from good, a spirit and pulse of good. (75–7)

For a spell too the poem's otherwise intricate syntax becomes less convoluted as the 'feel' of the poem is brought under control of the 'know'.

As in *Michael*, this poem has a number of interesting references to law. Here, though, the object is less to remind us of contractual obligations than to hint at a tightening strain of intimidation and regulation, that eventually crystallises as the threat to the beggars' right to roam. As an ingrained presence on the landscape, close bosom friend of the birds, the 'unpeopled hills' and the highway, the beggar comes within the compass of 'Nature's law' rather than mankind's. This law is that none, not even the 'meanest of created things', should be 'Divorced from good':

> A life and soul to every mode of being
> Inseparably linked.                                    (78–9)

As a son and close ally of nature, he is thus a figure of virtue (and Wordsworth's prayer in the final section makes this more explicit; see lines 165–8). Falling within nature's province also seems to imply that he operates beyond man's laws as proposed in the reforms to the Poor Law.

Line 160 suggests a connection with yet another legal system, an extension of this idea of his moral rectitude:

> let him bear about
> The good which the benignant law of heaven
> Has hung around him.                                (159–61)

The law of heaven takes up the reference to him as a 'spirit and pulse of good' (77), now implying the synthesis of soul and body, heaven and earth, spirit and matter. The suggestion that he comes under heaven's law – prior to man's of course – is endorsed by Wordsworth's later revision to line 80 where he inserted the statement that any man with a 'heaven-regarding eye' could be cast out of view 'Without offence to God' (line 84). Deference to God's law is further supported by the poem's religious diction: the Decalogue, soul, blessing, and 'hope in heaven'. All of these references and hints conjure up and sustain the impression of the ascetic old beggar as an errant mendicant friar exuding virtue and love (see line 152) and of Wordsworth as a man of the elevated pulpit administering pious orisons (see lines 134 and 155).

In January 1801 Wordsworth wrote to a real statesman with his pressing anxieties about the workhouse provision in rural communities. Sending a copy of *Lyrical Ballads* to Charles James Fox, he drew attention to some of the poems that touched on the issue. As a Whig politician – later the Prime Minister – Fox might have been expected to oppose the greater use of workhouses, or 'Houses of Industry', on grounds of compassion. But Wordsworth's case is based on his view that the social fabric of the working class was now being undermined by expanding industrialisation and heavy taxation (to finance the war with France). In addition to the deepening poverty brought about by these factors, he argued that the palliatives adopted – chiefly the workhouse – actually made matters worse by diminishing the strong sense of personal independence among workers and by splitting up their families:

> In the mean time parents are separated from their children, and children from their parents; the wife no longer prepares with her own hands a meal for her husband, the produce of his labour; there is little doing in his house in which his affections can be interested, and but little left in it in which he can love.   (14 January 1801)

As we might have expected, Wordsworth champions the upland poor as a particularly desperate case for attention (he also drew Fox's attention to *Michael* to illustrate this). Fox eventually replied, somewhat obliquely, and indicating that he did not care for blank verse, he preferred 'When we are seven' and 'The Idiot Boy'.

Returning to the poem, line 28 introduces a third kind of law, the 'moral law', and it is within a broad concept of justice that Wordsworth insists on the responsibilities of the community towards the homeless. Indicative of this is the poem's overt references to morality, but also to the idea of being constrained (for example, 'binds' and 'pent-up' in lines 81 and 173) – a clear contrast with the beggars' manifest liberty. He charges that while the politicians desire to restrict this 'happy wanderer' they themselves remain unconstrained, 'restless' (68). The dreaded outcome is again the disruption of the natural order of the society, symbolised in the extract by the binary image of the free movement of a wheel lodged in the runnel of its own habitual use (lines 55–6).

The anonymity accorded the aged beggar by Wordsworth permits him to be located in a variety of spheres of being. But, above all, it is in the view of the beggar as a man of the community that the poet hazards his case. His arguments – the 'know' of the poem – tend to come over as clouded by the overdone political rhetoric; see from line 67 on in the extract. As well as driving a firm wedge into the pastoral lyricism of the poem, the bombast here weakens the very points that the rhetoric seeks to promote.

We (as the statesmen) are entreated to spare such beggars, on the grounds that they are harmless, neither a 'nuisance' nor a 'burthen' to others (though Wordsworth's deliberate protestations ironically imply that they are). Far from being a social encumbrance they are, so Wordsworth asks us to believe, a positive benefit to it. This is of course quite an ironic, mischievous twist, suggesting that by making themselves an object of neighbourhood donations they are in fact being charitable to it!

The first stage of Wordsworth's argument comes in the second section of the poem, beginning 'Him from childhood' (22), where we see the beggar's good influence on three others, causing them to act out of character. The horseman leans carefully down with his cash donation, the toll-keeper makes a special effort to open the gates, and the irrascible Post-boy makes an abnormal detour around the deaf old man. Another important political element is that the beggar does not actually solicit alms but simply makes himself available for local disbursements, thus playing down the nuisance charge.

However, Wordsworth foregrounds the old man's chief contribution as a teacher. He is in fact a figure of nature (of the 'unpeopled hills' and the 'small mountain birds'). For the poet his educative function is simply an extension of nature's. This sort of role is also played by the 'frugal dame' of 'Nutting' (and see *The Prelude* [1805], IV, 55). Yet here the process of nurture is quite implicit, accidental even, indicated by Wordsworth's periphrastic terms 'some' and 'perchance':

> minds like these,
> In childhood, from this solitary being,

This helpless wanderer, have perchance received ...
That first mild touch of sympathy and thought          (101–6)

He is an educator too of the 'unlettered villagers', prompting them
to 'tender offices and pensive thoughts' (163). By a devious somer-
sault, his lowly station actually raises the dignity of these untutored
bucolics and, in the process, he elevates himself above them as a
presence of no trivial influence on these good people's lives.

The passage argues many such instances of his conducive magnet-
ism. We have noted already how he 'creeps / From door to door'
performing as a living archive of 'Past deeds and offices of charity'
(82), binding the present to a mythical past more enlightened and
gracious towards its tramps, signifying a golden age more expansive
and magnanimous to mankind as a whole. He is a 'silent monitor' too
(115), a litmus paper of society's humanity, its conscience.

As if to shame its reader, the above extract strives to connect
people, times and places in the manner of the tramp himself. Even
the 'easy' rich may benefit since, in a perverse sort of way, his own
poverty points up their affluence, 'peculiar boons' (118) – and ''tis no
vulgar service'. But the wise and educated have profited from his
magisterial influence while charitable individuals (line 98) may have
been initially prompted through encounters with such needy persons

In which they found their kindred with a world
Where want and sorrow were.          (107–8)

Unless the beggars and others are allowed to roam free, society may
be reduced to the brutish Burkean misery of 'selfishness and cold
oblivious cares' (87). The poor, too, as represented by the old man,
partake of charitable acts emblematised by the crumbs cascading
down to the small waiting birds (lines 18–19; a useful comparison
here is with Wordsworth's poem 'I know an aged man', which focuses
on the inmate of a workhouse).

In the heart of society's corpus, Wordsworth feels and knows, is a
matrix of love, 'virtue and true goodness' (97). The lyrical sections at
the start and finish of the poem illustrate that local folk readily
accommodate the beggar, it is only the 'restless' politicians and land-
lords who raise objections. The old man acts as the bonding mortar

of the community. In yet another irony of the poem, he is instrumental in binding the 'farms and solitary huts / Hamlets, and thinly scattered villages' (88–9).

Wordsworth's central thrust is that, as the Fox letter suggests, it is charity that holds together the community. His argument in the extract above is essentially that, without the possibility of love, charitable acts and even the fundamental idea of community itself would break down. He 'compels / To acts of love' (91–2) and he exhorts the 'statesmen' to do likewise.

Is this the 'blind love' of Michael again? I think the answer must be yes because those 'acts of love' are not the result of reason or deliberation ('unpursued'; 95) but of unthinking habit or tradition. Yet, later, reason may be seen to sanction these acts of kindness and love, leading to further virtues (see 91–7), suggesting that impulse or deeply ingrained 'feel' is prior to and more steadfast than reason or 'know'. However, in the final analysis, Wordsworth would like to argue that love unites both elements, thus dispelling their apparent dissonance. The aged, anonymous figure transcends the two:

> The mild necessity of use compels
> To acts of love                                                    (91–2)

### 'The Fountain'

'The Fountain' is one of a group of 'Matthew' poems in *Lyrical Ballads* that have as their central figure a wise old man based in part on William Taylor, Wordsworth's former head teacher at Hawkshead Grammar School, who enthusiastically encouraged pupils to compose as well as to study poetry. Wordsworth later claimed that Matthew is, in effect, a composite of several early teachers and, viewed across the range of 'Matthew' poems, he does emerge as a quite complex figure. In addition to 'The Fountain', the 'Matthew' poems in *Lyrical Ballads* include 'Lines written on a tablet', 'The Two April Mornings', 'Expostulation and Reply' and 'The Tables Turned' (which is discussed in Chapter 5; see also *The Prelude*, 1805, X. 489–514), where Wordsworth visits Taylor's grave).

**The Fountain**
**A CONVERSATION**

We talked with open heart, and tongue
Affectionate and true,
A pair of Friends, though I was young,
And Matthew seventy-two.

We lay beneath a spreading oak,                    5
Beside a mossy seat,
And from the turf a fountain broke,
And gurgled at our feet.

'Now, Matthew, let us try to match
This water's pleasant tune                         10
With some old border-song, or catch
That suits a summer's noon.

Or of the church-clock and the chimes
Sing here beneath the shade,
That half-mad thing of witty rhyme                 15
Which you last April made!'

In silence Matthew lay, and eyed
The spring beneath the tree;
And thus the dear old man replied,
The grey-haired man of glee.                       20

'Down to the vale this water steers,
How merrily it goes!
'Twill murmur on a thousand years,
And flow as now it flows.

And here, on this delightful day,                  25
I cannot chuse but think
How oft, a vigorous man, I lay
Beside this fountain's brink.

My eyes are dim with childish tears,
My heart is idly stirred,                          30
For the same sound is in my ears,
Which in those days I heard.

Thus fares it still in our decay:
And yet the wiser mind

Mourns less for what age takes away                               35
Than what it leaves behind.

The blackbird in the summer trees,
The lark upon the hill
Let loose their carols when they please,
Are quiet when they will.                                         40

With Nature never do *they* wage
A foolish strife; they see
A happy youth, and their old age
Is beautiful and free:

But we are pressed by heavy laws,                                 45
And often, glad no more,
We wear a face of joy, because
We have been glad of yore.

If there is one who need bemoan
His kindred laid in earth,                                        50
The household hearts that were his own,
It is the man of mirth.

My days, my friend, are almost gone,
My life has been approved,                                        55
And many love me, but by none
Am I enough beloved.'

'Now both himself and me he wrongs,
The man who thus complains!
I live and sing my idle songs
Upon these happy plains,                                          60

And, Matthew, for thy children dead
I'll be a son to thee!'
At this he grasped his hands, and said,
'Alas! that cannot be.'

We rose from the fountain-side,                                   65
And down the smooth descent
Of the green sheep-track did we glide,
And through the wood we went,

And, ere we came to Leonard's Rock,
He sang those witty rhymes                                        70

> About the crazy old church-clock
> And the bewildered chimes.

In his Preface to the 1802 edition of *Lyrical Ballads* Wordsworth reflected that Matthew was one of his 'less impassioned' individuals. Yet he is no less complex for his phlegmatic nature. In addition to encompassing a number of different sources Matthew (and the poem itself) operates on a multiplicity of levels: literally an old man on an afternoon stroll, he also figures as teacher, poet, sage and mage, personification of old age, the father, the son and a ghost too. With the sudden appearance of the spring at his feet he might suggest the person of Moses – or perhaps even the Deity. The short poem also hints at different humours: from silent repose at the start, to 'glee' (20) and 'tears' (29), to resignation (59) and perhaps enervation (64).

The opening stanza of the poem announces Wordsworth's continuing interest in the dialogue of youth and age, and the possibility of forging links between the two standings:

> We talked with open heart ... (1)

As we noted of the old Cumberland beggar the old man is a projection of Wordsworth himself in old age, just as 'Nutting' and 'There was a Boy' are remodellings of his youth (indicatively Wordsworth placed 'Nutting' immediately after 'The Fountain' in the second edition of *Lyrical Ballads*). Matthew, himself a poet, is a composer of 'witty rhymes' (15 and 70) and so makes an entelechy of Wordsworth's future self, a perception of what may be, a future about which the boy seeks some assurance.

The opening lines are also keen to insist on the honesty between the 'friends', with 'open heart', 'Affectionate and true'. The simple metonymic elements of line 1 are echoed by the apparent simplicity of diction and the frankness of the ballad measure. At the same time, a highly regular metre is echoed in the short and direct phrase structures, usually occupying one or two lines only. Taken together these elements reinforce a sense of freshness in the poem's meditations, as well as an idea of candidness, though occasionally the strictness of the ABAB rhyme scheme tends to strain the composure of its syntax.

The 'spreading oak' (5) connects us with that 'old oak', the Clipping Tree, of *Michael* (179) and with it the usual associations of great age and sturdiness, even of Englishness, apply here. Accordingly and inevitably, we are invited then to see the gurgling fountain as the complementary trope for youth. Although the fountain operates as a more complex symbol, we can note the familiar Wordsworthian dualism developing from the outset: Matthew as reticent, oak, static, stable, father, synchronic; the youth as provoker, stream, dynamic, restless, son, diachronic.

So languid is Matthew that he must be stirred from his oaken torpor, to be prodded into open life. The second stanza hints at ideas of movement and release from this with 'spreading' (5) and 'gurgled' (8). The poem too begins in a sort of rootedness ('We lay') and it is after the youthful poet's arresting 'Now' (9) that it moves forward to emulate the fountain itself by its flow: in the final stanzas the pair are united in a 'smooth descent' through the woods to St Leonard's Rock. Wordsworth's rousing 'Now' also jerks the old man into the present moment with some youthful urgency.

As the youth, Wordsworth appears desperate to stir the old man back into conscious life. To this end he tricks Matthew into one of the 'old songs' (11) and the puns on 'catch' in the same line draws attention to this ploy (as well as to the theme of holding back). The youth's 'catch' is to bring the old teacher to life by recapturing the past. 'Spring' in line 18 is also, of course, another important pun, whose sense of sudden release is a counter to 'catch'. Spring and catch are modalities that also recall 'Nutting' and *Michael*. Importantly it points us to the possibility of renewal (both as the fountain and, conventionally, the season) a possibility that is momentarily realised in lines 31–2.

Time is a high-profile theme in the poem, with a plethora of allusions to transience and decay, as well as to infinity and immortality. A strong awareness, a 'vital anxiousness' for the transience of youth and even of life itself, ripples beneath the surface. In the early part of the poem Wordsworth dallies with allusions and half hints: summer, the church-clock and the chimes, April, spring, old man, grey-haired, a thousand years. The dear old man is history but apart from the biographical details (which Wordsworth warned would elucidate nothing in the poem) the poem is not historicised by context, as *Michael* and 'The Old Cumberland Beggar' are. It is timeless and yet Wordsworth keeps tugging it back from immortal universals to a particular place and moment:

And here, on this delightful day. (25)

The particular moment, however, carries with it presages of death – 'We lay' (5), 'In silence Matthew' (17), 'I lay' (27). Like 'The Two April Mornings', this poem moves back and forward across time to link together different moments. So, in stanza 7 Matthew's memory connects with himself as a young man, a 'vigorous man', as Wordsworth is now 'Beside this fountain's brink' (28). The word 'brink' points to the frailty of the mortal form but also to the idea of his having recently reached early manhood, a threshold filled with 'vital anxiousness', seeking to link, to unify the Matthew of that moment with the Wordsworth of this.

I mentioned above that the opening to 'The Fountain' tries to urge simplicity and honesty. Yet this appeal actually belies the opposites of these virtues – complexity and deceit – that are strong matters in the poem. The surface ingenuousness confers the impression that the poem tries to shun figurative language. However, this is partly because we have become so familiar with Wordsworth's dual system of real and metaphorical mountains, fountains, gurgling streams, groves, sturdy old oaks and baffling piles of rocks. Natural materials do double service: on the literal level and as gateways onto the figurative other worlds of a symbolic domain. It is also in part the result of Wordsworth's brilliantly adroit phrasing that readily coaxes and controls the poem's semantics, opening and directing its effects. Thus, in the sixth stanza, the personification of the spring surprises with a transitive verb

Down to the vale this water steers (21)

At this point, 'steers' is a bold stroke, but then we recall that this man (Matthew) is renowned for his 'witty rhymes', his half-mad songs with their 'catches' like body swerves.

One such body-swerving catch comes in his famous (and witty) crux in the ninth stanza,

> Thus fares it still in our decay:
> And yet the wiser mind
> Mourns less for what age takes away                    (35)
> Than what it leaves behind.

The item 'still' teasingly takes up 'idly' and 'lay' from the previous stanza, momentarily blocking the forceful spring, flowing but 'leaves behind' in its course. However, 'decay' is a hard thought, imposing a sudden thematic blockage on the rising mood.

Humans have memory and the trace of the past weighs heavy upon them. This is what age 'leaves behind' for us, unlike for those birds in the tenth stanza, and the rest of nature, free from 'foolish strife' (42). 'The Two April Mornings' is the very illustration of the grief of memory when Matthew recalls the life of his daughter, but also in Wordsworth's recall of the life of Matthew and the sorrow of loss. Yet where 'The Two April Mornings' is the bright illustration, 'The Fountain' is the metaphysics that precedes and underpins it.

Memory is what age leaves behind. It is important to remember, though, that because memory is the storehouse of the past it is the accumulated culture of that past. As the old Cumberland beggar and Michael (and the Leech Gatherer too) also demonstrate. The boy here, as a kind of wizard's apprentice, conjures up the ancient grey-beard magus, a Merlin figure of wisdom and knowledge, the syn-thesis of bookish and natural learning. Having, in stanzas 10 and 11, apparently discoursed with nature itself he now passes on his insights.

In this respect Matthew might usefully be compared with the 'frugal dame' of 'Nutting', the adjacent poem in this volume. She is an adjunct of Matthew's schooling (she is the boy's house matron) and gives 'advice / And exhortation' (9–10) and after disguising him as a humble beggar, initiates him into the mysteries of nature and he hears – as here too – the murmuring of the brook. The label 'frugal dame' connotes a pas-toral divinity, and a natural teacher. In the fourth stanza of 'The Tables Turned' Matthew urges the boy to quit his books and:

> Let Nature be your teacher                              (16)

but as a school teacher too he really is the fusion of two camps: Rousseau's affective and experiential learning theory with the eigth-teenth century's fixation with bookish rationalism.

Having conjured up Matthew as magus, the youth seeks guarantees about the future and old age. As in 'Ode: Intimations of Immortality' his 'vital anxiousness' seeks some reassurance about mortality and a straw of hope before 'Shades of the prison house' begin to close in on his youth. His 'obstinate questionings', in effect, pursue forbidden knowledge and Matthew's subtly eminent response is less to do with nostalgia or mourning the past or even the complex sorrow of the twelfth stanza. His sober revelation is that old age does bring the prized fulfilment and rest from strife. The boy must look to nature for wisdom, the hidden or arcane wisdom, and then at the end of the poem the old artificer leads the youth away through a sort of sacred grove to descend to the Dantesque underworld.

Unlike natural creatures mankind is 'pressed by heavy laws' (45). This too is hard. On a fairly simply level these heavy laws mean, of course, that we do not have the same freedom as the birds (which 'Let loose their carols when they please', l. 39) or of the merrily wander-ing stream (compare 'Tintern Abbey's 'wanderer through the woods', l. 57). Their old age is 'beautiful and free' (44), while we are oppressed and 'cannot chuse' (l. 26; a phrase repeated from 'Expostulation and Reply', l. 7).

This fatalism or 'prison house' of what we are, the given of what it is to be human, is the downside of our exquisite capacity for reason, for art, beauty and the affections. Yes, the birds are free but essentially dim-witted. Our lot is, on the one hand, of mercurial sensitivity but, on the other, the fever and the fret of strife, and the best we can do is 'wear a face of joy' (47).

Thus an important aspect of our 'heavy laws', Matthew argues, is that we are highly complex entities. With the birds what you see is what you get: they cannot do or be otherwise. Their motive is embodied in their actions. But to be human is to be capable of concealment and deception, to wear a mask. Matthew appears a 'man of glee' (20) with a 'face of joy' (47), but this is only an outward show based on a memory of how things were ('yore', l. 48). Old age is char-acterised by what life leaves behind, the curse of a vivid and inescapable consciousness of the past, a constant reminder that the best is now behind. Accordingly, our motives are less rooted in the immediate than in a variety of other circumstances: the past, the need to present a good face, our awareness of mortality in 'decay', even our awareness of this awareness. And 'heavy' refers not only to the oppressive, inescapability of these 'laws', but also as much to the 'gravitas' of them.

As an old man Matthew's position endows him with a clarity of vision. From his grey eminence he is able to gaze back at the whole span of a life. Like Michael, his wisdom bestows on him a clarity of vision, gained in part through the hard knocks of life, especially (in Matthew's case) the grief from having 'kindred laid in earth' (50). The social mask he wears is also intended to conceal this along with the pessimism that his great age has wrought on him.

At the same time, the face that he prepares for the faces that he meets has something of deception about it. In the Matthew poems as a group, the youth strives to penetrate this, to reach beneath the mask and arrive at the truth of a life not yet lived. Matthew's replies are of course terse and highly sophistic. In the middle section (stanzas 9–14, which Coleridge considered to be amongst Wordsworth's finest poetry) he talks on metaphysics in a riddling, most allusive language: for example the catch in lines 35–6 and again in stanzas 12 and 13. So the 'man of mirth' may wear a 'face of joy'.

As sage Matthew comes across as a sound authority on human psychology, identifying its strife and heavy laws, the tribulations of retirement, the lack of love in the world, while he sings of Nature's different lore and concocts witty rhymes. For the young man he is both memory and future. His revelations, however, are riddling, in spite of the petition for frankness in the opening lines.

By the fourteenth stanza, Matthew seems to have become abstracted, distrait, as his reflective metaphysics turn him inwardly to his personal memories. He has not given the youth the knowledge of age – and indeed now adds another puzzlingly wily rhyme. His reference to 'friend' in line 54 echoes the youth's in line 3, thereby saluting their special intimacy, open-hearted, no longer divided as teacher and pupil (though Wordsworth is still the acolyte).

On the other hand, stanza 14 focuses on a kind of failure of friendship. His days 'almost gone' Matthew speaks of his life having been 'approved'. This could mean that his life is now completed, reached its allotted span. But, more likely I think, is that it is self-critical, in fact suggesting Matthew's lack of fulfilment, having become merely acceptable. And then we have the second riddle of the stanza

> And many love me, but by none
> Am I enough beloved. (56–7)

This sounds like a sort of pass at the young man, perhaps to prompt the youth's disavowal or affirmation that we do all love him. It also implies Matthew's despair at not having touched sufficient lives. The hint of homosexuality lingers too: two male friends supine on the grass talking of their love one for the other. Another, equally likely contingency is that the poem expresses Wordsworth's own guilt that he did not adequately love or articulate his love for this father-figure while he was still alive.

On the surface at least, however, they are united. The opening to the poem points to their correspondence, youth and age coalescing. Memory too acts like this here: Matthew's own youth is remembered and made present, as the man also prefigures once more Wordsworth's putative future. Times past, present and future overlap, implying the eternity of generations.

This theme is succinctly and brilliantly expressed in 'The Rainbow' (1802), which ends with

> The Child is father of the Man:
> And I could wish my days to be
> Bound each to each by natural piety. (7–9)

This snippet also forms the proem to Wordsworth's mighty 'Ode: Intimations of Immortality' (1802–6) and to direct its reader to the consolation that our mortal lives are set in an eternal sea of immortality and also that the 'babe' is bound in with 'palsied Age' through a continuous dialectic.

This theme of securing a link between youth and age becomes a central and enduring issue of Wordsworth's whole work. This challenge lies at the core of his great masterwork *The Prelude* and it is a major interest in *Michael* and 'Resolution and Independence'. The 'Lucy' poems too focus on this idea, but equally expose the obstacles (as we saw in 'We are seven', for instance). In 'The Fountain' the connection is symbolised in the figure of the timeless fountain/stream gurgling at their feet, transcending their differences to murmur on for 'a thousand years' (l. 23 and again striking a comparison with the Wye in 'Tintern Abbey').

When the youth/Wordsworth replies to Matthew in stanza 15, his words endeavour to stress the unity of their relationship, 'both himself and me'. Yet the poem as a whole claims a more realistic tone by foregrounding the difference and its strife. Although Matthew has the natural piety that might bind his days in harmony, he is prominent too in revealing the strife intrinsic to human existence (implicit in our 'heavy laws'). This point is reflected in the poem's many dichotomies: silence and sound, youth and age, freedom and causation, stillness and movement, rising and falling, vigour and decay.

The old man's realist rejection of Wordsworth's filial offer is a sombre acknowledgement of life's tensions and he eschews simplistic remedy. This echoes a similar moment in 'The Two April Mornings', when he rejects the possibility of the blooming girl as a replacement for his dead daughter and 'did not wish her mine' (56). The youth's offer also foregrounds the discomfort of Matthew having survived his children. It thus emphasises the loss of immortality that offspring conventionally represent (compare 'Lucy Gray') and also the irrecoverability of Matthew's youth in all but memory. It is a necessary, if painful, rejection and it leaves the young Wordsworth having neither youth nor age but, as it were, in limbo.

If we accept Wordsworth's juxtaposition of these two Matthew poems as representing a chronological sequence, then significantly Matthew is already dead by the start of 'The Fountain' – as he was in 'The Two April Mornings',

> Matthew is in his grave, yet now
> Methinks I see him stand ...     ('The Two April Mornings', 57–8)

If, methinks, he is already dead in 'The Fountain' then this presence instils this poem too with an uncanny ghostly supernatural feeling in which Matthew is again recovered by memory. Another literary figure who sees fatherly ghosts is, of course, Hamlet in a play of filial piety, the son striving to be atoned with the father:

> And, Matthew, for thy children dead
> I'll be a son to thee!' ('The Fountain', 61–2)

The poem's the thing, and while Matthew is perhaps more akin to King Lear (another loser of daughters) he appears to Wordsworth to offer some provocative metaphysics by transcending to the mysterious bourn of nature. The youth had previously breathed life into Matthew, reviving him briefly as the old man acknowledges in line 30:

> My heart is idly stirred

and talks of his 'decay' in line 33. In line 59 the youth takes up once more the word 'idle' that perhaps hints at Hamlet in his malaise of indeterminacy, depending on Matthew for fatherly direction. Line 62 comes on suddenly in histrionic despair and brings the moment to its crisis, resulting in the dispelling of the ghostly king:

> for thy children dead
> I'll be a son to thee! (61–2)

They rise as one and the youth hears the old man's voice again singing his witty, crazy rhymes and catches (with overtones of Ophelia here too) and a noble father lost.

## Conclusions

All three of the poems discussed in this chapter have illustrated well the strong humanitarian tendency in Wordsworth's early verse. In showing his compassion for the social predicament and age of his particular characters, these poems also reveal his support for the values that they represent and incorporate, particularly fortitude, loyalty, humility, and the propriety of a hard physical existence.

At the same time, these poems demonstrate people living in close unity with a harsh upland environment that has inspired a strong sense of community. In this context Wordsworth is eager to bring home what he sees as the impending calamity for the rural scene to be brought about by pernicious changes in land tenure and industrial technology, threatening to destroy the traditional relationship between the people and the land.

Against this background of instability and hardship Wordsworth argues for the dignity, freedom and intrinsic worth of old age. However, he also uses the theme of age to extend and explore his familiar concerns with nature and human mortality, and to establish a dialogue between youth and age so as to draw out and clarify his own relationship to both.

## Further Research

Contemporary with 'The Fountain' is another of the Matthew poems, 'The Two April Mornings', and you will find it valuable to examine this poem in terms of the portrait of old age presented there. In particular, try to assess the symbolic function in the poem of Matthew's deceased daughter. What is the dramatic effect of the final stanza?

# 4

## Social Issues: 'the mean and vulgar works of man'

> A time there was, ere England's griefs began,
> When every rood of ground maintained its man;
> For him light labour spread her wholesome store,
> Just gave what life required, but gave no more:
> His best companions, innocence and health;
> And his best riches, ignorance of wealth.
>   But times are altered: trade's unfeeling train
> Usurp the land and dispossess the swain
>       (Oliver Goldsmith, *The Deserted Village*, 1770)

Wordsworth is often and popularly thought of as a 'nature poet', one whose primary concern is scenery, the mountains, rills and ghylls, wandering clouds and, of course, those daffodils. But the poet himself always regarded his true subject matter as the study of mankind itself.

His one-time ally William Hazlitt makes this focus clear in an essay of 1825. With thinly disguised irony his article sneers at the 'levelling' idealism that had motivated *Lyrical Ballads*,

> It partakes of, and is carried along with, the revolutionary movement of our age: the political changes of the day were the model on which he formed and conducted his poetical experiments. His Muse ... is a levelling one. It proceeds on a principle of equality, and strives to reduce all things to the same standard. ... He takes a subject or a story

merely as pegs or loops to hang thought and feeling on; the incidents
are trifling.    (Hazlitt, *The Spirit of the Age*, 1825)

We have already encountered something of Wordsworth's concern
and compassion for the poor, the dispossessed, beggars and vulnerable groups in Georgian England. Chapter 6 describes the political
and social background of that society about the time of the publication of *Lyrical Ballads*, and you may find it useful to read that chapter
alongside this one.

In this chapter I would like to examine in detail Wordsworth's
treatment of the effects of social conditions on family and community life, the relationship between the individual and his or her
community, and in broader terms his condemnation of social injus-
tices. The chapter will focus on three poems: 'The Convict', 'The
Female Vagrant' and 'The Thorn'.


## 'The Convict'

### The Convict

The glory of evening was spread through the west;
    On the slope of a mountain I stood,
While the joy that precedes the calm season of rest
    Rang loud through the meadow and wood.

'And must we then part from a dwelling so fair?'        5
    In the pain of my spirit I said,
And with a deep sadness I turned, to repair
    To the cell where the convict is laid.

The thick-ribbed walls that o'ershadow the gate
    Resound; and the dungeons unfold:        10
I pause; and at length, through the glimmering grate,
    That outcast of pity behold.

His black matted head on his shoulder is bent,
    And deep is the sigh of his breath,
And with steadfast dejection his eyes are intent        15
    On the fetters that link him to death.

'Tis, sorrow enough on that visage to gaze,
    That body dismissed from his care;
Yet my fancy has pierced to his heart, and portrays
    More terrible images there.          20

His bones are consumed, and his life-blood is dried,
    With wishes the past to undo;
And his crime, through the pains that o'erwhelm him, descried,
    Still blackens and grows on his view.

When from the dark synod, or blood-reeking field,        25
    To his chamber the monarch is led,
All soothers of sense their soft virtue shall yield,
    And quietness pillow his head.

But if grief, self-consumed, in oblivion would doze,
    And conscience her tortures appease,        30
'Mid tumult and uproar this man must repose;
    In the comfortless vault of disease.

When his fetters at night have so pressed on his limbs,
    That the weight can no longer be borne,
If, while a half-slumber his memory bedims,        35
    The wretch on his pallet should turn,

While the jail-mastiff howls at the dull clanking chain,
    From the roots of his hair there shall start
A thousand sharp punctures of cold-sweating pain,
    And terror shall leap at his heart.        40

But now he half-raises his deep-sunken eye,
    And the motion unsettles a tear;
The silence of sorrow it seems to supply,
    And asks of me why I am here.

'Poor victim! no idle intruder has stood        45
    'With o'erweening complacence our state to compare,
'But one, whose first wish is the wish to be good,
    'Is come as a brother thy sorrows to share.

'At thy name though compassion her nature resign,
    'Though in virtue's proud mouth thy report be a stain,     50
'My care, if the arm of the mighty were mine,
    'Would plant thee where yet thou might'st blossom again.'

Wordsworth's 'The Convict', probably written in 1796, first appeared in the *Morning Post* in December of the following year over the signature 'Mortimer', perhaps as a filler to meet Coleridge's contractual obligations to that paper (this was the signature that Coleridge himself frequently used for his verse there). At this time, convicts, dungeons and other issues of social injustice were highly fashionable topics in the popular verse of 1790s magazines, sporting such titles as 'On the Necessity of Solitary Confinement in Gaols' (1792), 'The Prisoner's Lamentation' (1795), 'The Female Convict' (1797). Such poetry was the literary extension of an intense public debate on the appalling conditions in English jails and 'houses of correction', rousing readers' consciences and emotions on the divisive question of prison reform.

Wordsworth's satire clearly originates from within the reformist stream of this current. Yet while indulging in some of the stock emotional reactions he also seeks to steer it into something of his own thematic direction. The poem works in at least three different ways: it is a straightforward plea for penal reform, it is a sort of Gothic romance and, giving some piquancy to these two, it is also an allegory of human mortality.

The poem's induction sets up a contrast between natural repose and freedom, and the horrors of the works of man, the jail. From the peaks of natural joy in the first stanzas, the mood abruptly plummets as Wordsworth confronts his instinctive reluctance to visit the convict. The word 'repair' in line 7 ironically anticipates and satirises the final thoughts of stanza 13: 'joy' becomes 'pain' (6), 'mountain' turns into 'deep' (7) while the free 'dwelling' sinks to the awful 'cell' (8).

In a Dantesque move the third stanza takes us into hell, via an obscure gate, through a gloomy cave of 'thick-ribbed walls', leading at last to the dejected and bent outcast. In claustral despair, lingering has become languishing. Such stark confinement is a grimmer empathic variation on Wordsworth's own remembered incarcerations, including 'Tintern Abbey's 'lonely rooms' (26) and the 'hermit's cave' and we might also include here the graves in the Lucy poems. Wordsworth identifies human mortality as a sort of jail sentence: in his powerful 'Ode: Intimations of Immortality', too, Wordsworth explicitly links human mortality and 'Shades of the prison house'.

Both 'The Convict' and the 'Immortality Ode' tap into an awful despondency of despair, though it is fair to say that in the former his approach is a more emotional one. Nevertheless the convict is 'outcast of pity' (12), dismissed of hope, except for the glimmer held out by Wordsworth's visit. The otherwise absoluteness of this convict's predicament is vividly tricked out in the words 'deep', 'sigh' and 'steadfast' – as well as by the more theatrical 'black matted head' and 'fetters'.

Among the poem's other key words is 'memory' and, although it does not actually appear explicitly until line 35, its significance is already felt by the third stanza. Here the convict is plagued by a twofold sting of memory: like the Ancient Mariner permanently cursed by the memory of his crime (stanza 6) and, again like the Mariner, he is beset by the prospect of oblivion. Given that in the eighteenth century common prisoners were generally locked up for life and abandoned to starvation and disease, the picture of the 'outcast of pity' in a 'comfortless vault of disease' (32) is understating the horrible reality. In addition to the 'thick-ribbed walls', howling mastiff and physical confinement, the convict is inescapably interned within the mental torment of irredeemable guilt.

As we might expect, the theme of confinement is deepened by claustral imagery and ideas: cell, overshadow, grate, fetters, o'erwhelm and pressed. Wordsworth's strategy in drawing these out is to broaden the poem with overtones of coercion and subjection. For example, stanza 6 hints at fate and this is taken up later, in line 45, with the ironically weighted reversal of the man as the 'Poor victim'.

The 'fetters that link him to death' (16) is more than a figurative nod at mortality and the prison house, and connects with other fetters and constraints in Wordsworth: Michael's irrevocable 'covenant' and his commitment to familial destiny, 'The Old Cumberland Beggar's theme of our being 'inseparably linked' – as well as numerous forces to chasten and subdue mankind with ties of family, morality, nature and social conscience. In Rousseau's words, mankind is 'born free, and he is everywhere in chains'.

Ironically, as the poet enters the labyrinth, the dungeon begins to 'unfold' (10). And then 'I pause' produces the poem's first moment of drama – the words themselves draw attention to the caesura that heightens the moment. As a whole the poem has a marked textuality and self-awareness that place the poet both within yet also outside the poem's events as though observing himself (as *he* observes the prisoner). For example, the numerous repetitions: 'stood' (2 and 45), 'pain' (6 and 23), 'turn' (7 and 36), 'heart' (19 and 40) and 'head' (13 and 28); 'deep', 'blood', 'care', 'consumed', 'wish', 'fetters' and 'sorrow' are all repeated. There are correlatives too: yield and resign (27 and 29), rest and repose (3 and 31) and quietness and silence (28 and 43). These echo through the poem with an eerie chiming effect while the straitness of the diction is in accord with the poem's central theme. On the other hand, Wordsworth freely sets up strong and explicit contrasts ('our state to compare', 46), for conflict and tension but also to help to define one state through the 'other' or to firmly confine the focus; for instance, light and shade (stanzas 1 and 3), king and convict (stanzas 7 and 9), silence and noise (stanzas 7 and 8).

The second sensation of the poem comes at the end of stanza 4. The labyrinthine syntax of the stanza eventually unravels into the melodrama of its final line, and:

> the fetters that link him to death                    (16)

This line, with its implicit physicality, draws together the poem's abundant imagery of the body. There is much seeing (lines 12, 15, 17 and so on), and listening (lines 4, 10, 14 and so on), as well as physical movements and some restless turmoil of changing positions: 'spread' (1), 'part' (5), 'turned' (7), 'pierced' (19) and so forth. The poem as a whole writhes within its own fetters. The word 'pressed' ought to remind us, of course, of Matthew's caution that we are 'pressed by heavy laws' and perhaps also of 'The Rainbow':

> And I could wish my days to be
> Bound each to each                                    (8–9)

Read in the context of Wordsworth's 'Immortality Ode', it is not difficult to interpret the convict here trapped in the shades of the prison house as yet another allegory of the human condition. Here, line 16, points to the fetters of human mortality, to death and, in parallel with the 'Immortality Ode', the opening stanzas of 'The Convict' refer to the growing loss of 'celestial light' as we penetrate deeper into the brooding shadows, of 'black' and 'blackens', consuming hope.

The dejected and obscure figure of the prisoner, bones consumed and 'life-blood' dried, is an apt (if deeply pessimistic) allegory of the fall of man, stressing mortal degradation rather than his capacity for the divine. There are strong echoes of the Miltonic Hell in *Paradise Lost*, Books I and II, ('the king of heav'n hath doomed / This place our dungeon', II.316–17), and Wordsworth's poem also taps into a religious dimension. So the deep sigh and 'steadfast dejection' of stanza 4 and the 'sorrow' in stanza 5 can relate to the fall of Adam and, by extension, to all mankind's mortal clay. This idea is picked up again later, in stanza 12's reference to this 'Poor victim', that we are all victims of original sin, the 'stain' of line 50, and hence forlorn regret that 'wishes the past to undo' (22).

The translation of the convict as the 'victim', together with the concept that we are all offenders, both clearly advance Wordsworth's liberal mission on penal reform. Yet stanza 5 now threatens to destabilize his case. ''Tis sorrow enough', line 17 transfers the emotion from the dejected convict and onto the poet as he gazes down on him. While the poem's strong physicality acts to reinforce its verisimilitude, lines 19 and 20 are also threatening:

> Yet my fancy has pierced to his heart, and portrays
> More terrible images there. (20)

The charge is perhaps that these terrible images together owe more to the poetic fancy projecting heightened feelings onto the dungeon scene recollected later than to scientific objectivity.

This aspect brings to mind Coleridge's cautionary deconstruction in 'The Nightingale', of how the poet 'filled all things with himself' (line 19) – pointing the finger at Romantic subjectivity and the pathetic fallacy. It is Wordsworth's extraordinary 'fancy' that enables his verse to visualise and empathise the position of the 'other' in the first place. But the suspicion that these impressions owe much to the subjective projections of a *particular* Romantic imagination weakens the social project with the possibility of an unreliable narration. Wordsworth again engages mind with physical phenomenon but the result – or the admission – is problematical.

The convict's fetters then shackle him to death. It is a life sentence, both literally and figuratively. The melodrama of these lines is also forward into the sixth stanza and:

His bones are consumed, and his life-blood is dried.          (21)

Wordsworth's habitual propensity for emotional rhetoric and periphrasis obviously diminishes the socio-political message (as it did in the pulpit section of 'The Old Cumberland Beggar'). Here the convoluted syntax of stanzas 7 and 8 and the emotional declamation in stanza 12 distract from and thus blunt the argument. In the sixth stanza, however, by working through the convict's own emotions Wordsworth is more successful in evoking the reader's compassion. The general but striking impression is of a man reduced by the physical pain of the fetters and 'disease' and the mental torment of despair and guilt to a depraved level of sub-human existence. We learn little of the man himself and this anonymity plus his dehumanising treatment renders him something of a wild monstrous thing in its lair like a minotaur.

An 'outcast' (12), 'victim' (45) and object of pity for Wordsworth, the prisoner anticipates other victims of injustice and other scapegoats: Coleridge's ancient mariner, of course, but also Byron's The Prisoner of Chillon (1816) and Manfred (1817), and Keats's ailing knight-at-arms in 'La Belle Dame sans Merci' (1819).

'The Convict' appeared only in the first edition of *Lyrical Ballads* and was replaced in future editions by Coleridge's 'Love'. Yet, ironically, both poems have intense overtones of the Gothic narrative and its incarcerated victims in thrall to their spiritual sensitivities as to villainous captors.

Stanza 6 draws this physical frailty to its highest pitch and also introduces the question of the man's crime (by way of his remorse and regret, and 'wishes the past to undo', 22). Although Wordsworth's intention is clearly to undiminish the crime (and thus transcend any easy notion of forgiveness), some readers have argued – and some still might – that this remorse actually demonstrates the effectiveness of this dreadful prison regime. This is harsh. Wordsworth's argument is that nothing justifies this dehumanising degradation. This is society's crime, 'its mean and vulgar works' that converts the perpetrator into the 'Poor victim' (45).

By the same token, the prisoner himself is anonymous. He is less a man than 'convict' and 'victim', with black matted head and 'deep-sunken eye' (41), and little else. This anonymity aptly reduces him – as the jail conditions have – to something less than human, perhaps animal-like by robbing him of the distinguishing marks of the humankind.

Anonymity is also a trade mark of the Romantic loner, the wanderer, for instance, the ancient mariner atoning for his sin, the heroic Cumberland beggar and the Gothic hermit in *The Prelude* (1850 IX.444 on). Usually outcast, victimised and rootless, as Wordsworth believed himself to be at times in his early manhood, the convict is one focus for the poet's reformist zeal. By obscuring the identity of the convict and empathising with the 'pains that o'erwhelm him' (23), Wordsworth hints that he (and by extension the reader) are equally the prisoner, imprisoned by agenbite of conscience and his duty to help.

Of course, these anonymities are there because Wordsworth at once insists on the futility and waste of the prison conditions. His view on prison is more positive: that the punishment should be measured to the crime and that punishment is in fact not enough – there should be rehabilitation too, as the final stanza indicates. Wordsworth's attitude here is all one with his wider philosophy at this time of his life, of the unity of mankind and the unity of nature.

Stanza 12 affirms Wordsworth's brotherly sympathy while the opening of the poem depicts that true natural balm from which the convict has been exiled (and deepening the painfulness of the 'Poor victim'). Both of these elements are foreshadowed in 'Tintern Abbey' in which Wordsworth's incarceration in the 'lonely rooms' of towns and cities is haunted by a sense of nature's power to bring about a 'tranquil restoration'. As if to reinforce this relationship (and the remedial role of nature) Wordsworth carefully juxtaposed the two poems in the first edition of *Lyrical Ballads*.

The anonymity of the convict is one reason why stanza 7 is likely to wrong-foot the first-time reader. It is a pivotal stanza, a quiet moment and yet another source of contrast set in the midpoint of the piece. However, following on the Gothic horror and pains of the first half, the references to 'synod', 'field', 'monarch' and 'pillow' come as a shock at first. The phrase 'blood-reeking' (25) takes its cue from the prisoner's dried-up 'life-blood' in the previous stanza but the clichéd dalliance of the king's chamber remains inchoate with the rest of the poem.

But if we set these images within the context of the French Revolution and the Jacobin 'fraternité', the stanza owes something of an allusion to the ghastly Bastille and its destruction in 1789 (the year before Wordsworth himself visited France). On these terms, the stanza begins to make some sense, something more than a private nightmare, drawing onto anti-monarchist overtones and the focus on prison as a contemporary revolutionary archetype of social injustice. In 1796, the moment of the poem's composition, Jacobinism is still strong enough and dangerous enough to inject this warning. But by 1800, Wordsworth's radical ardour was beginning to cool and the poem was omitted from the new edition of *Lyrical Ballads*.

Seen in any other light, stanza 7 obtrudes like the proverbial sore thumb. Working away beneath its gentle sibilants ('soothers of sense' and so on), the awkwardly disrupted syntax announces a thematic and emotional discord. The convoluted thought pattern extends into the succeeding stanza where 'doze' (29) satirises earlier ideas of sleep and oblivion, before 'tumult and roar' overcome the calm illusion reposing at the centre.

The style returns in stanza 8 to play directly on the reader's emotions too. The poem is a hotchpotch of emotions, split between an account of Wordsworth's shock and outraged awe at the circumstances (for example, lines 7, 17, 36, 45) and some melodramatic exertions to enlist the reader's affective response. The second half of the poem plays more earnestly on this attempt to manipulate us but the melodrama fails, as it must do, to elevate us into engaging and sharing with it. The result is that the poem lingers within the safe confines of the Gothic romance.

In terms of 'know' and 'feel', 'The Convict' remains firmly embedded in the latter. An emotive appeal is heavily dependent on circumstance and time. This poem appears within the contemporary context of the campaigns for prison reform by Romilly, Fry and others. The movement for penal reform in England really begins with John Howard (1726–90) on a roll of progressive movements with their roots in the Enlightenment and rationalist humanitarianism.

A major element in Wordsworth's case here is that the savage and barbaric treatment of the convict does not fit the crime – though this does not emerge with anything like clarity until near the end. The conclusion directs us to 'plant' the man, but this could be either in the sense of either rehabilitation in natural care or, more likely, transportation to the new colonies of Australia, the usual alternative to hanging. Some context might help us here.

In the England of 1800 an incredible 200 crimes were punishable by death. These included forgery, sheep rustling, stealing cash and, somewhat bizarrely, damaging Westminster Bridge – as well as murder and high treason, of course. The chief reason for this was that given the absence of a real police force, hanging was readily adopted as a deterrent, even for relatively trivial misdemeanours. One actual outcome of this obliquity was that petty criminals were often encouraged to commit murder to evade arrest. Samuel Romilly (1757–1818) eventually brought about the replacement of hanging with transportation or prison for lesser offences such as stealing cash and pick pocketing.

But, as eighteenth-century prison conditions were horrendously abominable, this was hardly likely to be an easy option. Wordsworth's descriptions of the 'comfortless vault of disease', though accurate, merely scratch the surface, while his sentimental tone does more to vent his own frustration and indignation at the horror than stir the contemporary reader. The contemporary prisons or houses of correction (originally set up to reform the work-shy) were houses of detention, warehouses of human misery with not even the pretence at reforming or rehabilitating inmates.

Foul and verminous, prisons were overcrowded breeding grounds for lethal diseases such as typhus and cholera, festering grounds for every form of human abuse in which all grade and ages of prisoner were pitched together into oblivion. Jailers were generally unpaid and thrived by extorting tips and bribes and selling basics to those convicts who could afford to pay.

By the time of Wordsworth's poem in 1796, John Howard's agitation for penal reform had stalled in the nation's reaction to the terror of the French Revolution and war. It was not to revive until Elizabeth Fry (1780–1845) successfully took up the challenge in the early nineteenth century, exposing the horrors of penal provision.

Wordsworth's denunciation of penal injustice is thus of and in tune with its era. However, its emotional strategy is of dubious efficacy and in fact understates the truth (as it perhaps must do). The anapaestic rhythm, though typical of protest verse in contemporary magazines, also works against the gravity of the subject (in 'The Dungeon', Coleridge's take on the same theme, blank verse carries a greater sense of earnestness).

The rising spring in this metre – with catalectic opening foot – runs counter to the cadences of the theme (this is, nevertheless, a difficult metre to pull off and its regularity here is quite a feat for Wordsworth). The demands of the rhythm also account for the abundance of conjunctions, determiners and demonstratives filling out the unstressed elements (stanza 3 is a good example).

The ninth stanza, with its 'fetter', 'limbs', 'weight' and 'pallet' returns the poem's attention to the physical realities of the jail, after the tortures of conscience in stanza 8. As we have seen before in *Lyrical Ballads*, one of Wordsworth's constant aims is to explore the relationship between mind and physical objects in nature. 'The Convict' offers a unique and strangely inverted challenge to this (the prisoner's cell is a sort of variation on the hermit's cave in 'Tintern Abbey', l. 22). For instance, stanza 6 alludes to the torments of the conscience and stanza 9 balances memory with fettered limbs.

However, the references to mental activity are outweighed by those to the physical. The implication is, of course, that the convict is reduced to the degraded rank of a savage beast held in a pen. Wordsworth's assault on prison conditions owes some of its inspiration to William Godwin's popular crusading novel, *Caleb Williams*, of 1794. The hero of the novel is imprisoned on a charge of robbery but, where Godwin seeks to show that the physical torments of prison are dwarfed by the mental, Wordsworth's mental agony is limited to the constant ache of conscience in a memory that cannot be bedimmed (and by the indistinct threat of the jail's mastiff).

Although Coleridge's 'Love' might not seem a likely companion piece, its lover, with his 'crazed brain' (60), suffers a similar kind of incarceration and also suffers most in mind. Here, the convict's stings of memory and conscience are surpassed in intensity by Wordsworth's own mental turmoil. This turmoil works through the poet's 'fancy' (in Coleridge's sense of the term), leaving a strong impression that the ordeal at the heart of the poem is in fact a projection of Wordsworth's own angst.

Having abandoned hope on the mountainside, the poet enters a species of Hell through a shadowy gateway, a cave of sorts (the poem has a number of comparisons with cantos II and III of Dante's *Inferno*). He enters oblivion, the realm of lost souls, to penetrate the depths of the human psyche via degradation and despair, approaches the centre of the human imagination ('self-consumed'), to reach what he had feared to discover: the horror, the horror of the Romantic imagination. This is only nebulously articulated here:

> A thousand sharp punctures of cold-sweating pain,
>     And terror shall leap at his heart. (39–40)

And the danger is more fully realised, for instance, in *The Rime of the Ancient Mariner* and in Mary Shelley's *Frankenstein*. The Gothic tale is only a pretext and a metonymy for the journey of self-examination and discloses the ontological insecurity underlying the Romantic consciousness.

Extending the medieval Gothic tangent, Wordsworth portrays himself as a grace-full crusader knight,

> 'But one, whose first wish is the wish to be good,
>     'Is come as a brother thy sorrows to share.' (47–8)

He is a brother knight, ministering to a fallen comrade-in-arms at the 'perilous gard', smiting the ogre of social injustice and its 'arm of the mighty'. Coleridge's knight and Wordsworth's supine victim make an interesting comparison with Keats's knight-in-arms of 'La Belle Dame sans Merci', and there is here too the occasional hint that the tormentor is female (for example, see line 30).

These strands, together with the faintly eroticising dimension in a Gothic tale of torture, surprisingly imbue the prisoner with a dimly stoic nobility. The overall effect of these possibilities, however, is to distract the poem's attention from its didactic purposes.

Wordsworth's wish, as the 'wish to be good', while it sounds treacly sweet and sentimental on today's ears is an expression of the humane sense of universal fraternity summed up in the 'one human heart', a 'life and soul to every mode of being / Inseparably linked' ('The Old Cumberland Beggar', lines 146 and 79). It is the same brotherly feeling informing Michael's stubborn commitment to his kinsmen and the Bard's rescuing hand in 'The Idle Shepherd Boys'.

In Wordsworth this impulse originates not in a rationalistic but in an affective source, but one that also recognises that at the root of man's difficulties is man's folly. Prisons are the work of man, 'mean and vulgar' of course, and in folly mark a divagation from the principles of nature, alluded to in the concluding stanza.

They are evidence of that same perversion of the 'wish to be good' that occurs in the frenzied sequence of 'Nutting', taking brief but manic hold of the boy until his riot leads to guilt, something to expiate. 'The Convict' illustrates well Wordsworth's fear that, without the balances offered by nature's salutary influence, there will be no safe check on man's instinct to exploit and even destroy the weakest of his fellows. The creative energy is also destructive.

Thus the motive for Wordsworth's visit to the convict as a brother, to be or to do good, is the motive too for composing the poem. The prisoner shows us the prison conditions in force, and the climax of Wordsworth's indignation arrives at the beginning of stanza 12 with the outburst of 'Poor victim!' (45). This reversal perhaps lays the poet open to the charge of naivety, but it does have the brilliant double effect of transposing the viewpoint. Hence the contemporary reader is to be mortified by both the prison conditions and the innocence of this victim of circumstances.

This ventriloquises William Godwin's doctrines and progressive theme that criminals are the inevitable casualties of wickedly disabling social conditions and the figure of the convict symbolises this miasma. Both 'The Convict' and Coleridge's 'The Dungeon' insist on a solution of reclamation and rehabilitation of prisoners by a civilised regime.

The opening to the final stanza, however, momentarily subverts this thrust by qualifying the possibility of clemency:

'At thy name though compassion her nature resign,
　'Though in virtue's proud mouth thy report be a stain' (49–50)

The prisoner is after all still convicted of an unstated crime in spite of his remorse and wishing 'the past to undo'. Wordsworth mercifully shuns the easy charm of John Bradford's 'But for the grace of God', proposing instead a Rousseauesque path of re-education through psychotherapeutic Nature:

Love of Nature leading to Love of Mankind
(*The Prelude*, 1805, VIII)

The final lines are a quiet supplication, and yet, even at this moment of relative optimism, they also acknowledge society's lack of readiness for this scale of moderation. As so often in Wordsworth, anger relents in the end to a prayer or a hope, and thus the theme becomes a personal rather than a social issue. This is signalled by the reappearance of the word 'care', in line 51 (from line 18), intimating Wordsworth's going forth into the world of mankind. Nevertheless, in the poem as a whole, his social commitment and sense of outrage at injustice are unmistakable.

In her *Tradition and Experiment in Wordsworth's 'Lyrical Ballads'*, Mary Jacobus dismisses 'The Convict' as simply typical of the pulp verse of 1790s popular magazines: 'he merely intensifies a topical theme'. But this is surely the point. In taking up a topical issue, Wordsworth does imbue it with the force of his broader vision consistent with the metaphysics of his mature verse. Taken in isolation the poem is not, perhaps, particularly good, but it derives its strength chiefly from an intertextual relationship with Wordsworth's wider metaphysics, especially his philosophy, as we have tried to show through reference to other poems.

### 'The Female Vagrant'

By Wordsworth's own account 'The Female Vagrant' was the earliest of the *Lyrical Ballads* to be composed. Begun in about 1791, he envisaged it as part of a much longer protest poem, *Salisbury Plain*, and in 1795 he revised and expanded it. However, after *Lyrical Ballads* had been projected, this plan was abandoned and the poem subsumed within the new collection. Even so, after first publication in 1798, Wordsworth revised the poem for the 1802 and 1805 editions, the cumulative effect of which was to tone down the original anger and protest that had first inspired its composition.

At about the time of the poem's initial composition Wordsworth, aged about 21, was himself almost a vagrant. In dire penury, he had wandered the lanes and by-ways of Cumberland and Wales seeking out vagrants and other drifters, beggars and peddlers, whom he treated with a strange mixture of fascination and reverence and whose tales later supplied a wealth of poetic characters and narratives, including 'The Old Cumberland Beggar', 'The Pedlar', 'Old Man Travelling', 'The Discharged Soldier' and *Guilt and Sorrow*.

These figures are another aspect of what the 1800 Preface describes as the 'low and rustic life', whose elemental honesty remains uncorrupted by the 'influence of social vanity'. Observing the effects of genuine misery and oppression at such close quarters had the expected result of intensifying his indignation against the establishment and social system that had produced them. Wordsworth vented his resentment in, amongst other poems, 'The Female Vagrant'. And yet his softening revisions of this poem over the next twelve years also chart the poet's gradual apostasy, a mellowing of his remonstrations, exchanging protest for the picturesque.

The mid-1790s were thus a period of great stress and insecurity for Wordsworth. It was the period of his greatest disjunction with society: unemployed, strapped for cash, isolated from Annette Vallon and their daughter in France, and alienated by an increasingly reactionary government hell-bent on war with France. At the time, he was progressively drawn towards the revolutionary ideals of men like Rousseau, Tom Paine and William Godwin (see Chapter 7 for further background).

Through his seminal work, *Political Justice* (1793), Godwin exerted a strong influence on the early politics of both Wordsworth and Coleridge. A central tenet of his liberal thesis was the belief that private property was the source of inequality and conflict within society. Crime is thus an inevitable consequence of the social oppression maintaining this status quo:

> A numerous class of mankind are held down in a state of abject penury, and are continually prompted by disappointment and distress to commit violence upon their more fortunate neighbours.
>
> (*Political Justice*, I.9)

As well as striking against injustice caused by the overall social system, Wordsworth's poem hits out at its particular iniquities: as he explained, his aim was 'partly to expose the vices of the penal law and the calamities of war as they affect individuals' (letter to Francis Wrangham, November 1795). 'The Female Vagrant' has two principal political thrusts: on one hand, against the dire poverty caused by agrarian decline, and on the other, against the wars, first with the American colonists and latterly with France. Discharged and maimed soldiers were beginning to swell the great number of rural vagrants and the dispossessed made homeless and landless by the changes in agricultural technological and by the Acts of Enclosure.

The poem is the chronicle of causes that machinate a helpless woman's humiliating disaster. At the same time Wordsworth skilfully unites the two thrusts outlined above by exposing how rural dispossession and poverty conscript their victims for the military. Nevertheless his compassionate narrative mode and social zeal still permit the woman to recount her own narrative with a mixture of raw indignation and poignant despair, exposing the deep personal as well as cultural cost of brutal government policies.

Having been raised a child of nature, by her 'good and pious' father, the woman's rural idyll is devastated by the rising breed of landowner whose acquisitive scheming undermines and drives them to destitution. She marries and for a brief interlude enjoys domestic happiness – until war and economic depression force her husband to join the army. She loses her entire family to the American conflict and plague – 'in one remorseless year' – and eventually undertakes a nightmare voyage home. Desperate and alone, she suffers starvation and delirium, and drifts from the city to the relative sanctuary of the 'wild brood' of vagrants and travellers. At the end, now 'Three years a wanderer', she turns away in tears to trudge a rootless and anonymous existence.

The extract I have chosen for analysis is stanzas 19–25:

> Some mighty gulph of separation past,
> I seemed transported to another world: –
> A thought resigned with pain, when from the mast                    165
> The impatient mariner the sail unfurled,
> And whistling, called the wind that hardly curled
> The silent sea. From the sweet thoughts of home,
> And from all hope I was forever hurled.
> For me – farthest from earthly port to roam                          170
> Was best, could I but shun the spot where man might come.
>
> And oft, robbed of my perfect mind, I thought
> At last my feet a resting-place had found:
> Here will I weep in peace, (so fancy wrought,)
> Roaming the illimitable waters round;                                175
> Here watch, of every human friend disowned,
> All day, my ready tomb the ocean-flood –
> To break my dream the vessel reached its bound:
> And homeless near a thousand homes I stood,
> And near a thousand tables pined, and wanted food.                   180
>
> By grief enfeebled was I turned adrift,
> Helpless as sailor cast on desart rock;
> Nor morsel to my mouth that day did lift,
> Nor dared my hand at any door to knock.
> I lay, where with his drowsy mates, the cock                         185
> From the cross timber of an out-house hung;
> How dismal tolled, that night, the city clock!
> At morn my sick heart hunger scarcely stung,
> Nor to the beggar's language could I frame my tongue.
>
> So passed another day, and so the third:                            190
> Then did I try, in vain, the crowd's resort,
> In deep despair by frightful wishes stirred,
> Near the sea-side I reached a ruined fort:
> There, pains which nature could no more support,
> With blindness linked, did on my vitals fall;                       195
> Dizzy my brain, with interruption short

Of hideous sense; I sunk, nor step could crawl,
And thence was borne away to neighbouring hospital.

Recovery came with food: but still, my brain
Was weak, nor of the past had memory.                          200
I heard my neighbours, in their beds, complain
Of many things which never troubled me;
Of feet still bustling round with busy glee,
Of looks where common kindness had no part,
Of service done with careless cruelty,                         205
Fretting the fever round the languid heart,
And groans, which, as they said, would make a dead man start.

These things just served to stir the torpid sense,
Nor pain nor pity in my bosom raised.
Memory, though slow, returned with strength; and thence        210
Dismissed, again on open day I gazed,
At houses, men, and common light, amazed.
The lanes I sought, and as the sun retired,
Came, where beneath the trees a faggot blazed;
The wild brood saw me weep, my fate enquired,                  215
And gave me food, and rest, more welcome, more desired.

My heart is touched to think that men like these,
The rude earth's tenants, were my first relief:
How kindly did they paint their vagrant ease!
And their long holiday that feared not grief,                  220
For all belonged to all, and each was chief.
No plough their sinews strained; on grating road
No wain they drove, and yet, the yellow sheaf
In every vale for their delight was stowed:
For them, in nature's meads, the milky udder flowed.           225

In a traumatic voyage that frequently echoes the mental horrors of Coleridge's ancient mariner, the woman is forced to endure misery and terror on the very brink of sanity. The 'mighty gulph' (163) is as much a physical emblem of her exile from the old life of home, family and security as the image of the ocean separating the Old and New Worlds (gulfs figure often in Wordsworth, frequently as an apocalyptic abyss). She admits in stanza 23 that 'of the past' she had now no memory and the 'gulph' is both cause and effect of the mental disruption, 'robbed of my perfect mind' (172). At the same time, 'transported' in line 164 implies that though completely innocent of any transgression she has fared little better than a convicted criminal.

One aspect of Wordsworth's skill in this ballad is again how he induces his words and images to operate freely in both literal and figurative realms in the same space. One instance of this comes in stanza 19 where the woman is becalmed in the doldrums, the analogue of her listless life, drifting and thwarted before the 'wind that hardly curled / The silent sea'.

Furthermore, the futility and despair of the ship's situation symbolise the ineffectual British war against American rebel colonists. These aspects take up and reinforce the rumours early in the poem, particularly stanza 14's embittered anti-war tirade: better to live like dogs in humility than join that other 'brood', the soldiery that 'lap ... their brother's blood' (126). With unexpected cynicism she had earlier berated the government's cynical policy to use war ('proud parade' and 'noisy drum') to 'sweep the streets of want and pain'. The change in voice here marks her entry into political as well as domestic realism.

In stanza 19 an important factor in her state of mind after the 'might gulph' is the woman's religion. Robbed of 'sweet thoughts of home ... from all hope I was forever hurled' (169), and she sinks into a new level of despair. It is not, however, easy to be precise about the nature of her religious belief. When, as a child, the family loses its home, her father urges her to 'trust in God' (61). Yet, while he immediately starts to pray, she concedes 'I could not pray' (62).

Is she then, like the ancient mariner, damned for her sin of despair? Her father made her kneel and pray when she was a young girl (14). Later, as she flees the coast she again resorts to prayer but then her prayers, like her tears, 'were in vain' (97). Yet, in spite of her father's devoutness, he is not saved and Wordsworth is eager to insist that the twin disasters of war and poverty are man-made and therefore their solution lies in his rather than in divine hands.

On the other hand, her narrative is sprinkled with religious diction, most notably in the tenth stanza:

> Four years each day with daily bread was blest,
> By constant toil and constant prayers supplied.          (82–3)

The lexical group is naturally a vestige of her father's deeply felt and (we imagine) puritan faith. This and the abundance of pietistic moral language (the depression was an 'evil time', 91) is worked by Wordsworth to define her as simple and modest, subservient and victim of enormous and overwhelming forces (Wordsworth assures in line 2 that she is 'artless').

But the woman is in no sense a martyr to these forces or 'fate'. She does not comprehend them, except that on a deeply private level she wills against them helplessly and passively. In they end, though, they reduce her to the desperate realities of a tramp, at the mercy of charity and chance. Further, her religio-moral language points to the source of shame she feels, intimated in line 171, 'could I but shun the spot where man might come'. She has become the victim of mankind's folly but, also, specifically of a male engendered world (and there is even a hint in line 158 that she may have been raped).

Her particular use of the word 'proud' – of the mansion (39), the war (93) and of rich men (122) – is also an engendered one, contrasting with her own feelings of modesty and humiliation before their power. These thoughts arise again in stanza 27 where they posit themes of deception and shame.

As in 'The Convict', the middle stanzas of the poem are concerned with the torture exerted on the mind by loss and hunger. In these middle sections, her mind is a confusion of swirling thoughts out of which she strives to discover some order, while at the same time expressing her original traumatic condition. At the point where her mental crisis deepens, with the 'mighty gulph' yawning before her she warns:

It would thy brain unsettle to hear. (130)

Incredibly, at this point she is quite lucid, even though 'robbed of my perfect mind, I thought' (172). These middle stanzas are a brilliant representation of the woman's madness, which in itself tends to deconstruct Wordsworth's assurance of an 'artless story' of a simple woman. However, her stated notion of a 'perfect mind' hits at the tremendous mental struggle in which tormented guesses and perceptions become checked and doubted by second guesses and tremors. These are manifested in her snatching after absolutes (for example, 'all' in lines 169 and 221, 'never' in 202, and 'every' in 224. She is literally and figuratively 'Roaming the illimitable waters round' (175) and, despite the fact that she is eventually becalmed, she insistently fixes the horror before us.

The major figurative methods employed by the woman/ Wordsworth are the metaphors of the war, the storm and above all the sea. Although now becalmed on a wide, wide 'silent sea' she is still wracked by uncertainty and deception ('I thought', 'so fancy wrought', and to 'break my dream', ll. 172–9). Her inability to separate horrible reality from horrible dream represents an intensification of an already awful experience.

This experience is exacerbated by the constant fear that the worst has not yet visited her, not finally. Grief is not permitted to doze in oblivion, in the comfortless vault of her mind. She feels instinctively that the calm of the 'silent sea' is only the prelude to a yet deeper cataclysm. Denied the home of a 'resting place' or even a 'ready tomb', she has become yet another archetypal Romantic wanderer, 'of every friend disowned' (176).

As a brilliant evocation of madness, the stanzas of the middle section (stanzas 16–20) are thus difficult to decrypt. They seem to function best if we interpret them as an analogue of the disintegrating mind – and even of society, within the broader political picture. Surrealistically, of course, they fuse the maelstrom of the woman's mind with the desperate turmoil of survival, harking back to the misery of the colonial war and plague, and further back to the machinations of the 'proud' landowner.

While speaking of the fever of her private 'madness' in the past, these stanzas also overlap with her time *now* as a vagrant, conveying the great insecurity of her life as an itinerant. I find these writhing stanzas more convincing than the explicit statements of madness in 'The Mad Mother' or 'The Idiot Boy' and are a great economy of writing of the horrors of her derangement and the fierce irresistible energy that magnifies it.

As in 'The Convict', once again Wordsworth makes a bridge between mental disruption and alienation with starvation, mind and body as a dangerously disrupted entity:

> And homeless near a thousand homes I stood,
> And near a thousand tables pined, and wanted food.     (179–80)

Amidst plenty, this want is essentially the want of something deeper, of a broad sense of 'care', the glue of society and Wordsworth is, in effect, warning of the dire consequences of division and disintegration in society. It is fair to say that he is more incisive here than in, say, 'The Old Cumberland Beggar'.

Like 'The Convict', 'The Female Vagrant' works dyadically: Wordsworth warns us of the consequences of the rapid increase in the number of vagrants but he tries to elicit our sympathy by equating poverty, homelessness and despair with madness, mind encumbered in body. Wordsworth regards the pernicious danger here as the possibility that the woman, symbolising the whole class of homelessness, might reach such a point of desperate poverty and starvation beyond which no help would be effective.

Whether he sees this as a ferment for revolutionary stirrings is unclear. It is more likely that he regards a laissez-faire society as at base unChristian, even uncivilised. Even the customary hope of regeneration would fail, for 'nature could no more support' (194).

The awful prospect of a catastrophic mental collapse ('It would thy brain unsettle to hear') exercised an increasingly vivid fascination on early nineteenth-century imaginations. It was manifested in the dreams, hallucinations, faery visions, opium nightmares and mental traumas present in the productions of Coleridge, Chatterton, Clare, De Quincey and the 'mad' Blake. Revolutionary Romanticism took on the daring adventure of interrogating the constraints of the Enlightenment's rationalism and via the subjective and the emotions sought to probe the supposed stability of human psychology. While this later gave rise to Victorian whimsy, the bizarre, the erotic and the plain aberrant, Wordsworth's study springs from a deep compassion and political earnestness.

Accordingly, the middle stanzas of the poem make a reasonable fist at conveying something of the experience of mental and domestic dislocation. The couplet at the end of stanza 20 goes further and is

Wordsworth's attempt to mortify the reader's complacency: in a land of great plenty the poor are allowed to starve.

Wordsworth's compassionate tale of distress and despondency is also a warning of how dangerously close to disaster the well-off can be. Although at the outset of the narrative the woman's family is relatively comfortably off in their 'hereditary nook' amid 'native bowers', history cannot safeguard their frail idyll against the massive forces of economic change. The lives of most of these smallholders are only a thread's width from the penury that strikes the central character.

The poem's opening four stanzas establish a strong identity of home and place. It is a controlled and ordered home, a Wordsworthian balance of natural and bookish learning. The poet sets up the innocence and heedless felicity of the young girl as a foil to the depth of later ruin and degradation. Her disaster deconstructs the very notion of 'home' as the secure, timeless bond with the land (with obvious echoes from *Michael*).

In line 168 the woman laments at having been hurled from the 'sweet thoughts of home'. However, in the following stanza comes the chilling realisation of her illusion:

> I thought
> At last my feet a resting-place had found                    (172–3)

But what or where is 'home'? Her distressing lot is that just as she becomes attuned to a new level of ruin, she discovers there is always worse to come. The horror is that decline appears to have no bottom line.

Lurking behind eighteenth-century social complacency is an ingrained faith in determinism: on one side, a rigid superstition about fate and, on the other, a rooted sense of divine ordination. Although the woman herself does not explicitly subscribe to either of these beliefs, she is the victim of them, driven into starvation, homelessness and insanity:

> Here will I weep in peace …
> Roaming the illimitable waters round                    (174–5)

As a victim she is less than passive. Much more than the possibility of action, she yearns for rest and peace. Misfortune has dissipated her appetite for action, while her sustenance and life depend on the caprice of 'hazard, or what general bounty yields' (255).

By line 180, after the 'mighty gulph of separation', practically all material trace of her personal history has gone. Widowed and robbed of her children, she leaves no mark and has no name. She loses her personal foothold in history and becomes very nearly a non-person.

Yet the poem opens with a profusion of material facts about the girl's existence, the familiar reference points of place: their cottage, field, flock and flood, nets, cliff, boat and oar. On the other hand these points have a different synecdochic aspect, ironically hinting at the cosmic forces that will overwhelm the woman, and they dissolve into those vast 'illimitable waters', anonymous and destructive like an army, on which she hopes pathetically for 'mercy' (116). This is not exactly the wholesome sea of immortality we find in 'Tintern Abbey' or the 'Immortality Ode', but a symbol of mutability, alienation and rootless desolation.

The theme of passivity is extended into stanza 21 with 'enfeebled', 'adrift', 'helpless', 'cast'. The woman's tone here echoes that of the 'The Complaint of a Forsaken Indian Woman', who is 'alone in the desart'. Now returned to England, the female vagrant is first forsaken then forgotten. She also shuns the 'spot where man might come' (171), which is her attempt to break out of the causal naturalistic, forces sweeping individuals before it. He usual responses to these are avoidance or acquiescence: patience and submission (90), prayer (97), wish (105), resign (118) and weeping (lines 120, 174 and 252).

Her humility contrasts with the 'proud men' (122), the centre of power in the poem depicted as wealth, might and arrogance. Rather than yield her dignity and integrity, however, she comes to adopt a strategy more by default than intention, hiding 'Unseen, unheard, unwatched' (121). She is 'enfeebled' by a society dominated by males: man acts, imposes, moves, changes and fights wars. The two main enfeebling forces in the poem are associated with men; namely, the enclosures by the man up at the big house and the war. Linking the two are the economic changes, especially concerning industry, that draw her husband away from his family home.

Although she is sick and hungry the woman is too reticent to beg:

> Nor dared my hand at any door to knock                    (184)

The title draws attention to the fact that this is a specifically female vagrant. But to what effect? Within the context of the late eighteenth century, this point further stresses her situation as a victim because, as stanza 27 implies, a man is more likely to resolve his situation through crime ('midnight theft to hatch'). Wordsworth's title has a specifically engendering force in contrast to the more common con-temporary ballad title on this theme, 'The Vagrant', that generally presupposes a male central character. By adopting this approach, Wordsworth also engenders the sway of its events: a male system in which the woman has no property, no trade or skill (the opening line of the poem also endorses this idea with 'my *father's* cottage' rather than 'our').

At the same time, the term 'female vagrant' might have suggested an immoral woman, a slattern. But, from the outset, Wordsworth is eager to determine that she is a casualty of fortune, an honest woman, 'brought up in nothing ill' (242) by an honest man, himself by 'hon-est parents bred' (11). Principles are what she values above all, and their loss hurts more than loss of family since her survival depends on some self-deception:

> Nor to the beggar's language could I frame my tongue.          (189)

This characteristic lies at the core of her being. Integrity is her real home, a bedrock to rest firm on as a vestige of the lost idyll of her childhood. Hence, although Wordsworth links poetry with madness, he works hard to assure his reader here (as he does in 'The Old Cumberland Beggar' too) that 'vagrant' is not equivalent to 'criminal'.

The woman is in complete fealty to fluctuating forces and causes beyond her comprehension (anticipating Hardy's Tess and Ibsen's women). She seems to have no opportunity of freedom, in the con-ventional sense, until the death of her men and then her freedom is merely a species of drifting. Instead of a true sense of choice she has before her only a void.

So passed another day, and so a third (190)

She is again highly conscious of time. Which is ironic since, having been adrift at sea, she has lived for long outside of it. The family cottage, the 'hereditary nook', incarnates the family history as it does for Michael ('live the life they lived'). Time and family memory deepens the feeling of loss and therefore of global injustice.

In personal terms, time is memory of the lost past, beyond the 'gulph of separation'. As part of her present narrative, she repeats the phrase 'Can I forget' (lines 19 and 55) and she is aware that the mindset of her childhood locality is now lost forever in the 'illimitable' void of her driftings. The memory is one more torment and a terrible warning that mental disruption is the inevitable outcome of physical dislocation, bringing flux, chaos and catastrophe.

Time is also, of course, context, both personal and public. In stanza 21 the woman has gravitated, like so many impoverished drifters, into the city and dosses near a tavern. At different points in the poem the city is characterised by poverty (187) and by disease ('foul neglect', fever and 'polluted air'; stanza 12). But Wordsworth judiciously glosses over its dissolute character and 'evil courses' so problematic in *Michael*. Yet, like *Michael*, the project of 'The Female Vagrant' is to foreground most dramatically the dire consequences of the contemporary flight from the land.

After the woman's marriage there follows a four-year interval of relative ease and fecundity (bearing three children in four years). Then, disaster ensues, along with unmistakeable portents of economic depression:

The empty loom, cold hearth, and silent wheel,
And tears that flowed for ills which patience could not heal. (89–90)

The brief ease then turns out to be a mere blip in the inexorable decline of the woman's fortunes. Although the poem starts out 'High o'er the cliffs' (8), by stanza 22 the woman has sunk to 'Near the seaside I reached a ruined fort' (193).

The contest between the 'cottage' and the 'mansion' is of course an uneven match and the outcome is a landmark in rural history. In the eighteenth century weaving (the 'loom' and 'wheel') was a vibrant cottage industry and mainstay of the rural economy and in the cohesion of the family. The local community revolved around the small-scale organisation of hand weavers. From about 1800 the expansion of factory weaving and spinning on the back of new technology and increased mechanisation led to the break-up of this pattern.

The massive new mills transformed self-employed men and women into mere paid hands. The family ties were further loosened by the shift-working practices and by the notorious moral reputation of the mills, a by-word for sexual laxity, cruelty, ill-health and horrific accidents. What enclosure had done for the agricultural community, was now wrought by factories and mills on the 'loom' and the 'wheel', swelling the tide migrating to overcrowded towns.

This is the context of Wordsworth's 'mean and vulgar works of man' and 'The Female Vagrant'. It is in bleak contrast to the poem's opening pastoral ideal with its natural learning, care and harmony. Care is a crucial idea in the poem, as it is in 'The Convict'. Once the 'new man' (as William Cobbet scorned the grasping, opportunistic landowners) has arrived, childhood, like common property, is at an end and care becomes transmuted into self-preservation.

As a young man Wordsworth found himself the victim of the mighty landowner Lord Lonsdale (whose son was, coincidentally, identified by Cobbett as the worst of these graspers), resulting in years of anxiety and relative penury.

After the traumatic sea voyage and the loss of almost everything, stanza 22 marks the depth of her humiliation and degradation. But once she is taken up in the care of human providence, the following stanza represents a sort of rebirth, opening significantly with the word 'Recovery', and the first sign of hope since the death of her father in stanza 10. Following the 'mighty gulph' she has no memory of the past, her personal and family history wiped clean from a 'Dizzy' and 'weak' brain.

But then, in a series of oxymoronic outbursts, she scolds her fellow-patients for their muttering ingratitude (203–6). This is a nice touch by Wordsworth, of course. The difference singles her out as a vivid character, against the grain. But this 'artless' woman appeases his readership as an ungrumbling, slightly obsequious recipient of the common care, no matter how begrudgingly proffered by the parish. Above all, her gratitude seeks to reassure the reader that the vagrant is not a social deviant – just as she is no work-shy sponger, scambler, losel or loafer (under the 1744 Vagrancy Act 'rogues vagabonds and sturdy beggars' were considered work-shy and were liable to be 'whipped until bloody' and forced to work in a house of correction). The poem insists that we see her simply as an unwilling member of a new and growing underclass of outcast and homeless.

At the end of stanza 23 the groans that would 'make a dead man start' implies that, unlike the 'artless' heroine, her fellow patients counterfeit their ailments. The presence of such idlers threatens to undermine Wordsworth's argument, though they do have the dramatic effect of stinging the woman out of her torpor (line 209). Stanza 24 traces the rising curve of her recovery as she emerges from hospital care and begins to return to the world, seeing it with fresh eyes:

> Dismissed, again on open day I gazed,
> At houses, men, and common light, amazed.                  (211–12)

Significantly, she shuns the town and heads for the lanes and trees, thus emphasising the importance of the word 'open' in line 211. A born-again tramp she connects with the 'wild brood' whose ready care through 'food, and rest' contrasts with her satire on 'homeless near a thousand homes', in line 179. Their hospitality, a sort of communism ('all belonged to all') puts to shame the cold-blooded vanity and miserliness of the 'new men' of the mansion.

Her 'rebirth' marks a relatively happy return to ameliorative nature, the 'rude earth's tenants' (218) who represent for Wordsworth a bedrock of primitive honesty and piety, as well as 'those elementary feelings' (245), as he claimed in the Preface to *Lyrical Ballads*. Plumbing the very abyss of society, she and the poet are assured by discovering in this class the basic human instinct of gregarious cordiality. Although now far from the 'thousand tables', she hits upon the mythical Land of Cockaigne, of plenty and harmony in nature's meads, a burn of idleness and luxury:

> No plough their sinews strained; on grating road
> No wain they drove, and yet, the yellow sheaf

> In every vale for their delight was stowed:
> For them, in nature's meads, the milky udder flowed.          (222–5)

With more echoes of childhood, her fellow vagrants offer ease and freedom, and their entertainments represent fun, the 'thoughtless joy' (6) of her childhood in the country. These rural unmaterialistic vagrants encapsulate a kind of homecoming in her return to nature.

In her surrogate family she at last rediscovers some stability in her life. The poem is in one sense about becoming adrift once the hereditary and communal ties of place become severed or dislocated ('By grief enfeebled was I turned adrift'; 181). Chief among these is the family and we can consider what this means to her (and to Wordsworth). A source of support, stability and love, it is archetypal security, a shared location and direction, a link with the past and a stake in the future. Disastrously, the woman loses two families and, motherless too, she has lived most of her life dependent on the male aegis. Her father has raised her and when her sweetheart is about to be sent away for work she appears to seize at him in a panic:

> For never could I hope to meet with such another.          (72)

As a woman, she herself has no trade and has relied on males for support, property and sustenance. After the loom and the wheel become redundant (89), she has no means of independence

> Ill was I then for toil or service fit          (249)

Subject first to a father and then to a husband, to the man at the mansion and to the war-mongers, she becomes happy once again when she is alone, a vagrant but free of the men who have defined her life, 'Roaming the illimitable waters round' (175).

### 'The Thorn'

For most of his life, as the poems generally attest, Wordsworth tended to live in small rural communities. These are often characterised in his writings and those of his close associates as centres of intense inquisitiveness: everybody knows – or thinks they know – what everybody else is up to.

In early adulthood he was himself sometimes the victim of pernicious local gossip, such as in Germany where it was believed that he and his sister were secret lovers.

There was also the celebrated and comic episode of 'Spy Nozy' referred to earlier (see Chapter 6 too). Wordsworth's personal experience of scandal-mongering left him acutely sensitive to its malignant effects. This knowledge and sensitivity finds its trenchant expression in 'The Thorn'.

My discussion of the poem will focus on three main areas: the character of Martha and her suffering; the character and language of the narrator; and the poem's symbolism.

Composed in the famously creative spring of 1798, 'The Thorn' originates in Wordsworth's discovery of a withered thorn tree on a walk in the Quantock Hills. Dorothy's journal records the occasion:

*March 19, 1798*  William wrote some lines describing a stunted thorn

...

*April 20, 1798*  ... Came home the Crookham way, by the thorn, and the 'little muddy pond'.

In 1964 Albert Gerard tersely enquired 'is the poem about a man, a woman or a tree?' This enigmatic poem, that has generated a substantial amount of critical polemic, is of course about all three – and much more. The extract I have chosen for analysis consists of the last five stanzas of the poem.

### XIX

I did not speak – I saw her face,
Her face it was enough for me;                                   200
I turned about and heard her cry,
'O misery! O misery!'
And there she sits, until the moon
Through half the clear blue sky will go,
And when the little breezes make                                 205
The waters of the pond to shake,

As all the country know,
She shudders and you hear her cry,
'Oh misery! oh misery!'

### XX

'But what's the thorn? and what's the pond?                    210
'And what's the hill of moss to her?
'And what's the creeping breeze that comes
'The little pond to stir?'
I cannot tell; but some will say
She hanged her baby on the tree,                              215
Some say she drowned it in the pond,
Which is a little step beyond,
But all and each agree,
The little baby was buried there,
Beneath that hill of moss so fair.                           220

### XXI

I've heard the scarlet moss is red
With drops of that poor infant's blood;
But kill a new-born infant thus!
I do not think she could.
Some say, if to the pond you go,                             225
And fix on it a steady view,
The shadow of a babe you trace,
A baby and a baby's face,
And that it looks at you;
Whene'er you look on it, 'tis plain                          230
The baby looks at you again.

### XXII

And some had sworn an oath that she
Should be to public justice brought;
And for the little infant's bone's
With spades they would have sought.                          235
But then the beauteous hill of moss
Before their eyes began to stir;
And for full fifty yards around,
The grass it shook upon the ground;
But all do still aver                                        240

The little babe is buried there,
Beneath that hill of moss so fair.

### XXIII
I cannot tell how this may be,
But plain it is, the thorn is bound
With heavy tufts of moss, that strive                                245
To drag it to the ground.
And this I know, full many a time,
When she was on the mountain high,
By day, and in the silent night,
When all the stars shone clear and bright,                           250
That I have heard her cry,
·'Oh misery! oh misery!
'O woe is me! oh misery!'


'The Thorn' superbly exemplifies Wordsworth's interest in the lives and business of people, focusing sharply on the relationship between an outcast, persecuted individual and the community that first mystifies her and then tries to clarify that mystery.

Although the linear plot is here largely displaced by concern for mind and 'atmosphere', the starting point of 'The Thorn' is a rambling old gossip's narrative about Martha Ray who, having been jilted on her wedding day by her duplicitous lover, Stephen Hill, has become deranged and wild. Alienated from her village, she is the victim of lurid tittle-tattle that claims she was pregnant by Hill and has subsequently murdered her baby, burying it beneath the 'beauteous' mound close by an ancient thorn and the ever-muddy pond.

Readers have generally found 'The Thorn' to be one of the most uncomfortable in the collection. This seems to be partly due to the theme of infanticide and partly because of the poem's silences and evasions. The first line of the extract – 'I did not speak' – vividly seizes on the tacitness of the narrator's discourse. The poem has a great many references to talking – say, aver, maintain, swear and so on – and speech is a vital element in the network of this community. But, crucially, so is the rumouring of the community and the narrator who, in some measure, represents it.

So here, at the dramatic climax to the whole poem, there is a brief painful face-to-face encounter between narrator and Martha. At last, we get the chance to find Martha after the long build-up of mystery and warning. But the narrator cops out:

> Her face it was enough or me                                    (200)

But this is not nearly enough for us. It is one more evasion, and the gossipy narrator turns teasingly away.

This manipulative narrator employs a range of evasive devices, including the use of other people as narrators, typified in phrases like ''Tis said' and 'Some say' (lines 137 and 216). In a poem much occupied with telling, saying and swearing, this is not a little ironic. The confrontation at last holds out the possibility of some clarification, but intense emotions and a storm intervenes so that the narrator's epiphanic moment transmutes into panic and the moment is lost.

We too desire to know more about this mythic Martha, which is why this moment is so important. Identified with the thorn tree, she is (like the thing itself) described as 'wretched' (9 and 38). The thorn is 'aged' (34) and 'forlorn' (9) but, with leaden irony, 'Not higher than a two-years child' (5). Withered and dry, she makes a contrast with the youthful mound's 'fresh and lovely' appearance (35). In line 139 she is portrayed as 'mad', though if we take our cue from line 11 of 'The Mad Mother' this seems to mean excessively and passionately engrossed, over-solicitous, rather than insane.

This said, her interminable melancholy undoubtedly drives her to eccentric, asocial behaviour as here, sitting:

> until the moon
> Through half the clear blue sky will go                       (203–4)

Cut off from the human domain, Martha holds plangent fellowship with nature,

> And she is known to every star,
> And every wind that blows                                     (69–70)

She visits the mountain at all times, in all weathers, and shelters in a small hut on the desolate mountain slope.

She has become one of the 'rude earth's tenants' of 'The Female Vagrant', one of the 'wild brood', and her mind seems to be deeply interfused with a deeper spirit of nature, in the 'little breezes' of stanza XIX, eerily recalling Lucy Gray, another dead child who 'whistles in the wind'.

Because of this isolation, eccentricity and distractedness, along with her strange communion with nature, she is construed by the villagers as a witch. In stanza XIX she dwells under the lunar influence and has this strange affinity with nature. A great mystery haunts the three objects on the mountain, betokening unnatural rites: a pond that never dries, a spooky tree, and a blood-red mound that quakes (239). Infanticide has been rumoured too.

Before the woman herself has appeared, the narrator discomposes us with his descriptions of the desolate terrain and paternalistic warnings to 'take care and chuse your time' (58). Yet it is not clear why he gives warning: who is the danger, we to her or she to us? In stanza X he encourages us to visit her. By this way of hint and equivocation, the narrator cunningly draws the reader into the complex of rumour and gossip.

He treats her in part as he might a mad dog, in part as a skittish freak. Like Stephen Hill, the narrator has a duplicitous attitude: at times he sides with the gossips and at others he derides them. All the same, in stanza XIX, his abject impression of the agonised woman sobbing before the moon and the elements is a genuinely compassionate one. It undoubtedly ventriloquises Wordsworth's own uncomfortable feelings about his 1792 abandonment of Annette Vallon, pregnant with his child. These feelings find parallel outlets in many other depictions of the forsaken woman (for example in 'Margaret', 'Ruth', 'The Female Vagrant' and 'The Complaint of a Forsaken Indian Woman').

In 1790s' magazine verse, seduction and betrayal of women were somewhat hackneyed themes in popular magazine verse. Yet Wordsworth takes up the challenge and instils his treatment with some convincing empathy. Martha's suffering (ritualised by her chiming lament of 'Oh misery! oh misery!') is almost palpable and it is this along with the poem's riddles that are likely to compel our imagination.

The poem reaches its emotional climax in stanza XIX, but the pre-
varication in line 200 quickly disperses the intensity (in spite of
Wordsworth's exclamation marks). Consequently, the questions at the
start of XX are an attempt to revive the reader's involvement. They
strive to achieve this by directly engaging the reader in the fabric of
the local gossip. Having slyly raised the listener's curiosity, the narrator deftly sidesteps the issue with:

> I cannot tell                                                                    (214)

This is, of course, the oldest trick in the gossip's handbook (repeat-
ing the device as used at the end of stanza XVI). And the phrase 'I
cannot tell' is itself ambiguous: meaning both colloquially 'I don't
know' and 'I shall not reveal'. Stanzas IX and XI, however, do expose
the narrator's strategy, advancing by stages:

| | | |
|---|---|---|
| *from* | 'I cannot tell' | (89) |
| *through* | 'I'll give you the best help I can' | (111) |
| *to* | 'I'll tell you all I know' | (114) |

And is the narrator a disingenuous participant? Most villainously. As
a pivotal figure in the narrative, he stands both within its 'events' and
outside of them, as he stands both within and outside of the community, a point that enables him to speak invidiously for and against it.

Because of this, the narrator is at the centre of knowing in the
poem in terms of himself and of his community, and in terms of the
reader too. Accordingly, the reader is invited into the network of
the community through the desire to know ('network' is a key word
in the poem, referring to the local people, the poem's own system
of repetition, and the mound: see line 40).

Knowledge (and conversely ignorance) is manifestly a significant
mover in the poem. It is referred to repeatedly and it is a member of
a cognitive cluster that also includes 'discover' (189), 'find' (197) and
'trace' (110). In addition, Martha's intercourse with Hill is another
expression of forbidden or secret knowledge within the terms of
the poem.

The word 'trace' here connects the cognitive theme in the poem
with the concept of communal 'desire'. This applies in a double sense

of trying to fill the gaps, the silences and the unknown, and in the sense of a going-outward, or 'care' in broad terms (and 'care' is a strong idea in all three of this chapter's poems). Where this falls short there is, naturally enough, a filling-in regardless. So in stanza XX we have, in response to the unanswered questions, 'some will say' and 'some say' while 'all and each agree' (that echoes 'As all the country know', in the previous stanza). Then, further on, we hear 'some had sworn' (232) and 'all do still aver' (240).

The poem is about, among many things, the power of a community to fix on and victimise the loner, to create its own narratives by hint and sign in a sort of creeping whisper. The claustral society marginalises and mythologises the jilted woman and, in a way, she is jilted by the village too. It persuades itself that she is pregnant and a child murderer, though strictly speaking these remain unproven fictions. The superstitions about the quaking grave-mound in stanza XXII are likewise fabricated on rumour.

The poem throws some light too on the lot of the old Cumberland beggar, the mad mother and the female vagrant. They are all victims of a species of 'care' as I have termed their curiosity, expressed as interest but modulates into prying and, by degrees (the 'creeping breeze', l. 212), into moralising gossip. In stanza XX the lacuna of the unknown comes to be filled with 'maybes' until eventually 'all agree'.

There seems to be absolutely no compassion for Martha from the wider community, only supposition, accusation and disdain. In the absence of certainty, what the villagers project onto the woman is its own imaginative aptitude for the lurid and the immoral. The scarlet moss that in stanza XXI is supposed to signify infant blood and in XXIII chokes the thorn tree, also symbolises the stifling effects of the rural community on Martha, that 'clasp', 'drag' and 'bury' her (stanza II).

The narrative workings of the communal mind parallel in large the process of the poem's author. But behind the collective imagination constructing the localised fictions is the collective conscious. In a note to the 1800 edition of *Lyrical Ballads*, Wordsworth asserted that the imagination is the 'faculty that produces impressive effects out of simple elements'. For this reason, the poet places the reader among the villagers (in contrast to 'The Female Vagrant' where we are held off) and like them we must fill the gaps and draw together isolated signs and hints into a cohesive fiction.

By imitating the creative process – 'some will say ... and each agree' – the villagers and the narrator are aligned with the poet. The warnings in stanzas VI and IX about ascending the mountain are also warnings about what to accept as the truth. The balladeer as village gossip has himself woven a fabric (or 'network') of fiction around a few natural objects and the reader is encouraged by his gaps to weave his or her own fiction:

> I cannot tell; but some will say                                   (214 and 243)

Interestingly, Martha's story has affinities with Greek tragedy. For instance, the narrator is the spokesman of the chorus-villagers, commenting on the action while he is also a protagonist of that action. However, the narrator (like the speaker of 'Goody Blake and Harry Gill') has an ambivalent attitude towards the central character. He has sympathy of course for her distress as the victim of Stephen Hill (and perhaps as a foiled mother) but he is also very cautious. While to him she is a casualty, she may at the same time be a witch and witches are notorious for infanticide (as vagrants and gypsies have equally been charged). His is typical of the attitude that banishes Martha but then feels sorrow for her exclusion.

Some of the poem's simmering tensions are generated by these two attitudes, but not nearly as much as that tension generated by those three resolute features on the hilltop. In 'There was a Boy' Wordsworth notes:

> the visible scene
> Would enter unawares into his mind
> With all its solemn imagery                                   (21–3)

In that poem too the 'visible scene' includes this mysterious trio of tree, hill and lake, Wordsworth's iconic wilderness. For the poet, just as for his narrators, the scene has entered the consciousness with such intensity that they have acquired powerful symbolic status. Repeated references to these objects are part of the poem's mesmeric litany, as stanza XX typifies:

> 'But what's the thorn? and what's the pond?
> 'And what's the hill of moss to her? (210–11)

But what are they to us?

Stanza XX tries to deal with these questions on the naturalistic level and according to local legend, tree, pond, hill equates to hanged, drowned, interred. But XXI begins to interrogate the troubling symbolic aspects of this 'solemn imager'. The narrator 'cannot tell' of course but he has heard and he can speculate, can 'think' and 'say'. This is about all anyone can do with symbols and their marvellous ambivalence is grist to the rumouring mill.

In one of the earliest comments on the poem, the curmudgeonly Francis Jeffrey dismissed the imagery most prosaically: an unfortunate woman goes to the top of a hill and 'all the rest of the poem is filled with a description of an old thorn and a pond, and of silly stories' (*Edinburgh Review*, April 1808). But this mundanity misses the whole point of Wordsworth's acute focusing of attention onto an almost occult location haunted by demons of suffering and guilt.

As he does in 'The Convict', Wordsworth restricts his scene to a very limited range of objects whose elemental simplicity permits them to operate in both the literal and figurative domains. Yet even in the naturalistic domain, this control produces a powerful effect; as John Watson has pointed out, the ghastly juxtaposition of the infant's blood, bones, face and spades in stanzas XXI and XXII underlines the chilling horrors of isolation for Martha.

In line 221 the narrator intimates that he has heard that the scarlet moss gets its colour from the blood of the dead infant. The scarlet directly connects the woman (via her cloak; line 63) with the mound, and with the thorn tree since the network of bloody moss is gradually enveloping everything on the mountaintop (the scarlet cloak stigmatises Martha just as keenly as Hester Prynne's 'scarlet letter' in Hawthorne's novel). Together the objects interact to such a compelling degree that they almost spontaneously allegorise Martha's awful predicament. But first we need to tease these items apart for individual discussion.

Beginning with the thorn itself, it is repeatedly emphasised in terms of its agedness: 'old' (1), 'old and grey' (4) and so on. The opening to the poem is ponderous with the narrator's easy ironies. For instance, like Martha, the tree seems never to have been young. A mass of knotted joints implies an arthritic old age, yet crooked, as something conventionally witchlike. Devoid of leaves and thorns, its very existence betokens something miraculously tenacious. This eeriness is all one with the weird episodes on this strange desolate mountaintop, including the bleeding mound and the shaking earth.

The thorn's association with Martha herself is endorsed by the narrator's persistent anthropomorphism: in early stanzas it is depicted as 'wretched', 'melancholy' and 'poor', which enhances the idea too that demons are busy at work on this thrillingly uncanny site.

Just such an alluring aura must have first captivated Wordsworth himself on his 1798 encounter with the tree, which happened during a storm. He later disclosed to Isabella Fenwick something of his motive in writing the poem:

> I said to myself, 'Cannot I by some invention do as much to make this Thorn permanently an impressive object as the storm has made it to my eyes at this moment?' I began the poem accordingly, and composed it with great rapidity.

The fact that it took the storm to galvanise Wordsworth's feelings into interacting with this spooky twig points to the anthropomorphic processes at work within the frail narrator (Wordsworth nevertheless took strenuous pains to distance himself from him).

Thus the thorn-tree is manifestly more than the sum of its defunct parts, and it transcends the normal bounds of the empirical, slipping into the supernatural at least in symbolic terms. But if it is the central symbol what does it symbolise?

Inhabiting its haunted locality, the thorn recalls the notorious eighteenth-century gibbet sites with their inevitable mythologies of guilt and human suffering. Mary Jacobus reminds us too that, somewhat enigmatically, 'The commonest of all literary associations for a thorn tree were illegitimate birth and child-murder.' The shabbiness and persistence of the tree translate as a constant and ironic reminder to Martha of the passion and turpitude of Stephen Hill and of their putative infant. For the villagers, the tree in its steadfast immanence symbolises some indefinable and ineradicable transgression against the universe.

This moral hue is a property shared with other ancient solitary trees in *Lyrical Ballads*, for example *Michael*'s sentinel Clipping Tree and guardian oak in 'The Fountain'. Their persistence on the landscape is for Wordsworth, like the mountains and the wisdom of old men, proverbial and salutary. Yet none of his other trees comes near the thorn for its simmering overtones of guilt and suffering.

The next in the poem's symbolic trinity is the mound. Although Martha's pregnancy was but rumoured and her baby realised merely as an 'if' ('There's no one that could ever tell'; 160), the murder of the 'child' is something 'all and each' are certain of. The evidence lies beneath 'that hill of moss so fair' (220). And yet in stanza XXI the narrator does not share the same strongly imaginative powers of his fellow-villagers:

> But kill a new-born infant thus!
> I do not think she could. (223–4)

But then there is that troublesome evidence of the 'beauteous hill of moss' (236). Put three disparate objects together with a mysterious unconforming woman and there you have it: guilty as rumoured.

The 'fresh and lovely' mound resplendent in its vibrant mossy colours (stanzas IV and V) contrasts adverbially with the cheerless, funereal thorn-tree. However, where the moss has striven to choke and topple the thorn, to the mound it is a beautifying gloss, clothing and, by extension, protecting the baby beneath. Because of the strongly symbolic atmosphere on the mountain top, the colours of Martha's hill 'Green, red and pearly white' (48) also appear obscurely emblematic, implying youth, vigour and chastity. The poem's repetition of the simile 'like an infant's grave' (52, 61 and 93) likewise work away to foreground the symbolism of tomb and womb for the reader as it is literally for Martha.

The mound is a stubborn presence in Martha's history. If she has killed her baby, then it is possibly a vain attempt to remove it from history, to eradicate the memory of its father's treachery. His treachery has echoes of and fulfils the same dramatic role as the sins of the landowners in *Michael* and 'The Female Vagrant', striking at and undermining the hypostasis of human relationships. Like Michael's abandoned stones, the small hill has become transmuted into the stuff of public myth, lingering as the perpetually deferred project, like meaning itself, a kind of stolen future (compare the 'Lucy' poem in this light too).

The whole of the local community seems to have become hypersensitised by the mysterious events and speculations spooking this mountaintop. Indeed Wordsworth's tale elegantly focuses on the mechanics of speculation, gossip, whisperings, in a tiny intensely involuted rural community. At the centre of this is a readiness for voyeurism and autosuggestion:

> Some say, if to the pond you go,
> And fix on it a steady view,
> The shadow of a babe you trace,
> A baby and a baby's face                                    (225–8)

The reflective pond becomes the correlative of the constancy of the thorn and the mound. The shock here arises in the baby's staring and accusing glance cast back at the inquisitive viewer. Local intensity, superstition and curiosity all converge in stanza XXI in the symbolism of the pond.

But our first encounter with the pond is quite undramatic, artless, expressed in slightly ludicrous mathematical intensity

> I've measured it from side to side:
> 'Tis three feet long, and two feet wide.                     (32–3)

The banal precision of these dimensions tries to fix the pond as a real entity, locating it in the hard realm of phenomenon. John Purkis defends them as arising from a 'desire to placate the scientific and Lockean tradition' of British philosophy. Contrasting with the ethereal mysteries on the mountain, the empiricism of this couplet is perhaps most useful in supplying a benchmark of reality to the poem (that Wordsworth's 1800 Preface endorses as axiomatic). It has the additional merit of satirising the whiff of officious solicitude in the narrator, his 'vital anxiousness'.

This point is paralleled by the vocative style of the narration as a whole. Recalling the style of *Michael*, this accosting manner draws the reader directly into the anxieties of the village, at the same time assuring us of the propriety of the narrator and the veracity and wisdom of the villagers' viewpoint. Ironically, however, this mode is his undoing since it eventually divulges his unreliablity.

John Danby has suggested that the three objects – tree, mound and pond – are undoubtedly symbols of human misery but actually go beyond this and operate as agents of it. The ineradicable presence of these natural objects does exert a truly causative effect on the minds of the villagers, who obsessively seek to vent their suspicions on Martha. Of the three, it is the pond that fits Danby's representation most literally:

> Whene'er you look on it, 'tis plain
> The baby looks at you again. (230–1)

The reflectivity of the pond draws in and confronts the reader as a member of a wider community. We may all be to blame.

Significantly it is a 'muddy pond' (30) and thus compares unfavourably with the healthier, free-flowing and regenerative waters gurgling through 'The Fountain' and the sweet murmur of the Wye in 'Tintern Abbey'. This muddy bog is a reservoir of paralysis and stagnation (anticipating the cesspool in Ibsen's *A Public Enemy*).

It is a perpetual source ('never dry', 31) of prurient speculation in the community, but ironically one in which the community actually discovers or 'traces' itself. It is 'plain' too that, in constructing its myths, it unwittingly projects its own imperfections and proclivity for iniquity. Thus, in this sense, the community is portrayed by Wordsworth as an agent of its own unremitting misery.

Bound in with these symbolic objects and Martha's narrative, the poem is also the story of the mysterious narrator himself. In a note added to the 1800 edition Wordsworth described him as 'loquacious', something like the retired captain of a 'small trading vessel':

> The Reader will perhaps have a general notion of it, if he has ever
> known a man, a Captain of a small trading vessel for example, who
> being past the middle age of life, had retired upon a small annuity or
> small independent income to some small village or country town of
> which he was not native, or in which he was not accustomed to live.

Why Wordsworth chose to compare him to a ship's captain is
unclear (his own beloved brother John was such a one), but being a
stranger and outsider he serves well as snooper but also as the reader's
intermediary. He continually denies any knowledge of what is going
on (see lines 155, 175 and 24) and this seems to be part of his strenuous efforts to insinuate his confidence on us.

In 'The Idiot Boy' the narrator is loving and anxious while in
'Goody Blake and Harry Gill' he or she is volubly didactic. But here,
in 'The Thorn', the relationship with the reader is subtle and shifting,
adding an extra dimension to this remarkable poem's attraction.

Like Stephen Hill, he has a double attitude towards Martha Ray.
His sympathy for her as victim of Hill's cruel desertion is tempered
by his suspicions of her behaviour since then (even though this may
be the direct result of the former). His readiness to impress his ignorance on us further complicates this ambivalence and this, together
with his gossipy tags ('they say' 'some say', and 'I've heard') makes a
virtue of his unreliability.

Paul Hamilton believes that the narrator wilfully holds back on the
facts about the 'child's murder' with the object of heightening the
'*frisson* of a sensational murder'. If this is so, then it also heightens
and foregrounds the textuality of the fiction, a textuality that makes
the business about the pond's precise measurements even more facile,
a comical attempt to authenticate the story.

If Hamilton is right, then this would reinforce a view of the narrator as a scheming disingenuous gossip. His weaving metadiscourse,
continually alternating between 'I cannot tell' and 'some say' and 'all
and each agree' indicates a much more sophisticated form of gossip
than is implied by Wordsworth's observation about retired sea
captains.

Such men having little to do become credulous and talkative from indolence; and from the same cause, and other predisposing causes by which it is probable that such men may have been affected, they are prone to superstition. (*Advertisement* to 1800 edition of *Lyrical Ballads*)

The mood of stanza XXII epitomizes the overall tension in the poem between knowledge, imagination and superstition. The mounting suspicions of the anxious villagers provoke them into forming a vigilante group armed with spades. The only means to certainty would be to excavate the 'little infant's bones', but their superstition undoes them with chthonic rumblings in the mossy mound (compare these rumblings with the spirit of the deep in *The Ancient Mariner*).

Superstition is, like autosuggestion, one method of filling the knowledge gap, but their clumsy efforts are thwarted. In fact, their failure will have the result of prolonging the whispering uncertainty.

> But all do still aver
> The little babe is buried there                                   (240–1)

(though the subterranean shakings are apparently not taken as proof of anything). Hence the reader too is thwarted and we are left with the narrator's arch and increasingly feeble-sounding 'I cannot tell'. This is indeed his own balladic refrain, the antiphonal response to Martha's wretched 'Oh misery!' Wordsworth exploits the cadences in these to sketch a sense of closure, leaving the troubled gossip-riddled community transfixed in its state of insecurity.

## Conclusions

The poems dealing with humanitarian issues in this chapter represent an experiment in the broadening of Wordsworth's thematic range. The poet's compassion for the victims of social injustice is manifest. At times this compassion is almost palpable, at others it borders on the sentimental, as in 'The Convict'. By 1798 and the appearance of *Lyrical Ballads*, Wordsworth's primary concern is not to overthrow the state that allows or perhaps encourages injustice, but to establish viable institutions that can genuinely support its victims while preserving the contemporary social environment. The result is that his treatment too easily attributes the causes of suffering simply to the caprices of 'bad luck'.

His portraits of the victims (what Humphry House dismissed as Wordsworth's ethical symbols') clearly reveal his humanitarian alarm at people reduced to subsisting at the level of wild beasts. He does not propose practical solutions but, at most, hits at the failure of existing ones. Among the consolations that he does propose is the psychotherapeutic benefits of nature, though in the horrors of 'The Female Vagrant' and 'The Thorn', this rings somewhat hollow.

Ultimately, the social poems are also poems of human psychology. 'The Female Vagrant' is a chilling expressionistic depiction of the horrors of a species of insanity *viewed from the outside*, while 'The Thorn' brilliantly explores with some penetration the dynamics between an insecure community and an outsider, filtered through a narrator hovering ambivalently between the two. It is in this area that Wordsworth is most effective: the social mechanics become a pretext for a groping towards a casebook account of the characteristics of loss, victimisation, suffering, abuse, alienation and so on within the scenario of the disintegration of the rural community.

## Further Research

In order to get a broader grasp of poems that touch on the eighteenth-century social context, have a look at 'Goody Blake and Harry Gill', 'Old Man Travelling' and Coleridge's 'The Dungeon'. In particular, you will find it useful to examine in detail 'The Complaint of a Forsaken Indian Woman' and compare the treatment of its central character with that of the woman in 'The Thorn'. How does Wordsworth's choice of narrator and narrative mode affect the reader's response to the woman in each poem?

# 5

## Nature and the Supernatural: 'the strangeness of it'

I am a perfect enthusiast in my admiration of Nature in all her various forms; and have looked upon, and as it were conversed with, the objects which this country has presented to my view
(Letter to Dorothy Wordsworth from Lake Constance, 6 September 1790)

On his momentous walking tour of the Swiss Alps in 1790, Wordsworth encountered in its dramatic landscape an awesome, harrowing beauty, the most extreme expression of that power and majesty in nature that had been his close and companionable form since childhood. As book VI of *The Prelude* declares, he was profoundly inspired by 'unapproachable forests', 'majestic floods' and 'solitudes sublime'; in short he was transported wholly and exultantly into the colossal realm of nature's 'awful power'.

Wordsworth was profoundly humbled, too in his encounter with this magnificent apotheosis of those mysterious presences and forces first intimated in the 'meadow, grove and stream' of Westmorland. It was, of course, another sublime defining moment in Wordsworth's moral, religious and artistic life, as well as in the history of English Romanticism.

Wordsworth is often credited with the rediscovery, even the reinvention, of nature. It is a commonplace to say that his idea of nature is far from the simplistic popular idea of nature as a pleasant venue for a day out, with twittering birds, crusty cowpats and even crustier farmers. Wordsworth's nature must be understood from the point of view of a richly complex metaphysical relationship between, on the one hand, the individual consciousness and, on the other, a mysterious transcendental reality inhabiting the objects and organisms of the empirical world. To get some perspective on his vision it would be advantageous to have a brief history of nature.

In ancient Greek literature, mankind and nature are essentially two discrete entities. Yet this axiom does not inhibit Greek writers from exploring what it is that separates us. For Aristotle we are superior to the beasts by virtue of a superior intellect. However, as Aesop's anthropomorphism and the figures of Greek literature reveal, we share a host of characteristics, such as a foxy disdain for sour grapes and the obduracy of mean-spirited dogs.

Roman Ovid extends this by investigating the leaky interface between us, while Virgil depicts nature as a bucolic retreat from urban tensions. The Romans also embrace the Greek earth mother Gaia, as Tellus. On the other hand, Epicurus and Lucretius expose the paradox that while poets may decry the civilised and urban for the rustic, their civilised art is intrinsically rooted in the values of the urban.

For Christians, nature is frequently idealised as a prelapsarian paradise, the Edenic golden age of mankind. This view of nature encapsulates a moral idyll, as well as the expression of the magnificent incarnation of the divine:

> The heavens declare the glory of God: and the firmament sheweth his handiwork.   (Psalms 19:1)

In the sixteenth century Shakespeare casts back to classical perspectives of nature and synthesises them with elements of ancient English folklore, most famously in *A Midsummer Night's Dream* and *The Tempest*. For him, nature is again a magic site of danger, flux and metamorphosis, yet also a mirror revealing correspondences between man and natural planes of reality – the roots of the naturalistic fallacy.

By the time of the Enlightenment this charismatic view of nature is to a large extent dispelled and, if man's superior intellect is to flourish, it must dominate the brutalising effects of nature. Nevertheless, even though the new aristocratic man is ordained by God to be His steward over creation, mankind takes refuge in his cities and towns. He delights in the landscaped garden in which nature has been properly regularised.

Behind this view there lurks the bleak, constipated pessimism of Thomas Hobbes. But with the appearance of Rousseau's spirited romanticist paradigm in mid-eighteenth century, a much-abused and maligned nature is rescued from her rationalist chains. Rousseau famously avers that:

> man is naturally good, loving justice and order; that there is absolutely no original perversity in the human heart, and that the first move-ments of nature are always right. (*Letter to Archbishop of Paris*, 1762)

By nature good, man finds his proper home in a pre-industrial, pre-property-owning condition of innocence, the natural life of the 'noble savage' free of depression, pollution, discord.

The English Romantics, led by the 'Lake School' poets, embrace this new philosophy together with its radical vision and political over-tones and gradually work to undermine the tired old decorums and straits of Rationalism, announcing a new spirit of 'Sensibility'.

Nature is not now regarded as a threat or an impediment but a sublime source of truth, a balm and a rich mode of creativity. Rousseau's view of nature becomes informed with the subjectivist-orientated metaphysics of Kant and Schlegel and both of these strands converge in the aesthetics of Wordsworth and Coleridge.

Nineteen years after the first appearance of *Lyrical Ballads*, Coleridge set out its broad thematic terms:

> During the first year that Mr Wordsworth and I were neighbours, our conversations turned frequently on the two cardinal points of poetry, the power of exciting the sympathy of the reader by a faithful adherence to the truth of nature, and the power of giving the interest of novelty by the modifying colours of the imagination.
>
> (*Biographia Literaria*, Chapter XIV)

This very much echoes Wordsworth's own view in the Preface to *Lyrical Ballads*, that the poetry was to be grounded in the natural events of 'common life', made interesting by a 'certain colouring of the imagination'.

The three trig points of composition for them were to be nature, truth and the imagination – which became a vital source of tension both in the verse and between the two men. Coleridge explained the focuses by which their work was to be apportioned:

> my endeavours should be directed to persons and characters supernatural, or at least romantic … Mr Wordsworth, on the other hand, was to propose to himself as his object, to give the charm of novelty to things of the everyday.   (*Biographia Literaria*, Chapter XIV)

Mr Wordsworth's poetry was to treat of nature, while Coleridge was to open up the world of the supernatural. The division of labour in *Lyrical Ballads* is nothing like as clear-cut as this statement may indicate, and Wordsworth himself freely drew on the supernatural in some of his verse (such as in 'The Idiot Boy', 'Lucy Gray' and 'Nutting'). However, to explore these important co-ordinates I have chosen to discuss the following poems in this chapter: 'Lines written in early spring', 'The Tables Turned' and *The Rime of the Ancient Mariner*.

## 'Lines written in early spring'

As we have seen in previous chapters, nature represents for Wordsworth a diverse and complex range of real and figurative agencies, including teacher, nurse, friend, muse, goddess, therapy, moral counsellor and regenerator. Often regarding himself as nature's bard and prophet, he constantly exalts nature as his tutelary deity,

> Wisdom and spirit of the universe          (*The Prelude*, 1805, II.427)

> with something of a Mother's mind
> And no unworthy aim,
> The homely Nurse doth all she can
> ('Ode: Intimations of Immortality', 79–81)

The anchor of my purest thoughts, the nurse,
The guide, the guardian of my heart, and soul
Of all my moral being.                    ('Tintern Abbey', 110–12)

In discussing the poetry, we should remember too that 'nature' incorporates human nature in its own array of facets: reason, affections, ethics and justice, creativity, love, awe, brutishness, insight, mind, animus and imagination.

### Lines written in early spring

I heard a thousand blended notes,
While in a grove I sate reclined,
In that sweet mood when pleasant thoughts
Bring sad thoughts to the mind.

To her fair works did Nature link                    5
The human soul that through me ran;
And much it grieved my heart to think
What man has made of man.

Through primrose tufts, in that sweet bower,
The periwinkle trailed its wreathes;                    10
And 'tis my faith that every flower
Enjoys the air it breathes.

The birds around me hopped and played:
Their thoughts I cannot measure,
But the least motion which they made,                    15
It seemed a thrill of pleasure.

The budding twigs spread out their fan,
To catch the breezy air:
And I must think, do all I can,
That there was pleasure there.                    20

If these thoughts may not prevent,
If such be of my creed the plan,
Have I not reason to lament
What man has made of man?

As its title implies, 'Lines written in early spring' was one of the products of Wordsworth's great creative blossoming in the spring of 1798,
during which he experimented in a variety of poetic forms and subjects.
About this time, too, there develops more clearly in his mind the idea
of the 'universal heart' (*The Prelude*; XII.219); this, in simple terms,
is his view of nature as the active will, deeply interfused within the
phenomena of the natural world, animate and inanimate. It is this
idea which inspired 'Lines written in early spring'.

The poem begins in physical though not spiritual repose. The
'grove' (2) or 'bower' (9) is the familiar Romantics' code for tranquil
disengagement from the world's tensions and pains (cf. 'Tintern
Abbey', line 6). Here, in the opening stanza, Wordsworth composes
himself as a preparation to propounding his 'creed' (22). Yet no
sooner has he settled himself physically beyond the cares of the world,
than he returns to them in contemplation.

The 'blended notes' of harmonising nature act powerfully on the
ear to subdue him, lotus-like into that sweet mood which presages
sadder (but also creative) thoughts on the world of man (3–4). As a
means of entering Wordsworth's 'creed', the opening stanza of the
poem attempts to subdue and prepare the reader's mind too, a literary parallel to nature's effects on the poet.

The second stanza takes up the opening idea of 'blended' in the
word 'link' in line 5, thus literally linking the two stanzas. Setting up
harmony as the keynote, Wordsworth personifies nature ('her fair
works') as an active and deliberative agency, while the opening lines
of this stanza reiterate one of the major ideas of the nature poems: the
unity of man and nature:

> To her fair works did Nature link
> The human soul that through me ran                    (5–6)

This revisits, of course, the 'power / Of harmony' of 'Tintern Abbey',
as well as the motion and spirit that 'impels / All thinking things'.

'Lines written in early spring' is equally preoccupied with thinking
and thoughts (meditation is referred to in one form or another in
every stanza), yet where 'Tintern Abbey' stresses the restorative power
of nature, this poem posits a slightly different angle on the theme;
namely the potential of nature to grasp the human soul and elevate it

to unwonted levels of reflection and insight, to the height of Romantic 'sublime'.

We can trace echoes of these ideas in 'Nutting' and 'There was a Boy', where the youthful poet is harrowed by nature's capacity to

> enter unawares into his mind
> With all its solemn imagery                    ('There was a Boy', 22–3)

Again there is the Wordsworthian duality of sweet leading to sad thoughts. But here, in 'Lines written in early spring', he is grieved by 'What man has made of man' (8). This poem avoids details, but we are likely to recall the wilful wrecking in 'Nutting' or the 'dissolute city' of *Michael* or the cruelty in 'The Convict' and 'The Female Vagrant'.

Although the details are absent here, the references to 'heart' and 'think' in line 7 are likely to bring to mind another of Wordsworth's dualities, of 'think and know'. This line reveals how the poet engages on a deeply sensitive level with the pain of what man has made of man. The full weight and intrigue of the line are left trembling in the silence between stanzas 2 and 3.

The final line of the second stanza, 'What man has made of man' with its engaging poise, draws the first part of the poem to a pause with a complex metaphysic. Nature's occult but penetrating action on his soul reminds Wordsworth first that he is a thing of nature himself, blended to nature's 'fair works' and then, extending this thought, that, as a human, he is also linked to other men and women. However, and ironically, this double alliance reveals to him less the possibility of their concord than their antagonism, threatening the ideal of the 'universal heart'.

Stanza 3 expels his melancholy and recovers something of his former mirth via the nature present before him. Nature has once more set somewhat to delight and distract. The primrose and the periwinkle fascinate his mind by their intertwining patterns, while the word 'bower' reinforces the atmosphere of intimate seclusion. Nevertheless, just as the poet discovers consolation in nature, the word 'wreathes' in line 10 unsettles with a solemn reminder of mortality (our 'heavy laws' again). Despite this, he evades this avenue through a new and significant direction,

> And 'tis my faith that every flower
> Enjoys the air it breathes.                              (11–12)

'Enjoys' here is perhaps discordant on the modern ear, as is the anthropomorphism implicit in it (offending Coleridge's satire on the poet who 'filled all things with himself'). At the same time, we may resolve this by thinking of 'Enjoys' as meaning 'deriving benefit from' or fitting its environment. In any case, while the word annoys, it does express well Wordsworth's deep delight in this setting, implying the spontaneity of the thought.

By using a term normally attached to animate nature, Wordsworth implies another facet of his mystical 'faith': once the individual is prepared to be at one with the spirit in nature, nature will reciprocate with the joy of that moment. Taking a broader perspective, he seems to say that if people would only adjust their deeply-held precepts, they stand to prolong such delightful moments into a reconstructed and happier life.

This combination of epiphany and rapture, akin to Gnostic ecstasy, is extended into the fourth stanza with its 'thrill' projected onto the birds. In another instance of 'feel and know', Wordsworth's recognition that animals also think establishes a primitive kinship with them, but at the same time their inscrutability ('cannot measure') divides them from him. After the thought comes the emotion, the 'thrill of pleasure', a celebration of the minutiae of nature calling out to him, revealing and reflecting his own happiness in its energy.

Throughout the poem, Wordsworth ascribes not only a causative agency to nature but also intentionality. This purposive agency is personified in line 5 with 'her fair works', the goddess nature, recalling the classical Gaia-Tellus. Hence, not only does nature *happen* to link his soul to the 'fair works' but, referring to lines 17–18, there is a purpose or a volition in nature

> The budding twigs *spread* out their fan,
> *To catch* the breezy air              (17–18; emphasis added)

'Spread' is one of Wordsworth's favourite words in *Lyrical Ballads* for denoting nature's impulse to disseminate influence as well referring to biological growth. Further, given that this is a spring day with the sap beginning to rise, it is plausible to translate the budding, trailing, wreathing, spreading of tuft, flower and twig, as a willed purposive struggle for survival and attention.

In 'Three years she grew' Wordsworth again talks of the impact of nature as a generator and a moulder. But sure enough he tries to take us beyond a view of nature that understands only a blind deterministic force. Nature's formative influences are catalogued, while nature herself is visualized as:

> an overseeing power
> To kindle or restrain. (11–12)

In 'Lines written near Richmond' the stream cunningly beguiles its unsuspecting spectators, whereas in 'The Fountain' the small birds do not merely respond naturalistically to their context but:

> Let loose their carols when they *please*,
> Are quiet when they *will*. (39–40; emphasis added)

More than anything, the expression of emotions (joyous, smiling, brooding and so on) in nature's inanimate objects (leaves, streams, mountains and clouds) reinforces an impression of nature as in adjectival possession of soul, mind and sensibility.

Thus, in line 16, the hopping and playing birds seem to Wordsworth to perform these actions out of the 'thrill of pleasure'. His conviction of this is re-stated in the following stanza where, in spite of doing 'all I can', he becomes united with nature, so much so that he becomes convinced that the whole scene, including the trees and even the 'breezy air', shared in the pleasure of that elevated moment as the 'universal heart'.

The use of the past tense 'was' in line 20 points to the possibility of at least two moments here: one is the occasion of the original experience of 'pleasure' in the grove, and the other, the later recollection of this in tranquillity (although, about 45 years after writing the poem, Wordsworth claimed that he composed it more or less simultaneously with the moment of hearing the birds). In the former he is fully absorbed in nature's vitality and in the other meditating and making meaning of it.

The latter point is confirmed in line 19 with his imprecation, 'I must think, do all I can'. The ambiguity in the second half of this line evidences a more general ambivalence or uncertainty at work in the poem. This ambivalence continues into the final stanza that opens with two hesitant conditional clauses. Withdrawn from society, he becomes profoundly introspective, uncertain, and confused.

In fact, line 21 ('If these thoughts may not prevent') is so loose as to be practically meaningless. The following line only gropes towards the hope that his 'creed' accords with Nature's plan, that is, that the whole of Nature's 'fair works' are in fact blended with the 'human soul' in the 'universal heart' – as stanza 2 proposes. If this is so then mankind, by holding itself aloof, discrete from the rest of nature, is a force for division and destruction, a 'reason to lament'. However, the poem ends inconclusively on a question mark, part inquisitive, part accusative, and a confrontation with the reader.

Wordsworth later revised the final stanza (in a moment of even greater tranquillity), thus imposing on the end of the lyric a narrower range of interpretative possibilities, though also invoking a stronger sense of closure,

> If this belief from heaven be sent,
> If such be Nature's holy plan,
> Have I not reason to lament
> What man has made of man!                    (lines 21–4)

The gains in closure and clarity need to be set against connotation and latency of meaning. Replacing the final question mark with an exclamation mark also reinforces the new finality, though it dissipates the poem's vital anxiousness and it loosens the reader's engagement at the very point where it had been most intense.

The poem's complexity of metaphysics and mood is engagingly induced in its simple diction. A reverential paean to nature and an elegy on mankind's strife and frailty, each is deepened by its difference to the other. Consistent with its balladic tone, its perspective is both subjective and tentative, framed in a near balladic metre and quatrain (the second line of each stanza usually replaces trimeter with tetrameter).

Nature, though, is also human nature and in addition to primroses and periwinkle Wordsworth presents the human response to nature, as well as the reflective and contingent in humanity. These qualifications help to restrain any tendencies to didacticism in the poem's voice. The discovery of happiness in nature's 'fair works' encounters the sombre recognition that man himself undermines the happiness in himself. Ironically, it is his capacity for reflection that both links and sunders man from nature, while recognition of this operates as a form of supernatural creed.

### 'The Tables Turned'

'The Tables Turned' is another composition in the 'Matthew' sequence of poems, a companion piece and riposte to 'Expostulation and Reply'. In the latter, Matthew urges a young Wordsworth to get his learning through books. 'Up! Up! and drink the spirit breathed'. In that poem Wordsworth steadfastly insists that nature operates more tenderly:

> we can feed this mind of ours
> In a wise passiveness.               ('Expostulation and Reply', 23–4)

But the poet is provoked into making a fuller reply to Matthew's proposition, and this is set out in 'The Tables Turned'.

#### The Tables Turned

AN EVENING SCENE, ON THE SAME SUBJECT

Up! up! my friend and clear your looks,
Why all this toil and trouble?
Up! up! my friend, and quit your books,
Or surely you'll grow double.

The sun above the mountain's head,                               5
A freshening lustre mellow,

Through all the long green fields has spread,
His first sweet evening yellow.

Books! 'tis a dull and endless strife,
Come, hear the woodland linnet,                                    10
How sweet his music; on my life
There's more of wisdom in it.

And hark! how blithe the throstle sings!
And he is no mean preacher;
Come forth into the light of things,                              15
Let Nature be your teacher.

She has a world of ready wealth,
Our minds and hearts to bless –
Spontaneous wisdom breathed by health,
Truth breathed by cheerfulness.                                   20

One impulse from a vernal wood
May teach you more of man:
Of moral evil and of good,
Than all the sages can.

Sweet is the lore which Nature brings;                            25
Our meddling intellect
Misshapes the beauteous forms of things;
– We murder to dissect.

Enough of science and of art;
Close up these barren leaves;                                      30
Come forth, and bring with you a heart
That watches and receives.

Wordsworth asserts that pleasant thoughts breed pleasant thoughts. The message is clear and up-beat. A playfulness is instilled from the opening of the poem and Wordsworth's 'Up! Up!' throws back at Matthew his own words. The early morning setting of 'Expostulation and Reply' has now, in 'The Tables Turned', become evening. With his mind rested, Wordsworth attempts to rouse Matthew out of his pensiveness ('clear your looks'). The poem begins with the stirring cheer of a practical joke, and the opening stanza establishes an amiable spirit of banter. But behind this there is a hint of Wordsworth's

didactic tone, which later aligns with nature's own role as preacher/
teacher.

We can trace the emergence of nature's pedagogical aspect in the
second stanza. First nature tranquillises with 'sweet delights', richly
colourful in the crepuscular landscape lit by refulgent evening sunlight. Nature delights, gives unashamed pleasure in its beauty, a
refuge from the sterility of books and cities.

This view of nature as a lure is taken up in the third stanza.
'Books!' the poet exclaims, summoning his friend out of his tranquil
reverie with some exasperation. Academic learning is 'dull and endless', offering no lasting insights into nature's or life's mysteries. The
next word 'Come' repeats the summons, attempting to draw the
friend and the reader into the charm of nature. Wordsworth makes a
error in placing a linnet in the woodland, but the important thing is
that it stands to him for the allure of nature, summed up in the word
'sweet' (11), one of his favourite words for nature's allure. And nature
is not merely beautiful, for:

There's more of wisdom in it.                                    (12)

(This idea is echoed in Book I of *The Prelude*, where he describes
Nature as 'Wisdom and spirit of the universe'; 1805, I.427.)

His raucous shriek of 'Books!' at the start of stanza 3 is not a blan-
ket denunciation of literature, nor of the imagination, after all the
poem itself is a literary text. But it is a clarion blast against the opinion in 'Expostulation and Reply' that argues that books are the only
important medium of learning.

In the 1798 Advertisement to *Lyrical Ballads*, Wordsworth recalled
that both poems 'arose out of conversation with a friend who was
somewhat unreasonably attached to modern books of moral philosophy'. The 'friend' was the young critic William Hazlitt, who visited
Wordsworth and Coleridge at Alfoxden in May of 1798 and who also
recalled the moment as a sort of epiphany for him:

> Wordsworth, looking out of the low, latticed window, said, 'How
> beautifully the sun sets on that yellow bank!' I thought within myself,
> 'With what eyes these poets see nature!' and ever after, when I saw the

sun-set stream upon the objects facing it, conceived I had made a
discovery, or thanked Mr Wordsworth for having made one for me!
('My First Acquaintance with Poets')

Stanza 4 begins with yet another rousing shriek, underlining this
dissident new vision. Identifying himself metaphorically with the song
of the throstle, Wordsworth now aligns himself and nature with the
role of teacher. On the literal level, the throstle 'preaches' indirectly,
advertising nature's euphony. But Wordsworth's song is unfeignedly
didactic, as 'a man speaking to men', sharing 'sensations and passions'
and, as his Preface insists, a poet has a didactic mission, a duty to
change as well as to record. To this end, in Wordsworth the words
'nature' and 'natural' are not merely descriptively neutral but norma-
tive, morally prescriptive. Poetry should not leave things as they are.

Line 15 extends this theme by combining it with religious rhetoric:

Come forth into the light of things                                    (15)

where 'light' takes up and parodies the sunlight of stanza 2 (and also
burlesques Matthew's own use of the word in line 5 of 'Expostulation
and Reply'). The summons is for Matthew to open himself up to
what Michael described as 'the gentle agency / Of natural objects'
(29–30). In a word,

Let Nature be your teacher.                                            (16)

It is worth noting, too, that Wordsworth was no idle educational
theorist. In 1795 he and Dorothy had put his Rousseauesque ideas
into operation when they agreed to 'parent' Basil Montagu's young
son (in exchange for free accommodation at Racedown in Dorset).
Dorothy explained their 'method':

> We teach him nothing at present but what he learns from the evidence
> of his senses. He has an insatiable curiosity which we are always care-
> ful to satisfy to the best of our ability ... we have not attempted any
> further steps in the path of *book learning*.   (letter, 19 March 1797)

Wordsworth's own theory of natural education was quite elabo-
rately formulated. Derived mainly from the philosophy of Rousseau it

was modified to accommodate Hartley's theory of associationism (see Chapter 2) and involved two main axes. A 'practical' education dealt with a basic appreciation of nature's beauty and power, together with an understanding of nature's logic (for instance, the dangers and joys of nature and creativity). Spiritual education, although starting out in this practical grounding, necessitates a closer intimacy with nature's 'wisdom and spirit'. Wordsworth elucidates this in *The Prelude* as:

> unconscious intercourse
> With the eternal beauty, drinking in
> A pure organic pleasure                    (*The Prelude*, 1805, I.589–91)

His emphasis here on 'pure organic' also stresses the importance of both moral probity and harmony, integrated with nature, and 'inseparably linked' with the 'universal heart' of the natural universe. It is of course, at heart, a statement of a religious position, in which Wordsworth transcends objective, physical nature into the sublime, the noumenal realm of God – though it is important to remember that he does actually identify Nature with God (as *The Prelude* makes plainer; see II.357 and 429).

In 'The Tables Turned' stanza 5 expounds nature's 'world of ready wealth'. Part Celtic sorceress, part Virgin Mary, and part Gaia-Tellus, Nature is venerated by the poet as an acolyte at her temple. She is the creative principle, figure of eternal regeneration, bounty and grace:

> She has a world of ready wealth,
> Our minds and hearts to bless –
> Spontaneous wisdom breathed by health,
> Truth breathed by cheerfulness.                    (17–20)

Line 17's 'world of ready wealth' points directly to this regenerative aspect as well as to her abundance. In the following line, the reference to 'minds and hearts' calls up Wordsworth's core duality of 'feel and know' where, since nature is the origin of them, she is also the synthesis of these two sources of wisdom (reconciling natural and bookish learning). The word 'wisdom' is, of course, important here too because taking up the same word from line 12, it implies that like the linnet, all of creation is suffused with Nature's powerful spirit. This spirit feeds back into the human observer as 'health' (19) and 'cheerfulness', or ecstasy (20).

Where stanza 5 introduces the theme of nature-as-teacher, the following stanza both deepens and broadens this, signalled by the phrase, 'Of moral evil and good' (23). In terms of theme, this is a highly compressed unit (in a highly succinct poem), and the whole stanza works as a brilliantly intense metaphor, so much so that it seems to 'breathe' its truths even before it is understood explicitly.

> One impulse from a vernal wood
> May teach you more of man                                           (21–2)

'Impulse' is a richly expansive idea within the sinewy morphology of this stanza. To gloss it would be reductively banal, but let us note a similar reference in 'Three years she grew':

> Myself will to my darling be
> Both law and impulse                                                (7–8)

The word here has breathtaking connotations of energy, life, creativity, freedom spontaneity and so forth. As 'spontaneity' it strikes a common chord with line 19 of 'The Tables Turned'.

To receive 'impulse' is to be energised ('im-pulsed') touched and initiated too into the ways of the occult mysteries in nature, enlightened by a coming forth into the light of things. 'Vernal wood' also strikes the right note of awakening, in this context a sacral evocation of the imagination.

Much of the early diction of the poem is concerned with clearing away the old ways, re-freshing in a new light. This idea of 'freeing' is paralleled by the new learning, steeping in the 'lore which Nature brings' (25). As the nectar of gods, this lore is, naturally, 'Sweet'. In Wordsworth's own lore, this regeneration is achieved through a variation on 'associationism'.

As we found in 'Nutting', but chiefly in 'Tintern Abbey', for Wordsworth an individual (particularly a child) learns by linking together experiences in the world. This occurs at its best when the person is not passive but his or her experiences in nature are consciously interactive and above all proactive. The mind seeks to fuse consciousness and feeling with the vital spirit or 'impulse' of nature. Beginning in humility, the process is a neo-Platonic religious experience, moving beyond the things themselves into 'the light of things' (15) with the ultimate goal of apprehending 'the beauteous forms of things' (27).

It is on this plane of sublime experience that the soul 'drinks in' the moral force of nature. In this way, nature is thus not simply a teacher but a moral teacher, coaching the whole united being in such harmonious form that he or she achieves a sort of fulfilment (or 'wisdom') within the world, a fulfilment which is intellectual and affective. For Wordsworth this is, of course, what is meant by the 'supernatural'. It obtains its clearest expression and celebration in 'Tintern Abbey' (see especially lines 32–4 and 48–50).

After these rarefied metaphysical ideas, stanza 7 comes as bathos. But, given these ideas, this is no surprise because Wordsworth now satirises rationality as the source of knowledge, our 'meddling intellect'. Some critics interpret this stanza as an attack against bookish learning, but it seems to me that the poet is criticising the Enlightenment's stress on analytical thinking as the exclusive route to wisdom, rather than books in themselves. Science and rationalist philosophy can unweave the beauteous rainbow by clinically objective analysis:

We murder to dissect. (28)

If we rely exclusively on the 'meddling intellect', devaluing the creative potential of the subjective, the imagination and our emotions, Wordsworth believes we are doomed to distort the 'beauteous forms of things'. Every truth is, as Coleridge would most assiduously affirm, a human truth: if we forget this then all we may hope for are two-dimensional definitions that ignore the spirit.

A brief pause is set between stanzas 7 and 8, in which the epigrammatic force of line 28 is permitted to resonate. And then, with a flourish, the poet calls time on 'science and art' ('art' as a artifice, deceit). With a smart and complex pun on 'barren leaves', he calls the bluff on the 'dull and endless strife' of analytics, despairing of their claims to absolute authoritative truths.

The 'barren leaves' of line 30 refer to the leaves of sterile book-learning, pursued in isolation of the living leaves of trees and plants. However, the line is self-reflexive and, at this point, Wordsworth brilliantly reveals the potential contradiction in his poem: that to continue on this course would be to use the same scientific attitude he has sought to demolish. Hence his call to 'Close up these barren leaves' of the poem itself. Poetry itself must follow the Romantic course of imagination, affection and feeling, though not necessarily to the complete exclusion of reason.

'The Tables Turned' is a great advance on 'Lines written in early spring'. Its language is direct and lucid, addressed through an engagingly succinct voice, combining a freshness of natural imagery with a sweet turn of irony. It blithely integrates what Hazlitt called 'seeming simplicity and real abstruseness'.

## The Rime of the Ancient Mariner

In his notebook for 19 April 1804, Coleridge recorded:

> at certain times, uncalled & sudden, subject to no bidding of my own or others, these Thoughts would come upon me, like a Storm, & fill the Place with something more than Nature. – But these are not contingent or transitory / they are Nature, even as the Elements are Nature / yea, more to the human mind.

It is intriguing that Coleridge should identify this barrage of thoughts with the confusion of a storm. The figure encapsulates both the fury of these 'Thoughts' and his helplessness before them. In spite of this, they steer him towards deep insight on a nature that is 'more than Nature'.

These thoughts originate in nature, 'even as the Elements are Nature', yet they lead his mind over this elemental threshold into a strange occult realm. This is the realm of the supernatural (or as Coleridge sometimes called it, the 'preternatural'). For him, as for the Ancient Mariner, it is arrived at through personal ordeal, an awesome journey, both outward and inward, to become conscious of a more profound reality.

In the first edition of *Lyrical Ballads*, *The Rime of the Ancient Mariner* was given prominence as the opening poem, itself placed on the threshold of a professedly experimental kind of poetry. As we have noted above, it was Coleridge's task to write of 'persons and characters supernatural', and his method of accomplishing this is not, like Wordsworth, to begin with nature but with the deep uncharted reaches of the human mind. To explore the allotropic facets of the human psyche he chose the analogue of a disastrous storm-wracked voyage, whose central character is haunted by terrifying monsters and zombies, tormented by guilt, illusion and degradation, impotence and despair, until in the end he achieves something resembling redemption.

The opening to this extraordinary tale has about it the ring of a modern thriller: an ordinary innocent man is waylaid by a seeming madman and is subjected to a fantastic account of a nightmare journey. On a mysterious voyage to the southern ocean, the Mariner violates his shipmates' taboo by killing a harmless albatross, for which he is at first castigated, then commended and later alienated as the instigator of their disaster. Scapegoat and pariah, he suffers terrible psychological torment as the punishment for his 'crime', until eventually and fortuitously he blesses the water snakes. Subjected to further anguish, his ordeals culminate in the sinking of the ship. He is rescued by the pilot's crew, yet in spite of his expiation he is denied a final absolution and is condemned to wander the earth eternally, recounting his dreadful tale with 'strange power of speech'.

The passage I have chosen for discussion is from part V of the 1798 text, lines 327–81 (stanzas 77–88). After blessing the 'happy living things' in Part IV, the Mariner has enjoyed some 'gentle sleep' and slaked his thirst. So light-headed had he become that he feared he had died and become a ghost. However, an explosion of fire whips up a storm, stirring the dead crew to work the ship's ropes.

> The helmsman steered, the ship moved on;
>   Yet never a breeze up-blew;
> The Marineres all 'gan work the ropes,

    Where they were wont to do:                      330
They raised their limbs like lifeless tools –
    We were a ghastly crew.

The body of my brother's son
    Stood by me knee to knee:
The body and I pulled at one rope,                  335
    But he said nought to me –
And I quaked to think of my own voice
    How frightful it would be!

The daylight dawned – they dropped their arms,
    And clustered round the mast:               340
Sweet sounds rose slowly through their mouths
    And from their bodies passed.

Around, around, flew each sweet sound,
    Then darted to the sun:
Slowly the sounds came back again,               345
    Now mixed, now one by one.

Sometimes a dropping from the sky
    I heard the lavrock sing;
Sometimes all little birds that are
How they seemed to fill the sea and air        350
    With their sweet jargoning,

And now 'twas like all instruments,
    Now like a lonely flute;
And now it is an angel's song,
    That makes the heavens be mute.           355

It ceased: yet still the sails made on
    A pleasant noise till noon,
A noise like of a hidden brook
    In the leafy month of June,
That to the sleeping woods all night         360
    Singeth a quiet tune.

Listen, O listen, thou Wedding-guest!
    'Marinere! thou hast thy will:
'For that, which comes out of thine eye, doth make
    'My body and soul to be still.'         365

Never sadder tale was told
   To a man of woman born:
Sadder and wiser thou wedding-guest!
   Thou'lt rise tomorrow morn.

Never sadder tale was heard                                      370
   By a man of woman born:
The Marineres all returned to work
   As silently as beforne.

The Marineres all 'gan pull the ropes,
   But look at me they n'old:                                   375
Thought I, I am as thin as air –
   They cannot me behold.

Till noon we silently sailed on,
   Yet never a breeze did breathe:
Slowly and smoothly went the ship                                380
   Moved onward from beneath.

This astonishing and elusive poem has generated a huge multiplicity of interpretative viewpoints: religious, political, psychoanalytical, sociological, biographical and so on. Most often, readings have espoused mythic, symbolic and/or allegorical constructions including colonialism, New Testament, nature, the Fall of Man, the artist in general, and the Romantic artist in particular. The great spread of critical viewpoints and witnesses is testimony and tribute to the charismatic openness and stimulating potency of the text.

Perhaps surprisingly for a poem in which the supernatural is an important feature, the events have a firm grounding in nature, both as a frame of reference and a foil. Coleridge himself carried out extensive research for the narrative, including accounts of eighteenth-century voyages of exploration and endurance. These included Captain Cook's *Voyage to the Pacific* (1784) and Captain Bligh's description of his epic journey to safety after the mutiny on HMS Bounty. In fact the vivid naturalism of some of the descriptions in *The Ancient Mariner* has been said to account for the high level of demand among seafarers for the first edition of *Lyrical Ballads*.

By the time the poem has reached line 327, the voyage has developed a separate, internal life of its own. Concentrating on the events within the vicinity of the ship cultivates a very localised sense of nature cut off from outside reference points. For instance, here we witness the ship sailing on without aid of the wind, powered and steered (we learn in stanza 89) by the avenging sea spirit nine fathom below the keel.

Free will is a significant theme in *The Ancient Mariner*, as it is elsewhere in Coleridge. But here it is frequently expressed as a thwarting of the Mariner's purpose or determination, usually by more dominant forces such as the slimy creatures and spirits, God, the elements, the weather, as well as other human beings. Drifting is set up early on as a key motif in the poem.

This impotence of will is evidenced in the futility of the helmsman's steering in line 327, a dead man at the wheel. Like his ghoulish shipmates he is merely going through the motions. They are hollow men, resembling automata or zombies, responding from slavish routine, as 'they were wont to do'.

This inert, mindless movement is, of course, what makes them a 'ghastly' and a ghostly crew. The point is endorsed by the terse, lifeless statements in the opening stanza of the extract, its end-stopped lines a simulacrum of the mechanical existence of the crew. In the following stanza ('The body of my brother's son') the ship's routine becomes something uncanny in the repetition of the phrase 'the body' and its grisly muteness. This image of the zombie-like body brings home, too, the desolating ostracism of the Mariner by his volatile sea-mates.

The lack of normal social dealings between the Mariner and the rest of the crew turns the focus onto the inward 'actions' of the man. The effect is to further accentuate the already severe mental torture resulting from confinement with this ghostly company and the loss of human society. This alienation from society and the breakdown of communication represent the archetypal Coleridgean nightmare. As we noted in 'Love', the great underlying fear of his hero is the failure of friendship and the loss of social companionship, both of which are instrumental in warding off the pervasive threat of madness.

By the time we reach line 333 it is surprising just how ready we are to accept as normal the horrors, monsters and grotesquely non-natural events encountered. Our whole frame of reference has become shifted and distorted and just when it seems there can be no worse, the Mariner is pitched further into the abyss of pain. The result is that to a great extent, we become inured to the supernaturalness of events and more ready to accept them. So even within the short span of the above extract, we witness dead bodies at work, while odd sounds pass round and through them, a skylark sings far out at sea, the ship is powered by a deep submarine spirit, plus musical sails, and the Mariner himself becoming invisible. Most readers would delineate these phenomena as supernatural but before trying to wring sense from them, it would be useful to get clear what is meant by 'natural' and 'supernatural' in the context of *The Ancient Mariner*.

Nature in *The Ancient Mariner* takes three principal forms. (a) The animals, weather, elements (there is a great interplay between these) and other features that make up physical nature, including the water snakes. The mariners regard all these as intricately related because, for instance, they regard changes in the weather as the result of slaying the albatross. (b) Humans and human nature: this overlaps to some extent with physical nature, for example with regard to basic needs (food, drink, society), but includes the poem's perceptions of nature, the metaphysics and supernatural, morality and the impulse to kill. (c) The natural laws and order in the world: these include the predisposition for regeneration, mortality and natural justice.

Behind all three rests the possibility of God, though religion is expressed more formally in terms of imagery; for example, the hermit, and the Catholic diction of the Mariner ('God himself / Scarce seemed there to be', 632–3).

The supernatural, in the form of goblins, magical events, strange curses and weird transformations, was familiar material in the traditional ballads and were usually employed for suspense and their striking emotional impact (for example, see Thomas Percy's *Reliques of English Poetry*, 1765). Wordsworth's 'The Thorn' and *Peter Bell* (intended originally for inclusion in *Lyrical Ballads*) both making striking use of the uncanny. However, this does not imply that the supernatural must be posited as the antithesis of the natural.

Indeed Coleridge explores the supernatural and its interface with the natural for its metaphysical potential, as well as for its strictly entertainment value. First, though, we need to distinguish the 'supernatural' from the 'uncanny', the latter referring simply to the 'odd', or uncomfortably strange, and the disruption of the natural order of things. Thus, the uncanny in literature might include ghosts, witchcraft, poltergeists and so on. Examples of the uncanny in *The Ancient Mariner* include the strange weather effects, the animated body in stanza 78, a talking ship in stanza 46, and, from the Pilot's point of view, the apparently dead body that talks in line 593.

A feeling of the uncanny, or the 'eldritch' (line 234) can be created simply through the poem's gaps, the absence of markers, lacunae and elision. For example, a nameless Mariner and his anonymous ship set sail on an unspecified mission to an unknown destination. Coleridge's weird and archaic diction and spellings also contribute to the poem's strangeness: 'loon' (15), 'freaks' (47), 'wondrous' (50), 'crazy' (598), 'witch' (125), 'elfish' (267), 'jag' (317), 'gan' (329), 'Lavrock' (348), 'swound' (397) and 'fiendish' (571), plus an assortment of demons, spirits, ghosts and ghouls. The uncanniness deepens in proportion to how these affect or control natural, the expected.

Crucially, in Coleridge, the uncanny consists of those figures and events that expose the supernatural at work in the realm of phenomenon, the natural and human world whose limitations and potentialities it seeks to highlight. The uncanny conveys and confirms to us the existence of the supernatural. As such, the uncanny transcends the normal order, the laws of nature. Thus dead bodies may reasonably labour in the ship's shrouds and lavrocks sing far out at sea:

> And now 'twas like all instruments,
>     Now like a lonely flute;
> And now it is an angel's song,
> That makes the heavens be mute.                    (352–5)

Wordsworth too was energised by the great potential of this marvellous tale. In fact, the poem was first planned as a collaborative effort between the two men during a walking trip in Devon, the chief object being to raise £5 from its publication. Wordsworth is credited with supplying some of the verse and the poem's moral crux involving the albatross and the avenging spirit's pursuit of the Mariner. In spite of this earlier enthusiasm, he turned against the poem (and the

supernatural in general), trashing it for the poor critical reception of
*Lyrical Ballads*.

> From what I gather it seems The Ancyent Marinere has upon the
> whole been an injury to the volume. I mean that the old words and the
> strangeness of it have deterred readers from going on.
>
> (Letter, 24 June 1799)

The poem radically challenges the Preface's insistence on subjects
springing from the 'common life'. In fact, on this criterion, *The
Ancient Mariner* sticks out like a sore thumb. Accordingly, in later
editions, it was removed to the end of the collection, though some of
Wordsworth's own contributions make use of the supernatural. As if
to undermine the poem still further, he took it upon himself to alter
the title in 1800 to *The Rime of the Ancient Mariner. A Poet's Reverie*,
thereby shifting the whole balance integral to the relationship
between the natural and supernatural in the poem. But as the poem
appears to defend itself:

> It had been strange, even in a dream                                    (325)

The uncanny is, of course, by definition strange (and the word
'strange' appears numerously throughout *The Ancient Mariner*). But
by comparison with the horrors and transformations of modern cin-
ema, *The Rime* is not to our eyes that strange. There are still days and
nights, the ship remains on the sea, and men retain their shapes as
men. A large framework of order endures and this order functions to
contrast with the uncanny, acting as the Other, the desired and primordial state of order continually deferred. As his Notebooks reveal,
Coleridge was fascinated by the binary contrasts (note the great number of oppositions in *The Ancient Mariner*) and in this poem he
employs the normal and the uncanny to define each other. Thus,
in the above extract, we discover that mysterious episode in which,
following the storm:

> Sometimes a dropping from the sky
>    I heard the lavrock sing;
> Sometimes all little birds that are

> How they seemed to fill the sea and air
>   With their sweet jargoning,                      (347–51)

The bird resembles, by turns, all instruments, a 'lonely flute', and then an angel's song. In other words, it passes through the same phases as the Mariner's own history: from a throng, through loneliness, to a glimpse of the divine. Other flashes of this uncanny imagery occur in stanzas 83 (leafy June), 108 (a 'meadow-gale') and 132 (snow laden ivy).

One reason for these is to suggest the spasms of a deranged mind grasping at the familiar as it sinks into chaos. Another is, as Frances Austin has pointed out, that these were a common feature of old travel books aiding their authors to strike points of comparison with recognisable features (Coleridge's especial favourite among such travel stories was Purchas's *Pilgrimage*, of 1613). Most significantly, however, these references help to maintain the normal frame of reference by which to crank up instances of the uncanny and supernatural (in this context it is interesting to note that Freud uses the term 'unheimlich' to denote the uncanny, literally the unhomely, defining it as 'that class of the frightening that leads us back to what is known and long familiar'.)

The reference to the lavrock, or lark, and 'all little birds' keeps us in mind of the broader creation and thus of that larger bird slain by the Mariner, the inception of this other voyage of the guilt-ridden mind. It was the shooting of the bird in stanza 20 that had forced a crack into the mysterious other world:

> We were the first that ever burst
>   Into that silent sea.                            (101–2)

The albatross itself had emerged from this other world, of the supernatural, 'Thorough the fog it came' (62) and, because the mariners treat it like a 'Christian soul' (63), it seems to possess the nature and amphibious power to move freely between the two realms, to transcend the natural habitat of the bird to the noumenal supernatural (just as the lavrock eerily begins in a leafy English lane and transmutes into an angel's song). The uncanny draws attention to this detail of the bird, while at the same time opening up its potential as a symbolic image.

The ease with which the bird slips between the air and the 'fog', the superb facility of Coleridge's symbol here, together with his curious untypical restraint, unlocks the poem's receptiveness to allegorical readings. The uncanny has a major role here because, complemented by Coleridge's silences, it helps to transfer the central experiences out of the purely naturalistic and into the sphere of the ambivalent (and the poem positively buzzes with ambivalence). For example, we are continually beset by questions of the status of the poem's events: which, if any, of the Mariner's experiences and observations are actual physical events, which imagined or fancied, which reverie and which hallucinations?

The answer must be a phenomenological one – though nonetheless happier for that – and that is that his experiences are real to himself. For instance, in stanza 106 ('Like one on a lonely road') he confesses to a terrifying dread that a 'frightful fiend / Doth close behind him tread'. Most of us have been down that lane, of course, in which it is to imagine the presence of the Other. The supernatural is the Other, that other place or mode of being, the archetypal apotheosis of truth and beauty that is reached by means of the imagination. The poem can be interpreted as Coleridge's reaching after the world of the sublime via the pathway of nature.

The Lake poet Robert Southey (Coleridge's brother-in-law) later claimed:

> Preternatural impressions are sometimes communicated to us for wise purposes. (*Sir Thomas More*, 1831)

The wise purposes in *The Ancient Mariner* are, on one hand, indubitably moral but they are primarily spiritual. Construing himself as a kind of prophet, the poet is prevailed upon to see, as Wordsworth, 'into the life of things'. In a form of metaphysical idealism, the Romantic poet boldly penetrates the cracks in the natural order opened up by the uncanny and into the supernatural reality beyond. However, in Coleridge this seeing into the life of things is seldom with an 'eye made quiet', but with a fiercely volatile eye aroused through a direct engagement with those things.

Hence the two journeys in *The Ancient Mariner*: the outer made through strange weather, fiends and the horrifying ordeal of physical isolation, 'Alone, alone, all all alone' (224); and the inner journey through guilt, alienation and eventually degradation and despair to confront the inner reality of humanity. There is no single, apocalyptic climax as in, say, Conrad's *The Heart of Darkness*, but by experiencing what it is like *not* to be a man, especially through rejection, the Mariner comes to discover more closely what it is to be human.

Wordsworth believed that the supernatural existed within the 'common life'. Coleridge is not altogether that clear but in *The Ancient Mariner* he projects a view of the supernatural like Southey's: as impressions from beyond common objects but communicated through them. Perception of the supernatural is of the same order as the operation of the imagination and relies upon it: it is an active spiritual communion with the 'sense sublime', and a coadunating process. For Coleridge there is no necessary sense of Wordsworth's presence 'deeply interfused' and manifested through 'serene and blessed mood'. Instead it is a deeply painful and problematic insight in which the troubled communicant is 'cursed' (207), 'stunned' (655), 'forlorn' (656) and 'a wiser but a sadder man' (657).

Our discussion has moved away from close reference to the extract, but this was necessary in order to explore the metaphysical overtones implicit in stanzas 77 and 78. Both of these – together with 79 – also relate to Coleridge's theme of the 'One Life' (see Chapter 8), while the word 'clustered' in line 340 seems to point us to this theme. Through his ordeal and until the ship finally sinks in Part VII, the Mariner continues to regard himself as integrally part of the ship's community. Even when he has been ostracised, cursed and abandoned by his shipmates and they are all by now dead, he insists on referring to 'we', for example, 'we were a ghastly crew' (332).

The voyage represents all of their lives lived together and the Mariner's contacts with the supernatural, via the uncanny occurrences on the ship, continue to link him with the dead crew, the souls of his ship as well as with the universal spirit. However, he is agonisingly conscious throughout of the disjuncture between his own life (and even Life in Death) and the separate life of the others – just as killing the albatross has divided him from other natural creatures, the 'happy living things' (274). Yet his imaginative acuity and sense of shared humanity unites him with them on a symbolic level and enables him to survive (despite the fact that the Mariner does not exhibit a particularly vital will to survive – the life force is more vigorously in evidence around him).

At the same time he does put his own life at risk when, Christ-like, he sheds his blood to save the crew, in stanza 37. The poem highlights a group ethic and endorses the notion that the selfish will uninhibited is a threat to the stability of the community. At the end, the Mariner still relies on the help of others for his rescue. This myth of self-sufficiency retailed in fictions like *Robinson Crusoe* is knocked down as a frail idea that would ultimately be self-destructive.

Coleridge's theme of community is represented first by the Wedding Guest and in the notion of marriage, together with the convivial wedding feast. Although here and throughout the poem the Mariner is inadvertently an agency for division, he valorises community above all things:

> O sweeter than the marriage-feast,
> 'Tis sweeter far to me
> To walk together to the kirk
> With a goodly company. (634–7)

An extension of the One Life idea is Coleridge's concept of 'cosmic harmony' a sort of supernatural self-regulating fellowship of Gaia-Tellus, which the blundering Mariner offends by his slaughter of one of its members. Consequently, the other creatures and the rest of nature close up against him in a collective vendetta.

Loss of community, along with loss of voice carries with them a biographical poignancy for the loquacious, convivial Coleridge. As we have noted already, the loss of society represents for Coleridge a horrifying personal nightmare (loss of voice implies fear of artistic impotence too). In the extract, this failure of the voice plus deprivation of society are pointed up by the strange, presumably incomprehensible 'sounds' issuing from the mouths of the sailors (and note the word 'mute' in line 355).

After all the suffering, anguish and recrimination, the Mariner redeems himself by sanctifying all of the creatures. However the final, simplistic moral ending, exalting the love of 'All things great and small' (648), is mawkishly facile and does scant justice to the marvellous epic that leads to this moment. The ending carries the unmistakable Coleridgean trademark of a hurried conclusion in which tone supplants sense. Given the rich complexity of supernatural, religious and moral themes, shadowed forth in the first six parts of the poem, it is little short of a travesty.

One of its effects is to overstress the piety of the moral fable. The reader is prepared for this in part by the digression in the Mariner's direction in stanzas 84–6 ('Listen, O listen'). By continually drawing attention to the fact that it is narrative even a fiction, the Mariner sets up the expectation of closure and the events lead to a moral one. What we actually get though is a confused and fragmented morality, leaving the impression that the poem is undeniably didactic in some way but about precisely what is indeterminate. Stanza 85 anticipates and eases the finale:

> Never sadder tale was told
>   To a man of woman born:
> Sadder and wiser thou wedding-guest!
>   Thou'lt rise tomorrow morn.                    (366–9)

Nevertheless, Coleridge expertly moulds the supernatural theme in line with the demands of the moral fable as the chaos on the ship is resolved. Another effect of stanzas 84–6 is to return or to remind us of something like normality, of where we started out, and we return in these stanzas to an interface with the normal human society of the wedding. Line 371 returns the reader and the Mariner to some idea of a fundamentalist truth in the phrase 'a man of woman born' as if grasping at some first principle as the basis of his rehabilitation.

The wedding is also a reminder of the religious theme in the poem so that the narrative at this point conflates (and confuses) the three strands that have emerged: body, soul and destiny. In stanza 80, after the 'sweet sounds' have been ventriloquised through the bodies of the dead sailors, they depart mysteriously:

> Around, around, flew each sweet sound,
> Then darted to the sun                                          (343–4)

The 'sun' has earlier been identified with God (line 93) and the picture of these sounds materialising and flying around echoes that in stanza 51, in which mariners' souls 'did from their bodies fly'.

But are these 'sounds' a figure for the souls of the sailors? It seems an unlikely substitution and the absence of a strong religious idea here limits the ending to a moral rather than a religious message. The Mariner is bothered that God had 'scarce seemed there to be' (633), although this statement implies that He ought to have been there and occasionally was. So the poem makes some respectful nods in the direction of religion (chiefly, as I have suggested, through its imagery and diction) and still it does not speak of Christianity so much as a mystical Pantheistic supernature.

The appeal of Pantheism never quite consumed Coleridge though by 1798 it was exerting a compelling fascination. Its basic charm of wholeness chimes in with his ideals of a unified theory and unity of vision, clearly discernible in his themes of Pantisocracy, cosmic harmony and the One Life. Following his resignation as a Unitarian minister in January 1798, initially for financial reasons, Coleridge suffered a crisis in his beliefs. The many references to drought in *The Ancient Mariner* allegorise this crisis and the poem as a self-fiction allows Coleridge to objectify, even to publicise his private dilemma of faith. The prolonged mental trial of the restless Mariner recalls the wasteland and fiend-tormented illusions of 'Love', whose knight 'Nor rested day nor night' (which itself is a trace of Christ's forty-day crisis in the desert).

Both of these inner journeys through drought and inertia express Coleridge own spiritual confusion. This is not to suggest that *The Ancient Mariner* is anything like a fully realised allegory of religious scepticism, but it seems to explore the private crisis through the safety of symbolism and allegory. By the 1790s Coleridge was more disheartened by his spiritual condition than by the failure of his political ideals. *The Ancient Mariner* became a poetic outlet for all his darker tensions, contradictions, revulsions and fears.

*The Ancient Mariner* investigates the nature and origins of evil and virtue. These are expressed not in explicitly religious terms but in the dialectic between the Mariner's impulses for destruction and self-sacrifice, and between the horrors of the supernatural and the majestic beauty of nature (such as the towering ice, fluctuating mysterious seas and nature's marvellous creatures).

The slaying of the albatross focuses on man's own fallible nature but it rehearses the biblical Fall. However, the poem is not principally a religious dissertation, of course. For one thing the conventional religious elements in *The Ancient Mariner* come over as an expression of literary faith rather than Christianity *per se*. For another, the Mariner seems more devoutly moved by the supernatural elements that appear to derive from either the natural world or from within his own psyche.

As a student at Cambridge, Coleridge had espoused Unitarianism under the influence of David Hartley and the chemist Joseph Priestley. For some time after leaving university, he had struggled with its thorniest orthodoxy: a belief in what was called 'necessitarianism', a strain of determinism which conflicted with his own intuitive belief in free will. His composition of *The Ancient Mariner* coincides with the lapse of his Unitarianism and the question of where his beliefs might take him. Rejecting the humanism of his friend William Godwin, Coleridge recorded the predicament in his notebook:

> As we recede from anthropomorphitism we must go either to the Trinity or to Pantheism    (February 1801)
>
> [*an anthropomorphite refuses to accept Christ as God in human form*]

This is also one of the issues at the centre of *The Ancient Mariner* and the Mariner finds himself between the two poles: doubting the divided Godhead of Christianity that scarce seems there to be, yet equally unable to accept a full-blown Pantheism from which a forgiving or superintending God is largely absent. Consequently, the poem is less engaged in the formal cruxes of Christian faith than in the vivid metaphysics of the su pernatural and its essential relationship with mankind (a disenchantment and a resolution which have similarities with William Blake's).

Coleridge paradoxically delighted in the mysticism of religion. *The Ancient Mariner* continues to exude an implicit belief in the existence of God, but it is never fully convinced of His omnipotence or benevolence (for instance, an innocent crew is annihilated on the mere toss of a dice). More visible are some darker spirits of retribution actively at work in the natural and human sphere. These are, of course, metaphorical projections of Coleridge's nagging pantheism (with a few of his personal demons) that he strives to reconcile with the monotheism of Christianity. This Christian God 'scarce seemed there to be' because it has retreated to a back room and given over the world to the administration of other powerful supernatural forces. Given this divided and warring universe, the Mariner cannot realistically hope to achieve full expiation but, Cain-like, is doomed to tread the ambivalent world inconclusively, sadder and not necessarily wiser.

## Conclusions

For both Wordsworth and Coleridge, nature is an intensely complex subject, not only in itself but in terms of its relationship with the themes of imagination and truth. For Wordsworth, nature is many things: an educator, a source of moral experience, a regenerative and creative energy, a goddess, a 'nurse', a friend. For him it is a spirit too, yet as a deity nature seems to him to exert a real and awesome presence, so much so that it induces in him an enervating jouissance (which sometimes seems to have even an erotic charge to it). For Wordsworth nature is a vital, allotropic agency, which is constantly revitalizing itself and its acolytes. Apocalypse, for Wordsworth, is a vision of the meaning of nature in history.

Wordsworth believed that the supernatural existed within the 'common life'. Coleridge, in *The Ancient Mariner*, projects a religious view of the supernatural as impressions from beyond common objects but communicated through them. Perception of the supernatural is of the same order as the operation of the imagination and relies upon it: it involves an active spiritual communion with the 'sense sublime', and as a force for harmony it is, like the imagination, a coadunating force. The supernatural is the apotheosis of truth and beauty that is arrived at by humans through the action of the imagination.

## Further Research

Reread Wordsworth's 'The Female Vagrant' alongside *The Rime of the Ancient Mariner* and try to clarify what the 'voyage' symbolises in each poem. To what extent are the central characters in the two poems responsible for the events that occur in their journeys?

Both Wordsworth and Coleridge regard nature as a unifying principle, yet both the female vagrant and the ancient mariner are seen to suffer at the hands of a highly divisive and inimical nature. How far would you agree with this conclusion?

# PART 2

# THE CONTEXT AND THE CRITICS

# 6

# The Politics of Wordsworth and Coleridge

Bliss was it in that dawn to be alive,
But to be young was very heaven! O times
In which the meagre, stale forbidding ways
Of custom, law, and statute took at once
The attraction of a country in romance –
When Reason seemed the most to assert her rights

*(The Prelude,* 1805, X.692–7)

As we have seen in previous chapters, the poems of Wordsworth and
Coleridge are highly sensitive to the social and political context of
their day. In this part of the book I want to explore this context, that
is the broad historical and literary landscape of the late eighteenth
and early nineteenth century.

The 1790s was not a blissful period for most of the country's
population in terms of social and economic conditions but, from
a later perspective especially, it seemed to Wordsworth a volatile
moment in human history, of social and literary ferment in this country and political revolutions in America and France. To a young man
at that time, his country might have appeared to be dangerously
poised on the threshold of a revolution with powerful explosive forces
coalescing into two confrontational armies: the 'meagre, stale' old
ways of the Enlightenment and establishment versus the radical new
doctrine of Romanticism. The decade had opened with tremendous

idealistic expectation on one side and ended with a decisive reaction on the other, and the minds of Wordsworth and Coleridge were profoundly changed by the transition between the two.

From early on in their lives both Wordsworth and Coleridge were eager to express their social and political consciences in their writings. Both poets had suffered poverty as well as domestic upheaval and this, together with their fierce moral sensitivities and youthful ebullience, encouraged a staunch commitment to the new reformist ideas, challenging long-entrenched political interests in Britain.

Together the revolutions in America (1783) and in France (1789) constitute the outward or formal climax to a century of growing social unrest at home and abroad. In England the late eighteenth century had been a period of increasing social and economic upheaval, especially in rural areas; it can be broadly characterised as a time of accelerated expansion in capitalised industry, the spread of densely populated urban centres, large increases in taxation and inflation because of war, as well as the extension of the practice of land enclosure by large and powerful estates. These factors, linked with expanding and increasingly visible poverty, led to the emergence in the middle classes of a radical new political spirit, led by activists such as Tom Paine, Mary Wollstonecraft and William Godwin (whose 1793 book *Enquiry Concerning Political Justice* made him the doyen of the democratic movement in England).

According to William Hazlitt, the loftier philosophy of Romanticism was also the rallying point for the disaffected as well as for the suppressed desire for deeper egalitarian reform. The new philosophy embraced empiricism and personal experience as the basis of truth, and emphasised action, engagement and personal responsibility in ethics.

Paradoxically, although in many ways Romanticism counters Enlightenment attitudes, it was itself a logical outcome of ideas and attitudes implicit to the latter, including the affirmation of reason (as the above quotation from *The Prelude* indicates). Thus, while *Lyrical Ballads* stresses nature and humanitarianism, these strands were already theoretically implicit in the existing culture. In England the great awakening of social conscience and humanitarian values had already been promoted by the dissenting religious groups (especially the Unitarians) whose ranks had originally included Coleridge, Hazlitt, Blake and Paine.


## (a)   *Wordsworth and the 'Rabble-rousers'*

Wordsworth is often perceived as a somewhat reclusive, meditative poet. However, as a young man in the 1790s, he had been impatient to become involved in radicalism. From the period of his time as a student at Cambridge University he had steeped himself in the new political ideologies and prepared political pamphlets. As a writer ambitious for public acclaim, he also recognised a public responsibility to express the new soul of man and to realise the conscience of the rising society.

In his own personal life he had directly experienced injustice at the hands of the aristocracy in the figure of Lord Lonsdale, who withheld moneys owed to the Wordsworth estate after the death of William's father in 1783. Two important consequences of this were the loss of the family home and a decline into relative poverty. Subsequently, Wordsworth was left with the firm conviction that injustice was endemic in the fabric of the English system. It is largely from this that his sympathy springs for the victims of this system: rural paupers, vagrants, the dispossessed as well as for other marginalised victims such as the mentally disabled. As we have seen in Part 1, *Lyrical Ballads* has many examples of these victims, but see also *The Excursion* (1802–14), with its account of a family's ruin as a result of disastrous harvests, war, illness and unemployment.

On the other hand, for most radical thinkers, events across the channel in revolutionary France were uppermost, both as a potential model and as an ally for their own campaign. Two key dates stand out here and are inexorably connected: 1789 as the start of the French revolution, and 1793 for the English declaration of war on France. Having in 1791 witnessed the aftermath of the revolution at first hand Wordsworth was exhilarated by the achievements of a revolutionary programme on such a deep and comprehensive scale (the 'dawn' referred to in the above quotation).

Initially, radical idealists like Wordsworth were deeply inspired by the overthrow of the *ancien regime*, promising a rosy new dawn of equality and universal suffrage (though 'universal' still tended to apply exclusively to males). In Britain the final decade of the 1700s saw the unlikely alliance of groups as disparate as the progressive Unitarians, fanatical Jacobins and the Society for Constitutional Reform (prominent among which were the republican agitators William Godwin and John 'Citizen' Thelwall).

At about this time, Wordsworth's own anti-monarchism displayed a fervently idealist colouration. However, his prose style was distinctly less prolix than that of some of his early verse:

> Oh give, great God, to Freedom's waves to ride
> Sublime o'er Conquest, Avarice and Pride
>
> > (*Descriptive Sketches*, 1793)

In his polemical 'Letter to the Bishop of Llandaff' of the same year he was necessarily more forthright

> At this moment have we not daily the strongest proofs of the success with which, in what you call the best of all monarchical governments, the popular mind may be debauched.

Although this letter was not published in his own lifetime, its thrust against the Bishop's apostasy bears a revealing insight on Wordsworth attitude at this time. The substance of his harangue is that a monarchical system leads inevitably to a sterility of the culture as all its classes acquiesce in its hierarchy. He scolded men like the Bishop and the political philosopher Edmund Burke as turncoats, reneging on their early democratic ideals, denouncing them as backsliding apologists for a 'debauched' regime that sanctioned social iniquities such as rampant political corruption, child-labour and slavery.

At the root of both of these positions is the same didactic zeal which also informed his literature: writing, intellect and the imagination were all to be enlisted in the cause of humanitarian reform (see 'The Old Cumberland Beggar' and 'The Convict' for examples). In the Preface to *Lyrical Ballads*, he famously defines the poet as 'a man speaking to men'. Therefore, he also asks there 'How, then, can his language differ in material degree from that of all other men?'

However, in the Appendix to the 1802 edition of the poems, he takes this further and censures the greater part of eighteenth-century poetry for its elitism and consequently its 'adulterated phraseology'. His plea for an egalitarian poetics springs from that reflex registered in the avowal of 'The Old Cumberland Beggar' that we have 'all of us one human heart' and are 'Inseparably linked'. His adoption of the traditional folk ballad as the predominant form in *Lyrical Ballads* likewise signals his declared populist design.

The Preface forges a vital connection between Wordsworth's revolutionary literary purpose and his political reformism. The disappointment of the latter resulted in the focusing of his fervour into new literary and religious enterprises. In his letter of June 1802 to John Wilson (see Chapter 8), defending his approach in 'The Idiot Boy', Wordsworth drew attention to the need to confront previously 'distasteful' subject matter: 'a great poet ought, to a certain degree, to rectify men's feelings', trenchantly echoing the Preface's manifesto statement that the poetry ought to have a 'worthy purpose'.

Literature was to become for Wordsworth the main arena in his pursuit of progressive reform. Action was sublimated to words and the words would now have to be taken for the deed. But not for long.

By 1805, Wordsworth was taking stock in *The Prelude* of his early fury at the injustice endemic in the country's social, economic and political fabric. He had also become, at least in part, dissatisfied with his own ineffectuality, his failure to act on his principles. But by then his early principles too were faltering.

> I lost
> All feeling of conviction, and in fine,
> Sick, wearied out with contrarieties,
> Yielded up moral questions in despair
>
> (*The Prelude*, 1805, X.897–900)

For many, the French Revolution revived memories of the execution of the English Charles I in 1649. John Milton had written steadfastly in support of the new republic under Cromwell and it might have been expected that Wordworth would emulate his great poetic model. However, he later whinged that politics had distracted Milton from becoming a great poet.

In spite of the irritation directed at the Bishop of Llandaff and Edmund Burke, Wordsworth gradually turned his own back on progressive reform and his former dogmatic Jacobinism. By 1821 he would write:

> *I* abandoned France, and her Rulers when *they* abandoned the strug-gle for Liberty, gave themselves up to Tyranny, and endeavoured to enslave the world. I disapproved of the war against France at its commencement.   (Letter, 4 December 1821)

Wordsworth's blissful idealism at the dawn of the French Revolution, buoyed by hopes of regeneration after the purge of a corrupt regime, had been dashed by the ensuing 'Reign of Terror'. Having swept the Bourbons before it, revolutionary *esprit* had become factionalised and imploded in an onslaught on its own ranks, culminating in the exe-cution of Robespierre in 1794, effectively the end of direct Jacobin influence.

In the previous year England had declared war on France in sup-port of the deposed aristocracy, and the fanatical patriotism aroused by this measure was the turning point for many former republican sympathisers such as Wordsworth. Increasingly disillusioned, and finding their own loyalties compromised, many of these sided with the English reactionaries or, like Wordsworth and Coleridge, simply abstained from the conflict.

## (b)   *Coleridge and dreams of Utopia*

If anything, Coleridge's politics were even more energetically caught up in the republican movement. With his dissenting, Unitarian cre-dentials, Coleridge's reformist sympathies date from university days and student riots at Cambridge (he was suspected of being a ringleader). Under the seductive influence of Paine and Godwin, he had become thoroughly intoxicated by the revolutionary roller-coaster of 1790s progressive idealism. On the other hand, Coleridge had never been fully 'on message' and his attitude tended to be more a matter of intellectual curiosity, with a mishmash of humanism, Hegelian metaphysics, mystical religiosity and raw passion – fermented together in the rich alembic of his mercurial imagination.

By 1796 Coleridge had attained a distinctly notorious reputation in the Bristol area for sedition, a reputation that was to lead eventually to the droll affair of 'Spy Nozy'. His pamphleteering and public lectures had stamped his circle as a sink of sedition and free-thinking, particularly as John Thelwall was such a close friend. So defamed was the group that in 1797, with national security in crisis, a government agent was sent to Coleridge's village, Nether Stowey. Following a tip-off from local gossip-mongers, 'Spy-Nozy', as Coleridge nicknamed the agent, was to monitor their movements around the area of the Bristol Channel where a French invasion had been expected (Coleridge's own account of this bizarre episode is related in *Biographia Literaria*, Chapter X).

Coleridge's republicanism was really all one with and sprang from a deeply felt humanitarianism wedded together with his strong collectivism, and the quest for 'cosmic harmony'. These elements found early expression in the project for a 'Pantisocracy': an experimental scheme dreamed up in about 1794 with fellow-republican Robert Southey and others to purchase land in America and establish a small self-governing commune. This was to be founded on 'all that is good in Godwin'. On his birthday in 1794, Coleridge's letter to Southey set out some practical thoughts on the details of daily Pantisocratic life:

> Let the married women do only what is absolutely convenient and customary for pregnant women or nurses. Let the husbands do all the rest, and what will that be? Washing with a machine and cleaning the house … That the greater part of our female companions should have the task of maternal exertion at the same time is very *improbable*; but though it were to happen, an infant is almost always sleeping, and during its slumbers, the mother may in the same room perform the little offices of ironing clothes or making shirts.   (21 October 1794)

Not surprisingly, women were to be an indispensable element in the poetic community.

However, the quixotic Coleridge could drop a project with the same passionate ardour with which it was first taken up (Southey complained 'You spawn plans like a herring'). So by early 1795, having failed to attract the necessary subscriptions and with its chief author preoccupied by a fresh love affair, the Pantisocracy scheme lost its appeal (although it did materialise for others, albeit on a less ambitious scale).

The ease and passion with which Coleridge's proposals could soar and subside applied equally to his politics. His republicanism, fiercely ablaze in 1796, was stone cold by 1799. In his poem 'Recantation' of 1798 he publicised his growing disillusion with the French Revolution, now symbolised as a mad ox:

> 'The ox is mad! Ho! Dick, Bob, Mat!
>    'What means this coward fuss?
> Ho stretch this rope across the plat –
> 'Twill trip him up – or if not that,
> Why, damn me! we must lay him flat                    (103–7)

In the Utopian *The Destiny of Nations*, a series of fragmentary episodes, Coleridge had seized on France as the model for future nations, the 'warrior maid'. This was all well in theory, but the bloody aftermath to the Revolution along with the increasing danger of invasion by the French, focused his mind with a more reactionary take on the reality.

1793 had seen the suppression of the moderate Girondins in the new French administration and this growing extremism had placed English progressives in a testing predicament (aggravated by Prime Minister Pitt's increasingly hard-line measures). In his discussions with Thelwall, Coleridge too became aware of the widening gulf between himself and his Jacobin associates.

By 1795 war and a deepening pessimism over national survival activated a national backlash with a surge into patriotism and a widespread retreat into the right-wing. Moreover, reactionary mobs had attacked the homes of French sympathisers. The government strengthened internal security with emergency Acts against 'treasonable conspiracy' and 'seditious assembly'. By 1797–8, the year of *Lyrical Ballads*, with England's allies rapidly succumbing to French expansionist aggression, the nation was in the grip of a catatonic panic (in 1800 a frenzied mob in Hartlepool had hanged a monkey convinced that it was a French spy). Confronted by Napoleon's seemingly invincible momentum England had withdrawn its Mediterranean fleet and only a storm in Bantry Bay had thwarted a French force of 15,000 joining up with Wolf Tone's Irish insurgents. Given the very real and horrifying prospect of an invasion of the French reign of terror, it is not difficult to understand the political apostasy of both Coleridge and Wordsworth.

## (c)   *1798 and after*

For many readers, *Lyrical Ballads* stands as a huge landmark, as the starting point of English Romanticism and a new paradigm in literary theory (perhaps even the beginning of literary theory *per se*). On the other hand, it also marks the crucial point of departure in the ideological attitudes of its two authors. By 1798 Coleridge's interest had moved away from radical French politics in the direction of German metaphysical aesthetics, and the deeper study of Romanticist principles. In July 1799, on his return from Germany, he was still vilified in the British press as a Jacobin sympathiser, but this position was by then finished. His letter to Wordsworth makes clearer the malaise of former idealists:

> My dear friend ... I wish you could write a poem, in blank verse, addressed to those, who, in consequence of the complete failure of the French Revolution, have thrown up all hopes of the amelioration of mankind, and are sinking into an almost epicurean selfishness.
>
> (September 1799)

While the 'amelioration of mankind' retained its appeal to his religious sensibility, physical revolution was no longer the means of bringing it on. Coleridge's regular articles for the *Morning Post* also reveal just how far he had shifted towards centrist politics, urging the radicals to soften their extremism if only to head off the Tories' assault on liberty:

> these are times in which those who love freedom should use all imaginable caution to love it wisely ... Good men should now close ranks.
>
> (*Morning Post*, 12 December 1799)

Love of freedom as a concept had ousted love of revolution. By the time of *Lyrical Ballads* both poets were beginning to espouse something of the reactionary beliefs of William Pitt and Edmund Burke, both formerly denounced as political apostates. Faith in revolutionary action had become supplanted by a trust in the gradual evolution of a liberal parliamentary democracy, supported by progressive educational reform. The truth was that patriotism and an 'almost epicurean' sense of self-interest had softened their appetite for a fight.

The course of both political lives is a chronicle of continuing animadversion. In 1812 the assassination of Spencer Perceval, against a background of violent opposition to social and economic injustice, was the final straw for a good many reformists who began to believe that emancipation, social equality and fraternity were dangerously synonymous with anarchy. The painter John Constable was such and declared with some fear that England was gradually being ruled by the 'dregs and rabble of society'.

As a Young Turk, Wordsworth had unequivocally embraced the French Revolution as the great practical hope for the betterment of mankind. As an older eminence, he came to demonise the impoverished class of his countrymen whose dignity and improvement he had formerly sponsored (compare his attitude in the Preface and the 'social' poems of *Lyrical Ballads*). He believed that this class represented a threat to order and stability, which was best maintained by strong rule from above. In 1833, in the wake of the Great Reform Bill he complained

> My opinion is, that the People are bent upon the destruction of their ancient Institutions, and that nothing since, I will not say the *passing*, but since the broaching of the Reform Bill could, or can prevent it. I would bend my endeavours to strengthen to the utmost the rational portion of the Tory Party.   (Letter, 15 November 1833)

Thus the old enemies, the aristocracy, in the guise of the House of Lords, and the Tory Party came to be seen by him as guarantors of national freedom.

Among former admirers and fellow writers, Wordsworth was never forgiven for his tergiversation. Mary Shelley called him a slave to the aristocracy and in 1818, when John Keats visited Grasmere in adulation, he was horrified to discover 'Lord Wordsworth' out canvassing for Lord Lonsdale, the local Tory candidate. Hazlitt, an early admirer and friend scorned his 'dereliction of his first principles', his backsliding on the ideals of *Lyrical Ballads* as much as of his politics. And as late as 1845, with Wordsworth's star firmly fixed in the Pantheon, Robert Browning famously and deeply reviled him as 'The Lost Leader':

> Just for a handful of silver he left us,
>> Just for a riband to stick in his coat . . .

# 7

# *Reading and Writing in Eighteenth-Century England*

Yes, in those wanderings deeply did I feel
How we mislead each other, above all
How books mislead us

(*The Prelude*, 1805, XII.205–7)

A thrilling time for political activity, the turn of the century was a key moment in the history of literature, criticism and the printed word in general. Wordsworth's Prefaces to *Lyrical Ballads* are infused not only with a strong awareness of his reader but also with the overt intention of changing the reader, indeed they aver that the great artist creates the taste by which he or she is to be judged.

Implicitly he thus sees his work as very much addressing not merely a dilettante audience but a broad corpus of readership, 'mankind' as a whole in fact, one that he hopes to win over on the grand scale. In particular he sets out his mission as a crusade against the 'triviality and meanness' of contemporary writing, ousting it with his own 'sublime notion of Poetry'. He stresses the importance of moral purpose in a work but laments of his own time:

> The invaluable works of elder writers, I had almost said the works of Shakespeare, and Milton, are driven into neglect by frantic novels, sickly and stupid German Tragedies, and deluges of idle and extravagant stories in verse.   (Preface to *Lyrical Ballads*, 1800)

To discuss the remarks of Wordsworth against the context of his own time we need to get a handle on the world of books, readers and writing in England in the eighteenth century, looking in detail at changes in the practices of English publishing and in literacy in the period and their effects on the world of writing.

### (a)  *Publishing, printing and book-selling*

By the start of the 1790s, writers had available to them a wide range of possible publishing outlets and readership for written work unforeseen a 100 years previously. He or she could approach a newspaper publisher with poetry or prose, with the prospect of reaching an enormous readership. However, unless they were an established writer or celebrity, there was little prospect of payment for their publication. The national reviews offered a much better chance of paid writing, whether for new 'imaginative' work, for miscellaneous articles or reviewing the work of others. Wordsworth himself had published some early verse in magazines and in 1794 had even planned to publish one himself (under the title, *The Philanthropist, a monthly Miscellany*). In a letter of June 1794, he complained of 'the trash which infests the magazines'. Coleridge too had published 'Lewti' in the *Morning Post* (though because of this it was precluded from the collection), but had no hang ups about the press as a source of finance or communication. Throughout his career, he was continually either editing, publishing or planning to publish periodicals (such as *The Friend* and the *Courier*).

The eighteenth-century rise in the periodical was driven by a variety of factors. Chief among these was the fact that they were exempt from newspaper tax (in 1800 this was $3\frac{1}{2}$ pence a sheet, rising to 4 pence in 1815). This placed newspapers beyond all but the well-off, yet as the periodicals would not include news, they had to be filled with something, and something popular. The high rate of tax was aimed at stemming the rise of politically radical newsheets. William Cobbett's right wing *Weekly Political Register* (started 1802) evaded this by omitting current news. Even with the tax, the sale of newspapers more than doubled from about 20,000 in 1750 to over

48,000 per day in 1790. This naturally opened up a whole new area of livelihood for an aspiring writer, although established writers could afford to look down on it as hack work. Wordsworth himself, although he often resorted to the press to campaign on current issues, shuttered himself against the new wave:

> All the periodical Miscellanies that I am acquainted with, except one or two of the Reviews, appear to be written to maintain the existence of prejudice and to disseminate error ... I will not prostitute my pen. (Letter, 23 May 1794)

On the other hand, the rise of the reviews represented a unique and highly volatile phenomenon in English letters. The rapid acceleration of titles created a rich vibrant and astringent milieu that coincided with the appearance of *Lyrical Ballads* and provoked the English Romantic movement (though for the most part it was fiercely opposed to it).

By the end of the eighteenth century, practically the whole of literary criticism was in the hands of two small reviews, the *Monthly* and the *Critical Review*, whose critiques generally amounted to little more than summaries or 'puffs' written by publishing hacks. Within a decade, belligerent, tough and gossipy new magazines had transformed the face of reviewing. Cobbett's committed Tory *Political Register* was matched by the brilliant, Whiggish *The Edinburgh Review* of the same year, and there followed a second generation of the new breed with Leigh Hunt's energetically radical *Examiner* of 1808, which advanced the cause of the Romantic poets, followed by the Tory *Quarterly Review*. Were it not for the dawn of these mighty organs, little or nothing of the writings of William Hazlitt, Thomas De Quincey, Leigh Hunt, Cobbett, Jeffrey and Lockhart might have survived. The new generation of critics began to see the establishment of literary criticism as an intrinsically meaningful and systematic intellectual activity.

For books, an established writer could expect to receive a lump sum in exchange for the rights to his or her work, although a newcomer would likely be asked to pay a subsidy towards the production and/or distribution costs (they would typically have to be sponsored too by an affluent and influential patron). A wealthy author might publish him/herself after coercing their friends and associates to subscribe to the published work – with money up front for their subscription.

The gradual lapsing of the Licensing Act resulted in a rapid increase in the numbers of printers and presses and a subsequent proliferation of forms and markets for their products, not just books and magazines, but in the day-to-day materials of tickets, advertising bills, signs, posters and so on.

Gradually the present-day division between the publisher, printer and bookseller emerged. In the early eighteenth century a 'bookseller' usually paid for a book to be printed and bound as well as dealing with the retail selling and distribution of it. Sales were often through a single bookshop (especially in London and cities such as Bristol where Joseph Cottle printed and sold *Lyrical Ballads*), but also through a developing network of provincial booksellers as well as through itinerant vendors and by subscription.

With regard to book publishing, easily the largest single category was that of religious items. Chief among these was, of course, the Bible and the Book of Common Prayer and both the Bible itself and biblical commentaries actually represented popular reading. From 1750 to 1800 approximately 240 religious books per year were published and theological works amounted to about 25 per cent of reviews in, for example, the *Gentleman's Magazine*. Biblical commentaries went through an amazing number of editions, including one by Matthew Henry (*An Exposition of All the Books of the Old and New Testaments*) that went through ten editions by the end of the eighteenth century.

Linked to this spiritual reading, philosophy books too were a rapidly growing corner of publishing. Although literate readers might make the Bible their first choice for piety and moral guidance, philosophy books presented a bold challenge to received ideas about the world. This market gathered increasing momentum on the back of the growing interest in empiricism (after Newton, Hume and Locke) and the controversies between Bishop Berkeley and 'common sense' realists such as Dr Johnson on the nature of reality. During the eighteenth century, 'natural science' too was emerging as a discrete subject, and the growing interest among the affluent laity became expressed as a high demand for cyclopaedias such as that of Ephraim Chambers, and for books on natural history, including George

Buffon's inspirational *The Natural History of the Horse* (1762) and White's *Natural History of Selborne* (1789).

Although Wordsworth, in particular, sought to caution society's great faith in books ('books mislead us'), he too was very much of his period. The new fascination in science, and botanical books in particular, signalled that growth of interest in nature and landscape that Wordsworth and Coleridge would extend and transform. Both poets were closely involved too in the political controversies of the late 1700s, at a time when the government was increasingly ready to curtail the freedom of the press. As is often pointed out, the 1790s dawn with blissful revolutionary promise and sets in reaction, fear and repression. Edmund Burke, bitter opponent of the French Revolution, considered that an unregulated free press actually threatened rather than protected civil liberties. Improving popular literacy with access to an 'anarchic expansion' literature pointed up the 'French danger'. Thomas Paine's *The Rights of Man* (1791–2) threatened the bastion of ruling interests, while the works of Mary Wollstonecraft and Mary Hays were treading on the forbidden lawn of male polemics.

In philosophy, science, politics – as in religion – bliss was it to be in this new dawn of publishing. Romantic literature also sold well at the turn of the century, in particular gothic and sentimental works (as Jane Austen's parodic *Northanger Abbey* attests). A torrent of best-selling novels streamed forth, indicating literature's great potential for big profits. Sir Walter Scott's poetry published by Longman's was very successful: *The Lay of the Last Minstrel* (1805) sold 44,000 copies by 1830, while in 1814 Byron's *The Corsair* (published by John Murray) sold over 10,000 copies on its first day. Eventually Byron's massive popularity edged out Scott, who then turned to novel-writing, achieving a major success with *Waverley* (begun in 1805) and opening up the fashion for historical fiction (Wordsworth too uneasily accused Byron of 'poaching on my Manor', letter, 24 June 1817).

### (b)   *Effects on writers*

Another important consequence of the lapsing of the Licensing Act was that legal copyright no longer obtained in print culture publications. Naturally, blatant piracy and plagiarism also spiralled, posing a serious threat both to the health of the growing publishing industry but also to the gradually improving income and autonomy of the writer.

A Copyright Act in 1709 set out to re-establish protection, but was largely ineffective since it had little practical power and left serious loopholes gaping for the entrepreneurial opportunist to exploit (for instance, Dublin was excluded from its provisions). In 1744, matters worsened when the House of Lords ruled that copyright could not be retained in perpetuity. The fact of copyright in a work is crucial for publishers and authors in that the former can only fork out reasonable sums for a work if they are certain of controlling long-term rights in it.

To protect their interests, booksellers (and later printers and publishers) began to set themselves up into 'congers', small groups with mutually protective agreements on rights in printed works. These grew into strong cartels that eventually stabilised the market, but had the effect of fixing high retail prices by managing and monopolising sales and distribution in an expanding market.

Even with these changes, gifted new writers still had great difficulty in seeing their work reach print. Publishers made their greatest profits in a strong backlist of standard and classic authors, such as Chaucer, Shakespeare, Milton and Dryden. The most lucrative rights consisted of two major fields: religious works (including the Bible and the Book of Common Prayer) and dictionaries (especially Greek and Latin). Two examples will illustrate the relative weight of these: in 1779 the copyright for the popular poet, Stephen Duck, was auctioned for £22 while that of a French/English dictionary went for £800 (Bristol publisher Joseph Cottle paid 30 guineas for the copyright of the first edition of *Lyrical Ballads*). The closing decades of the century, however, saw an end to the London monopoly on classic titles as regional publishers printed and sold these throughout the provinces.

After the 1774 ruling on copyright, the relationship between the writer and their publisher began to change noticeably. Until this time it was the norm for a poet to receive no payment at all for their work. This reflected in part the commercial reality that modern poetry did not sell that well, but also the artistic reality that poets were either themselves wealthy individuals or had wealthy patrons to support and promote them (a common view prevailed that to prostitute one's talents for base lucre was exceeding unseemly). In truth, the only writers who might expect a living wholly by their pens were dramatists, and then principally through theatre receipts (both Coleridge and Wordsworth experimented in this field; only Coleridge achieved any success as a dramatist with *Osorio*, after it was revamped as *Remorse*).

With the steady growth of magazines from the 1750s and the seemingly insatiable appetite for reading, the future for writers to earn an independent living became extremely promising. When Constables set up the *Edinburgh Review* in 1802, the owners insisted that all contributors would be paid. Some regarded this as hack writing while others, such as Southey and Hazlitt used this source to become independent and finance their work in *belles lettres*.

Robert Southey earned between £600 and £800 per annum for his work on the *Quarterly* magazine while William Hazlitt worked for the *Morning Chronicle* for about £200. In a letter of February 1812, Wordsworth gave among his ambitions for writing the prime one of being able to support his family solely by his pen, though he never quite pulled this off. Even so he still refused to fawn to the literary journals, either for work or to boost his sales (which in a roundabout sort of way acknowledges their great power to do both). In 1830 he went as far as to describe one review critic as 'a miserable maggot crawled out of the dead carcase of the Edinburgh Review!'

The increase in print culture was itself part of a fashionable rise in education and self-improvement. Another off-shoot of this and a valuable source of income for writers was the public lecture, which, as well as providing direct finance, also enabled a writer to promote his name and works. Wordsworth confessed he was utterly incompetent in this area of public contact, but the more congenially theatrical Coleridge took to it (principally as a result of the urging of Humphrey Davy at the Royal Society) with varying degrees of commitment and success.

The fact of the matter was that while history books and the classics became profitable, poetry and novels were still difficult to shift, although Wordsworth and Coleridge both hoped to do well out of

*The Ancient Mariner* and then *Lyrical Ballads*. Even at the fashionable end of the market, authors were at the mercy of the powerful publisher and it was not until the 1790s that authors began to secure profit-sharing deals on their books. This important step opened up the way towards a professional class of writer as well as the modern role of publisher (Walter Scott is generally regarded as the first professional novelist and Byron the first professional poet capable of supporting themselves wholly from their work).

### (c)  *Readers: education and literacy*

During the eighteenth century the population of England doubled while the number of readers almost trebled. Members of the wealthy social classes plus professional and merchant ranks, numbering perhaps about 10 per cent of the population, represented the literate elite by and for whom the mainstream print culture was produced. The proportional increase in the privileged groups, especially, led in turn to an increase in the school population and subsequently in the demand for textbooks. At the same time, a relative improvement in transport and re-organisation of London publishers and booksellers resulted in a more efficient distribution of printed matter throughout the country.

Education was one of the key concerns of the broad Romantic movement. The education of the middle and upper classes was still largely in the hands of private tutors and the 'public schools'. Although there was little in the way of public provision of education in the late eighteenth century (not until the 1830 Act would this become a reality in England), even the poor could educate their children after a fashion. Payment of a small fee could get them 'educated' by an odd assortment of largely untrained minders and dames, and anyone who wished to could set up a 'school'.

However, the century witnessed an increase in the provision of charity schools, led chiefly by Isaac Watts, the hymn writer, and the Evangelical moralist Hannah More (whose *Strictures on the Modern System of Female Education* was a reactionary reply to Mary Wollstonecraft, stressing maternal and domestic roles for young women). The broad aims of charity and Sunday schools were to strengthen the prevailing social order and to promote the reading of religious material, especially prayer books and moral tracts. Opponents, meanwhile, warned that educating the poor would have the knock-on result of equipping radicals and spreading subversion by making labourers dissatisfied with their lot. And they were, by and large, correct. The increased demand for printed matter together with increasing refinement of readers ultimately did lead to the dissemination of political culture among the oppressed, opening the path towards nineteenth-century social and welfare reformers.

The poet John Clare (1793–1864) remembered his own impoverished family circumstances and sketched a first-hand account of his 'education' around 1800:

> Both my parents was illiterate to the last degree, my mother knew not a single letter, and superstition went so far with her that she believed the higher parts of learning was the blackest arts of witchcraft … there was often enough to do to keep cart upon the wheels, as the saying is, without incurring an extra expence of pulling me through school … As to my schooling, I think never a year passed me till I was 11, or 12, but three months or more at the worst of times was luckily spared for my improvement, first with an old woman in the village, and latterly with a master.    ('I was born at Helpstone')

Clare, the son of an unemployed farm labourer in Northamptonshire, had little more than a very rudimentary schooling, but basic literacy enabled him, like many others, to become by and large self-taught, working through all manner of printed scraps, ballads, advertising, religious works and cheap reprints of the classics.

It will come as a surprise to no one that standards of literacy in pre-industrial England correlated strictly with social and economic class. Acquiring even basic literacy depended on local educational opportunities, religious faith, gender and family background. At the start of the 1790s, the writer Isaac D'Israeli (father of Benjamin) announced the 'new republic of letters', but the statistics for literacy do not altogether support this claim. Although literacy is difficult to define and measure, by 1790 it was approximately 60 per cent among men and

40 per cent among women, and the highest levels prevailed in market towns and the more affluent suburbs of cities. Even this humble figure was greatly undermined by the upheaval at the outset of the Industrial Revolution.

However, with the gradual widening of even a simple literacy and the inception of cheap books, the possibility of self-education among the poor became feasible. In towns especially this possibility was given a major boost by the emergence of public libraries. One land-mark development here is the opening of the British Library in 1759, combining the collections of Sloane, Cotton and others, although access was in practice limited to that literate few with adequate means to pay the subscription and the leisure time to use it. Subscription libraries spread rapidly across the country, a sort of mutual commu-nity that clubbed together to buy the stock and limited borrowing to its members. Circulating libraries, on the other hand, were set up for profit by individuals and companies, opening to all who could afford the fee (for instance, in 1770 the Minerva Press shrewdly opened a circu-lating library in London with a lending stock of about 8,000 books). Where the subscription libraries had the earnest endeavour of carrying high quality literature, the circulating libraries' emphasis on profits meant an emphasis too on popular works, especially fiction. The latter also stocked history, biographies and travel books and exercised a strong moral and political control over their holdings (and thus eventually over its publishers).

Endowed libraries represented a third important area in the spread of print culture. These were often set up by political interest or occu-pational groups such as the clergy or factory labourers. The appearance of the Mechanics Institute in the late 1700s led to the rapid spread of their own 'endowed' libraries and reading rooms, serving the poor and working readers and further stimulating the growth in publishing.

The spread of libraries was concentrated mostly in cities and larger towns. Poorer country readers still depended largely on circulating cheap publications and ephemeral material among themselves. Wordsworth noted that among this group he found:

> half-penny Ballads, and penny and two-penny histories, in great abundance; these are often bought as charitable tributes to the poor

> Persons who hawk them about (and it is the best way of procuring them); they are frequently stitched together in tolerably thick volumes, and such I have read.   (Letter, 5 June 1808)

Wordsworth then goes on to add that, while most of the contents of these 'chapbooks' are wholesome, they often contain superstitious and lewd material (but adds his regret that he lacks the talent to write for and profit from them).

Among the poor and especially in rural areas, another method of disseminating literature was the widespread practice of reading aloud to unlettered groups. This continued at least into the early 1800s indicating that the contents of written materials reached a far wider audience than the raw figures or printing would imply.

Although there were no significant advances in printing technology to speak of, production of cheaper news and book print as well as the growth of trade bindings (a whole edition of a book being bound) helped to reduce the price of reading. Daily newspapers appeared for the first time in the early eighteenth century and in spite of stringent government tax, there was huge growth in newspaper titles and sales during the century (arguably the most popular daily paper in the 1790s was London's *Public Advertiser* with sales of around 3,000 a day).

In the general market for cheap printed material, there was also an unremitting expansion, including news-sheets, songs, pamphlets, chapbooks and broadside ballads. These were hawked – as Wordsworth points out above – by itinerant pedlars (the 'chapmen'). Chapbooks included popular rewrites of famous classics, shortened, simplified and bowdlerised for a semi-literate market. The most frequently treated titles were *Pilgrim's Progress*, *Moll Flanders*, *Robinson Crusoe* and *Gulliver's Travels*, which became folk myths and whose events often departed far from their originals (one chapbook of 1797 had reduced *Moll Flanders* from about 400 pages in the original to a mere eighteen). Other folk myths were also the regular fare of this extremely popular form of printed fiction: *St George and the Dragon*, *The Adventures of Robin Hood*, *Jack and the Beanstalk* and *Accounts of Lancashire Witches* give a flavour of the material. As Wordsworth points out in his letter, these books often bound in together an exciting miscellany of adventure stories, ballads, smut, superstition and zodiacal predictions. Although greatly disparaged by the learned (as well as by the illiterate), the chapmen played an enormous part in the spread of printed material throughout the country to fill the great vacuum generated by a huge growing market.

### (d)   *The Ballad revival*

In his Preface to the 1800 edition of *Lyrical Ballads*, Wordsworth recorded that he hoped the book would be the antidote to those 'idle and extravagant stories in verse' that:

> are now acting with a combined force to blunt the discriminating powers of the mind, and unfitting it for all voluntary exertion to reduce it to a state of almost savage torpor.

Among the literature generally approved of, were the classics, both Greek and Latin, and during the eighteenth century these also shared very much in the rising tide of print culture. For most general readers and schoolboys, however, these were now consumed in popular translations. The same applied to Germanic and French classics, whose translations were mostly carried out by women writers. Yet, although the classics were usually regarded in Augustan letters as superior to English, one of the surprising results of extensive translation was in fact to make the vernacular increasingly popular as *the* language of art, poetry in particular.

Hence Wordsworth's exhortations to use plain ordinary English diction and syntax in poetry were an extension of this growing movement, just as his fervent promotion of nature as a theme grew alongside a contemporary fascination in botany and the collection of field specimens. In fact, as we have seen above, many of the poetic genres and subjects in *Lyrical Ballads* were already appearing in the popular magazines of the late 1700s. Wordsworth himself, and Coleridge, had published verse in these magazines.

The period was also one of revival for the literary ballad form. Folk ballads had long been a strong element of the oral tradition among the poor and labouring classes, a means of preserving and transmitting a shared mythology as well as oblique political protest, drawing on legend and local folklore. The 1790s fashion in magazine writing was for the literary ballad with vivid storylines and character, the uncanny especially if wrapped in a fake antiquarianism – all of which can be traced into *Lyrical Ballads* (for instance, the Lucy poems, 'The Thorn' and *The Ancient Mariner*). Wordsworth acknowledged the early influence (on 'The Idiot Boy' especially) of the ballads of Gottfried Bürger that had been appearing in English translations in the early 1790s (for instance in the *Monthly Magazine*, where Coleridge hoped to place *The Ancient Mariner*) and other key ballad inspirations included Thomas Percy's celebrated *Reliques of Ancient English Poetry* (1765), James Macpherson's highly influential *The Works of Ossian* (1765) and the ballads of William Hamilton and William Mickle.

The renewed interest in folk and literary ballads is one possible outcome of the drive towards the democratisation of literacy and learning. Equally important is the appearance of the working class or 'plebeian' poets. These are often seen as an alternative poetic culture, but it is in fact a pastiche of its patrician models, and the poets involved usually depended heavily on the approval of wealthy patrons. Foremost among them are John Clare, Stephen Duck (the 'Thresher poet') and Mary Collier (the 'Washer-woman poet'). Most of these poets were self-taught and earned their crusts in most unliterary occupations (as did William Blake and John Keats). Others included John Bryant (pipemaker), Henry Jones (bricklayer), Ann Yearsley (milkwoman) and William Brimble (carpenter). Recent literary discussion has elevated the reputations of some of these writers – chiefly from the point of view of historical or gender studies. But it has to be said that, with a few exceptions, their work is obstinately mediocre.

The Preface to *Lyrical Ballads* itself advocated the 'humble and rustic life' for its subject matter while the 1798 'Advertisement' privileges the 'language of conversation in the middle and lower classes of society'. At the same time, as ambitious writers seeking to make money from *Lyrical Ballads*, Wordsworth and Coleridge both still depended on the patronage of the wealthy for their survival: Raisley

Calvert's legacy of £900 rescued Wordsworth in 1795 and Thomas Wedgwood's annuity of £150 from 1798 enabled Coleridge to devote himself to poetry. The collection did not make either of them wealthy – even though the first edition had sold out within a year. So poor were its prospects that, after purchasing the rights to the collection, Longman's gave them to Joseph Cottle. However, in 1800 they had a change of mind and paid £80 for the rights to publish the new edition of 2,500 copies.

# 8

# *The Poet as Critic and Theorist*

> You desire me to communicate to you copiously my observations on modern literature, and transmit to you a cup replete with the waters of that fountain. You might as well have solicited me to send you an account of the tribes inhabiting the central regions of the African Continent. God knows my incursions into the fields of modern literature … are absolutely nothing.
>
> (From a letter from Wordsworth to William Matthews, 13 August 1791)

In addition to their deep and abiding commitment to the practice of verse, Wordsworth and Coleridge were both preoccupied with developing poetic theory. In this chapter I want to discuss their early ideas on poetics, looking closely at two key documents: first, Wordsworth's Prefaces to the 1800 and 1802 editions of *Lyrical Ballads*, and then Coleridge's reply to this, in *Biographia Literaria*, published in 1817.

## (a) Wordsworth and 'pre-established codes of decision'

At the front of the first edition of *Lyrical Ballads* there appeared an unsigned 'Advertisement', which served as a preface to the collection in which Wordsworth proclaimed the aims of the collection. It was part apology and part strident fanfare, a strident broadside against late eighteenth-century literary taste on which he and Coleridge hoped to gatecrash with their new poetics. With not a little bravado, Wordsworth declares that contemporary taste with its 'pre-established codes of decision' is stifling poetic progress. He warned his unsuspecting readers that the poems ought to be considered as experiments. The gist of Wordsworth's argument falls into two main areas: subject matter and language.

In contrast to the prevailing idea that poetry must address certain conventional topics, particularly classical themes, Wordsworth declared that in principle poems could and therefore ought to concern 'every subject which can interest the human mind'. From our twenty-first-century viewpoint it is easy to overlook the truly radical implications of what Wordsworth was claiming.

So ground-breaking was this attempt at freeing poetry from contemporary shackles that the Advertisement felt obliged to propose some notes towards a new definition of poetry and even of art as a whole: poetry was to be concerned with the 'natural delineation of human passions, human character and human incidents' in marked contrast to the contemporary fixation on stereotypical subject matter, themes and values. In doing this Wordsworth was, of course, hoping to set up the terms, his own terms, by which the poems should be judged, as a counter to 'pre-established codes of decision', which were based on fixed expectations and the Neo-classical view that a work qualified as art only if it measured up to fixed criteria.

In essence, English Romanticism was proposing a break from this objectively determined eligibility in favour of a more subjective assessment of art, that is through the individual observer, eventually leading to a relativist view of literary criticism (though this was to be some long time in the coming). Yet Wordsworth does not go quite the whole hog on this and adduces the view of Joshua Reynolds that taste and judgement in literature are still dependent to some extent on training and experience without which 'judgement may be erroneous'.

William Blake, William Cowper, Robert Burns, Thomas Chatterton and others had already started the ball rolling here. But the old guard was not readily going to accept this type of paradigm shift without a fight and it closed ranks against the theory.

The mainly hostile reviews of *Lyrical Ballads* had no stomach for its subversive view of language or the simple ordinariness of its characters.

Of his proposal the most radical was in relation to the language of verse. Underlying Wordsworth's 1798 Advertisement is a serious questioning of the eighteenth century's *objective* view of art. As well as adopting classical themes and attitudes, eighteenth-century poetry was expected to deal with them in Augustan forms (including the 'personification of abstract ideas' which Wordsworth later vilified). It was further expected to use accepted and lofty modes of discourse based on Greek and Latin models especially in terms of diction and syntax.

Revolutionary in both the political and literary senses is Wordsworth's announcement that the poems of *Lyrical Ballads* set out to explore how far the conversational language of the lower classes could be used in verse compositions. This attempt at simplifying the language of poetry confronted both the idea that there was a correct register for verse but also a correct class of poet for writing it. In a period of intense edginess over democratising currents across the channel such a proposal constituted a highly provocative signal.

Wordsworth's statement adroitly anticipates the likely charge that the 1798 lyrics were in fact so revolutionary as to disqualify them as poetry altogether (for a discussion on how innovative these were see Chapter 10). Thus his broadside attack on conservative taste did not stop at subject and language, but queried the very concept of poetry itself, 'a word of very disputed meaning', and this germ led Wordsworth to develop his more detailed theory of poetry in the Preface to the 1800 and 1802 editions.

The second, expanded edition of *Lyrical Ballads* appeared in 1800. Its highly controversial subject matter and treatment prompted a 17-year-old Glasgow student to write a long and now famous letter of criticism on *The Idiot Boy*. John Wilson, who later served as editor of the highly influential *Blackwood's Magazine* and university professor and became a close friend and supporter of Wordsworth. In general terms he admired the poem but took particular exception to its central character.

His letter begins by rapturously commending the poet's 'language of nature' and the depth and authenticity of the feelings expressed in the collection, followed by a euphoric litany of praise for the verse. Wilson precociously supports Wordsworth's views on the freedom of subject matter but, somewhat inexplicably to us, he slates *The Idiot Boy* on the grounds that 'in the choice of subject matter you have committed an error' (that is, the figure of the idiot boy himself) although he conceded that the poem is 'executed in a masterly manner'.

Wordsworth used the reply to his young admirer as the opportunity for a reaffirmation and clarification of his views in the Preface. After reiterating his conviction that nature is in childhood the chief initiator and nourisher of the feelings, he addresses Wilson's particular hostility to the 'distasteful' subject matter of *The Idiot Boy*. First he stresses the point that taste is variable, subjective and culturally relative. He agrees that poetry ought to give readers pleasure but argues that this can be done by exploring the deeper character of human nature, examining ourselves on a profound spiritual level. The examination should not be limited to members of a particular social class and may include children, the poor and disabled.

Wordsworth believed that this 'levelling' aspect had been one of the great achievements of *Lyrical Ballads*. But a poet had a larger duty:

> he ought, to a certain degree, to rectify men's feelings, to give them new compositions of feeling, to render their feelings more sane, pure and permanent, in short, more consonant to nature, that is, to eternal nature, and the great moving spirit of things.
>
> (Letter to John Wilson, June 1802)

By valorising the didactic role of poetry, Wordsworth revisits a perennial chestnut concerning the true purpose of literature: literature he argues, should not restrict itself merely to reflecting society, as the mirror up to nature, but must also try to change it. Poetry, like nature, can stimulate and nourish the feelings but also manipulate them, hinting too that this duty also has religious and political dimensions to it.

The strong sales of the first edition of *Lyrical Ballads* encouraged Joseph Cottle to publish a new edition, expanded into two volumes, in 1800. Wordsworth used the occasion to blazon his own name (excluding Coleridge's) on the cover and to introduce the new book with a detailed Preface (expanded in 1802), recapitulating the collection's original aims and reflecting on poetic style and the nature of the poet.

Wordsworth's Preface is now often regarded as the first genuine attempt to place on a reasoned foundation the technicalities of poetry and the relationship between author, text and reader. In setting down many of the issues of modern literary studies, it is often acclaimed as a seminal, ground-breaking document in the theory of literature and of modern poetics.

The Preface begins by reiterating the experimental nature of the first edition, to see how far a poet could employ the 'real language of men' in literature. Then, after slighting and minimising Coleridge's involvement in the first edition, Wordsworth expands on this point, adding that he is now interested in using the psychology of learning as a means of exploring education and as a basis for poetic form:

> The principal object then which I proposed to myself in these Poems was to choose incidents and situations from common life, and to relate or describe them, throughout, as far as was possible, in a selection of language really used by men; and, at the same time, to throw over them a certain colouring of imagination, whereby ordinary things should be presented to the mind in an unusual way; and, further, and above all, to make these incidents and situations interesting by tracing in them, truly though not ostentatiously, the primary laws of our nature: chiefly as regards the manner in which we associate ideas in a state of excitement.

He was to seek realism in events and in the language, but a realism that is modified for literature's sake by the poet's imagination. He was not trying to present images in the ways that the new, exact sciences were already doing, but in an imaginative form that reflected the ways in which nature has its greatest impact on our experience, to present received impressions through the filter of the poet's subjective creative imagination.

The key word here is 'associate', because we have noted already (in discussing 'Tintern Abbey' and Coleridge's 'The Nightingale') the importance which Wordsworth attached to using Hartley's theory of associationism as an account of the psychology of form, 'the manner in which we associate ideas in a state of excitement'. Since imagination in its encounter with nature was thought to absorb impressions via the mysterious workings of associationism, it made sense to Wordsworth to exploit this mechanism as a means of ordering the content in a written text. In this way, Wordsworth hoped to set literature and its effects on a basis of natural logic. Throughout his writing, he repeatedly returns to this idea that for writing to be good and morally effective it should emulate the form of nature.

On the theme of realism, the cornerstone of his theory is a primitiveness derived from rural culture. He argues that he adopted the 'humble and rustic life' as the subject matter for his verse because he believes such a primordial existence preserves the basic elemental feelings of mankind as well as a genuine freedom of expression and truth of experience. In other words, rural life and values were untainted by the nightmare horrors of urban and industrial values then encroaching on and enslaving man's soul (the 'encreasing accumulation of men in cities').

Wordsworth's earnest moral tone permeates practically everything he writes – both here and in the verse. However, Wordsworth's next point is that, while each of the poems in *Lyrical Ballads* has 'a worthy purpose', he claims that he did not set out with a specific, preconceived moral design, adding famously:

> For all good poetry is the spontaneous overflow of powerful feelings.

Does this mean, then, that simply anyone driven by overwhelming emotion might successfully compose poetry? Wordsworth claims not, on the grounds that poetry of value may only be produced by someone ('a man') 'possessed of more than usual organic sensibility'. A poem is created from this emotion when it is 'recollected in tranquillity', tranquillity being a semi-mystical form of repose which can be likened to that sublime moment in 'Tintern Abbey' when

> with an eye made quiet by the power
> Of harmony, and the deep power of joy,
> We see into the life of things. (48–50)

Once more art aspires to the condition of nature. A poet could only be someone of exceptional gifts, particularly of natural holistic sensitivity, in tune with both nature and his fellow man.

If poetry is to have a worthy purpose, then this begs the decisive question of what that purpose might be. In a letter of June 1794, the revolutionary Wordsworth writes that it is the duty of authors to promote social justice.

His 1800 Preface repeats and extends the mission statement of the original Advertisement (and echoes his reply to John Wilson): that art (like nature) should strengthen and purify the reader's affections; the object is to elevate the reader's mind to the 'perception of beauty and dignity'. Overcrowding in the cities has produced in the degraded minds of 'men' a desire for novels of cheap sensation, tragedies and idle verse.

Throughout the whole of the manifesto there is a strong reactionary moral standpoint. On the one hand, his democratic beliefs at this time welcome the broadening readership in the land and the increasing spread of literature, but behind them lies the dread that the new readers are being diverted away from 'beauty and dignity' into cheap novelettes and 'idle verse'. For Wordsworth, a poet is not merely a man gifted with exceptional 'organic sensibility', important though this is. As a 'bard' he has a duty too, both to literature itself and to his society:

> He is a man speaking to men: a man, it is true, endued with more lively sensibility, more enthusiasm and tenderness ... than are supposed to be common among mankind.

Paradoxically, a poet is ordinary enough to understand and communicate with his or her fellows but extraordinary in terms of his ability to see and understand his fellows and to articulate his own distinctive vision of society and his dedicated role in it. This is not going as far as Shelley's view that the poet is a sort of visionary seer or prophet; nor is it Keats's image of the poet as society's 'soul-making' physician. Yet Wordsworth's view does anticipate both of these writers by regarding the poet as especially gifted and with a enormous responsibility to his or her society:

> the Poet binds together by passion and knowledge the vast empire of human society, as it is spread over the whole earth, and over all time.

The poet must be of his own time in terms of his experience but of all time in terms of his writing. In the 1800 Preface he now includes his own reasons for being a poet: because he desired to express 'the most valuable object of all writing ... the great and universal passions of men ... and the entire world of nature'.

But what is a poem? Taking up his point in the Advertisement again, the poet's subject matter is still defined as whatever 'can interest the human mind'. But in tackling a definition of a poem, Wordsworth reopens a can of worms which is still very much open today. And the controversy it raises provoked him to add a coda in the form of an Appendix to the 1802 edition.

The difference between poetry and prose is not, he argues, a linguistic one. However, linguistic points are one of the few features that the Preface does dwell on in depth. Among these Wordsworth most famously declares that his own poetry has minimised 'poetic diction'. Consistent with his antipathy towards 'pre-established codes of decision' he rejects 'poetic diction' as legacy of the fixed and classical view of poetry: that is, predictable themes executed in a standardised poetic language and clichéd tropes. The worst outcome of this has been to set up a barrier between the reader and the 'genuine experience' existing somewhere behind the text. Well before the 1790s, poetic language had degenerated into a stale and hackneyed idiom alongside a rigidly canonical subject-matter (Wordsworth himself cites examples of this from Alexander Pope and Dr Johnson as typical offenders).

Wordsworth's poetic fundamentalism, stressing truth, naturalness and bucolic values denies the urbanite affectations of eighteenth-century poesy and in its place proposes good honest fustian: the language of the lower classes ('my style is distinguished by a genuine simplicity'). But further, and more irritatingly for Coleridge, he asserts most strongly that there can be

> no essential difference between the language of prose and metrical composition.

In order to bring poetic language closer to the 'language of men' it should be purged of affectation and thus the moral feelings will be 'corrected and purified'. One way to realise this is for a poet to write prose and then 'poeticise' it, though the most effective formula is for the author to select the *appropriate* subject matter and the language will inevitably be determined by this.

All of the various prefaces to *Lyrical Ballads* were written by Wordsworth. At the centre of these articles of faith is his drive to take hold of literature and to redefine its key areas: the poet and his or her purpose, the nature of poetic language, and the subject matter. The intensity and breadth of the articles lay open Wordsworth's profound commitment to poetry, yet, at the same time, they also suggest a desire to control the reader's response to new writing and, at the back of this, lies an important idea which he attributes to Coleridge, that:

> every great and original writer must himself create the taste by which he is to be relished; he must teach the art by which he is to be seen
> (Letter to Lady Beaumont, 21 May 1807)

While many critics dispute the extent to which we can attribute the Romantic revolution in poetry directly to Wordsworth, his prefaces represent the clearest contemporary attempt to articulate the new literature movement and to influence its direction.

### (b)   *'five hundred Sir Isaac Newtons':*
### *Coleridge's literary theory*

> And Coleridge, too, has lately taken wing,
>    But like a hawk encumbered with his hood, –
> Explaining metaphysics to the nation –
> I wish he would explain his Explanation.   (Byron, *Don Juan,* I.ii)

After *Lyrical Ballads* had first appeared, Wordsworth expressed only one serious disappointment with the poems collected there: the inclusion of *The Rime of the Ancient Mariner*, whose language contradicted his injunction for everyday events narrated in modern simple language,

> From what I can gather it seems that The Ancyent Marinere has upon
> the whole been an injury to the volume, I mean that the words and the
> strangeness of it have deterred readers from going on.
>
> (Letter to Joseph Cottle, 24 June 1799)

For future editions it was, as we have already noted, despatched to the
bilges of the book, as the final poem of volume one, in spite of
the fact that *The Ancient Mariner* had started out as the collaborative
enterprise of the two friends.

In *Biographia Literaria*, his encyclopaedic reflections on life, philosophy and literature, Coleridge expounds his own view of the gestation of
*Lyrical Ballads*. A classic of literary theory as well as a personal odyssey,
the *Biographia* started out in 1815 as a short preface of 'five or six pages'
to introduce a collection of his poetry, but expanding exponentially
until, by 1817, it was published as a two-volume work in its own right.

The great spur to the book was Wordsworth's own volume of verse
published in 1815 as *Poems*. *Biographia* was designed partly as a rival
to this volume, but since Wordsworth's new book also reprinted the
*Lyrical Ballads'* 1800 Preface, Coleridge was now stirred to respond
with his own literary theory.

Chapter XIV sets down the 'two cardinal points' of what was their
shared view of poetry at that time: 'adherence to the truth of nature',
but a nature intensified through the 'modifying colours of the imagination'. In *Lyrical Ballads* Coleridge was to work on 'persons and characters supernatural' and to present them with sufficient inward truth
as to provoke in the reader 'that willing suspension of disbelief ...
which constitutes poetic faith'.

In *Biographia Literaria* Coleridge suggests that the numerical
preponderance of Wordsworth's poems in *Lyrical Ballads* was due to
Wordsworth's being the more industrious of the two. This is only
partly true: Wordsworth consciously took over the work to lock out
Coleridge but, at the same time, Coleridge's interest had cooled con-
siderably. After Tom Wedgwood (brother of the pot man, Josiah) had
endowed him with a generous legacy, he no longer depended on the
money that *Lyrical Ballads* had been expected to generate.

Wedgwood's annuity freed Coleridge to devote himself to his most cherished enterprise, a concentrated study of metaphysics as the philosophical starting point of poetry; in short a universal theory of Romantic poetics. Along with Wordsworth's Preface, Coleridge's search marks the first modern attempt to regularise literary theory both as an intrinsic, academic enquiry and as the practical basis for the composition of texts.

*Biographia Literaria* is part of the fruit of that sponsorship which enabled Coleridge to get clearer some of the literary and philosophical ideas that inform his early verse. To expand on his earlier design, he plundered his notebooks, lectures and journalism, and his voluminous marginalia on philosophy, especially ancient Greek and the recent German Romantics. Some of his ideas have already been discussed in the chapters on the poems, most noticeably his theory of the imagination.

In the *Biographia* Coleridge sets himself a gargantuan task of uniting all of his philosophy into a coherent system, to synthesise ideas into the philosophical equivalent of the 'One Life'. This is a massively ambitious project, which he could never realistically hope to achieve. Add to this his dilatory habits, sloppy working practices, fondness for contradictions and digression, plus a general disorganisation and we have the baffling, maddeningly inspiring, brilliant and humanitarian Coleridge. Of this he was himself too much aware:

> what I could have done, is a question for my own conscience. On my own account I may perhaps have had sufficient reason to lament my deficiency in self-control, and the neglect of concentering my powers to the realisation of some permanent work.   (*Biographia Literaria,* Chapter X)

In spite of this, the book contains some flashes of inspiration which illuminate Coleridge's early ideas on literature. However, before examining the *Biographia Literaria* itself, a useful place to begin our discussion is a series of letters he wrote to William Sotheby during autumn 1802. In one of the letters Coleridge claims that the Preface to *Lyrical Ballads* was to be written by himself, though in another he maintains that half of what Wordsworth did write was the 'child of my own Brain' and continued to disagree with the Preface. However, in 1802 he complained to Robert Southey that he found Wordsworth's Preface confusing.

The importance of the Sotheby letters lies in their discussion in small scale of some of the themes of Coleridge's later writing. For example, in his letter of 13 July 1802, Coleridge set down that a great poet must also be a great metaphysician and that Shakespeare was the model of this. A poet must also be an individual of passion:

> In my opinion every phrase, every metaphor, every personification, should have its justifying cause in some *passion* either of the Poet's mind, or of the characters described by the poet.

So far there is no real conflict with Wordsworth's views in the Preface but it is noticeable how much more stress in Coleridge is placed on the passions. However, his next point clashes profoundly with Wordsworth's view that poetic language should restrict itself to everyday speech. Because poetry has a 'passion' within itself as poetry, Coleridge argues, it fully justifies creative experimentation in the form of 'new combinations of Language'. This crux lies at the heart of the controversy of *The Ancient Mariner*. Where Wordsworth is content and intent on reflecting everyday linguistic forms, Coleridge sees the whole point of poetry as energetically developing new forms, language as a progressively versatile medium.

Imagination, therefore, is a more important and stimulating source of truth than the slavish reproduction of Newtonian reality. According to *Biographia Literaria*, the latter is merely the mechanical workings of the Fancy

> The more I understand of Isaac Newton's works, the more boldly I dare utter to my own mind ... that I believe the souls of five hundred Sir Isaac Newtons would go the making up of a Shakespeare or a Milton.   (Letter to Thomas Poole, 23 March 1801)

In a long letter to Sotheby of 10 September 1802, Coleridge makes some illuminating notes towards his definition of imagination. Using theological imagery, he first likens the elusive faculty of the imagination to religious inspiration or as a spirit inhabiting the mind, before he breaks into the more familiar terminology of the *Biographia*: the fancy, or 'aggregating Faculty of the mind' contrasts with:

> *Imagination*, or the *modifying*, and *co-adunating* Faculty. This the
> Hebrew Poets appear to me to have possessed beyond all others – &
> next to them the English. In the Hebrew Poets each Thing has a Life
> of its own, and yet they are all one Life.

What we have here is not only the well-known distinction between
the passive and active mental powers, but also Coleridge's famous
principle of the One Life, united and convivial.

The letter shares Wordsworth's belief that to intensify the One Life
we ought to experience nature at first hand, to feel the uniqueness of
each element and its connectivity:

> A poet's *Heart & Intellect* should be *combined, intimately* combined
> and *unified*, with the great appearances in Nature.

And while a poet such as the highly influential William Bowles has
sensibility, a great poet such as Wordsworth has passion – fifteen years
later, in *Biographia Literaria*, Coleridge continued to think of
Wordsworth as the quintessence of the great poet.

The opening three chapters of the *Biographia* constitute a straggling,
discursive preamble to his main theory. Among these, his stated aims of
settling the 'controversy concerning the true nature of poetic diction'
and of defining the 'real poetic character of the poet' reveal the extent
to which his discussion is provoked by Wordsworth's comments.

Eventually Chapter IV takes the discussion into a more resolute
direction. He acknowledges the deep impression made on him by
Wordsworth's 'The Female Vagrant' and how it stimulated his distinction between 'fancy' and 'imagination', which most critics had
conflated. But where Wordsworth wished to distinguish them as they
appeared in poetic practice, Coleridge set out to examine their
differences in origin.

The following chapters delve into the intellectual background
starting from first principles ('metaphysics and psychology have long
been my hobby-horse'). The foundations combine Aristotle's metaphysics, a critique of Hartley's associationism, Spinoza on pantheism,

Bruno's cosmology, Schelling on Kant, as well as the empiricist philosophy of John Locke and David Hume.

His philosophical remarks, like his literary remarks, are a sort of mid-life reassessment of his youthful allegiances, a coming of age. The same applies to his religious and political axioms. He uses the book to set down firmly that as a Christian, with a strong belief and love of Jesus Christ, he has finally abandoned the Unitarianism of his youth. Having seen the later course taken by the French Revolution he had also discarded all Jacobin sympathies. One of his most intensely modern philosophical statements comes in Chapter XII, *A Chapter of Requests*, where his equation of existence and epistemology appears to anticipate Heidegger's existentialism,

Truth is correlative to being.

Refining the views from the Sotheby letters, Coleridge now challenges some of Wordsworth's claims in the Preface to *Lyrical Ballads*. His first objection is that Wordsworth confuses the imagination with the fancy. As we have seen, Coleridge's view of the imagination is that it embodies an '*esemplastic*' power, to combine and shape impressions, ideas, etc. stored in the memory, and this power is coadunating, that is, aggregating or working towards a unity. As we have noted in Chapter 2, the fancy simply brings forward from the memory our accumulated impressions. On the other hand, according to Coleridge, Wordsworth believes that the fancy does have some power to 'evoke and combine'.

Coleridge proceeds to divide the imagination into the Primary, the power working behind artistic creativity (which is a God-like creation from nothing: 'a repetition in the finite mind of the eternal act of creation'), and the Secondary imagination, which is the power to dissolve received impressions and recombine them in a new form.

Coleridge now uses this discussion of the imagination to introduce his objection to many of the Preface's claims and ideas. Two interrelated points in particular stand out. The first is the prickly question of what constitutes a poem. Poetry, he argues, is not the same as prose since it is written in metre and rhyme, and exploits possibilities in sound and quantity in its phonemes. Moreover, poetry is not usually written primarily for transmission of 'scientific' truth and its formal elements can be enjoyed as much as its contents.

These are not easily defensible as distinguishing marks and, as if to concede this, he adds that poetry can exist without metre, citing the Bible as an example of poetic prose. Having driven some way down a cul-de-sac he resorts to a circular argument: poetry, we find in the end, is what poets write. Not many of us would want to argue with that. But, further, a poet writes poetry when he 'brings the whole soul of man into activity' and imparts to his writing:

> a tone and spirit of unity, that blends, and (as it were) fuses, each into each, by that synthetic and magical power, to which I would exclusively appropriate the name of the Imagination.
>
> (*Biographia Literaria,* Chapter XIV)

It is the enchanting magic of the Imagination that forms writing into the 'one graceful and intelligent whole' that is poetry.

The second major departure from Wordsworth's Preface is on the issue of the appropriate language of poetry. In Chapter XVII, Coleridge begins by agreeing that poetic language had become sloppy and hackneyed by the end of the eighteenth century. 'Poetic diction' was then a pejorative term for mere artifice. But one objection to the proposed solution is that everyday and rustic language can be applied only to a limited type of poetry, that dealing with rural issues. Another problem is that rustic people *per se* do not inevitably represent models of good morality, Furthermore, their language does not readily admit of poetic discussion of advanced philosophical or abstract ideas.

He believes that Wordsworth's precept that poets should adopt the ordinary language of country people is, finally, impossible. To be able to speak like a rustic he would have to be a rustic, and therefore not a poet. Few these days would agree with the sociology of this distinction and as philosopher-poet Coleridge has in mind something more to do with education. Given his 'definition' of poetry above, Coleridge seems to be saying that because poetry aspires to reach and enunciate the sublime or divine essence of human existence, in 'one graceful and intelligent whole', your average unlettered hayseed is unlikely to match up to requirements.

He concludes this part of his argument by reasserting that Wordsworth was wrong to prescribe that poetry should or indeed could be written in ordinary language. Since the defining characteristics of poetry include its non-realistic metrical rhythms and heightened language (he later described poetry as 'the best words in the best order') verse could never use the ordinary language of the 'humble rustic life'.

Chapter XV identifies four characteristics necessary for a poem: verse of musical delight; subject matter of public interest; striking images – which should be brought into unity; and a poem ought to embody a 'philosophy', that is, thoughts, knowledge or emotions.

The *Biographia*'s discussion of verse closes with an assessment of the 'defects' and 'excellencies' of Wordsworth's poetry, concluding with a typical Coleridgean tribute of self-less homage, ranking him in 'imaginative power' with Shakespeare and Milton.

This book above all demonstrates Coleridge's serious claims to be a philosopher especially as he applies his vast experience and intellect to an astonishing breath of reading. It displays an unpremeditated richness of mind and sensibility. Coleridge was at the centre of a very impressive range of contemporary minds: at various periods his circle of acquaintances included some of the real intellectual giants of the age, artists, scientists, editors, radical thinkers and so on: Humphry Davy, John Thelwall, Charles Lamb, John Keats, William Hazlitt, Leigh Hunt, Lord Byron, Erasmus Darwin, Joseph Banks, Wilhelm von Schlegel, Robert Southey and Percy Shelley.

Of a quite brilliant and creative mind himself, Coleridge readily made himself available to new ideas, and the new artistic ideas of the day centred on German Romanticism. While he cannot be credited with introducing Romanticism itself into Britain, the theoretical foundations of the movement in this country were almost exclusively established and promoted by Coleridge (it is often remarked that he furnished the intellectual support for Wordsworth's poetic theory). This was in large measure due to his unique familiarity with contemporary German philosophy, especially the work of the Schlegel brothers, Friedrich von Schelling, J. G. Fichte and Gotthold Lessing who find their influence in the *Biographia*.

*Biographia Literaria* did not enjoy a warm reception on publication, but then it is an exceptional kind of book. Seeking to coadunate philosophy, literary theory, memoir, religion and psychology with autobiography it has shades about it of Tristram Shandy, Don Quixote and Hamlet ('I have a smack of Hamlet myself, if I may say so', he confided in 1827). Yet there is an excitement about this 'rag-picker's bench' – it is the sort of excitement that is frequently found in the best work of Nietzsche or Wittgenstein whose methods he often anticipates.

# 9

# Dorothy Wordsworth and the Lake Poets

> Dorothy Wordsworth, the Sister of our great Poet, is a Woman of Genius, as well as manifold acquirements; and but for the absorption of her whole Soul in her Brother's fame and writings would, perhaps, in a different style have been as great a Poet as Himself.
>
> (Coleridge, letter of 26 August 1833)

In this letter, written a year before his death, Coleridge speculates, as many have done since, on what might have been Dorothy's success as a writer had she not lived in the shadow of her brother's fame. Although she vehemently rejected any idea of herself as a serious poet, her journals and letters do reveal that 'in a different style' she was in fact a highly gifted poetic writer. Coleridge's letter strikes at three of the key elements that recur in discussions about Dorothy: her devoted dedication to William, her contribution ('absorption') to his success and the possibility of her own success as a poet if circumstances had been more propitious.

Although most of Dorothy's friends recognised her outstanding literary gift, the only work published in her own lifetime was short extracts from her journals and letters that her brother appended to his own published poems, or redrafted and incorporated into his tourist book *Guide to the Lakes* ('Excursion on the Banks of Ullswater'). Her journals were not printed in their own right until selections appeared in 1897. In truth, they were generally written with no view to publication, as simple responses to and records of the life around her, written in a cursive copperplate, sprinkled with lists, impromptu memos, domestic accounts, drafts and bits of verse, reflecting her own random moods and stream of consciousness.

The journals make no claims to conventional literary fluency or merit but record her penetrating perceptions and emotional responses with imaginative insight, what her biographer Ernest De Selincourt describes as a 'veritable transcript of real life'. Even when Dorothy's close companions encouraged her to publish, she could become adamantly self-effacing; writing to her close friend Lady Beaumont about 'Recollections of a Tour made in Scotland' (1803) she protested her ignorance:

> Do not wonder if you or Sir George should detect some inaccuracies, often misspelt and even miscalled, for I never looked into a book, only bore in my mind my own remembrances of the sounds as they were pronounced to us.

The letter then goes on to recount a comic story in which, by the force of her compassion and simplicity of heart, she utterly wrecked one of Coleridge's jokes – and these two characteristics are the ones which most often strike her contemporaries both about herself and her writing. And, while most people visit her writings in order to explore Wordsworth and his work, they usually come away with some remarkable insights on Dorothy herself. Having said this, I would like to start a discussion of the woman, by way of her journals and poetry in addition to her letters, by first looking at her relationship with William and Coleridge.

### (a)   *Dorothy among the poets*

From her early teenage years Dorothy's cherished hope was to set up home with her brother. She had no aspirations of becoming a poet and insisted to her friend Catherine Clarkson: 'I should detest the idea of setting myself as an author.' The third child and only daughter of John and Ann Wordsworth, Dorothy was aged seven when her mother died, and was sent away by her father to live with her 'aunt' in Halifax where she stayed for the next five years. For a period of fourteen years she boarded in the houses of various relatives with varying degrees of happiness, often working as a sort of unpaid domestic servant, and receiving only a token formal education. At last, in 1795, her long-held ambition for her home was realised when she was reunited with her beloved William and they settled together at Racedown in Dorset.

This year marks a coming of age and, in choosing to keep house for William, she sets herself at the very hub of the nascent English Romantic movement. Her writing expresses a deep elation at her freedom to roam the hills, woods and seascapes, liberated from aunts, uncles and her own minority. As well as setting up and regulating their household, Dorothy fervently helps to foster artistic friendships in a congenial home environment, which becomes at different moments the haunts of intellectuals the like of William Hazlitt, Charles Lamb, Robert Southey, Thomas De Quincey and John Thelwall.

*The Prelude* testifies abundantly to the therapeutic benefit which this reunion had on Wordsworth's outlook and development, following the despair of his revolutionary ideals, and Dorothy devoted herself to his recuperation, both as a brother and as a poet. After their 'separation desolate', Dorothy is embraced as 'A gift then first bestowed' and their reunion is celebrated in 'a joy / Above all joys' (*The Prelude*, 1805, VI.211–18).

The year of their reunion was momentous in another respect following William's new acquaintance with Coleridge, the other major influence on his artistic development at this time. When the Wordsworths moved to Alfoxden in 1797 to be nearer to Coleridge, the latter described their specially close association as 'three persons, but one soul'. Furthermore, Coleridge's letter, quoted above, acknowledges her profound stimulus to his own intellectual and imaginative life.

It was at Alfoxden, Somerset, that Dorothy began to keep her famous journals, beginning in January 1797 (or at least the surviving fragment begins then) and maintaining it until May of the following year. After their unhappy period in Germany in 1798, the Wordsworths realised another treasured ambition, that of a return to the English Lake District, when they took the lease on a cottage close to the shores of Grasmere. Here, at what later became known as Dove Cottage, they established a settled residence and in her new journal Dorothy elatedly detailed the great busy, brimming life of the neighbourhood, its fascinating characters, her friends and visitors, the poets, the surrounding countryside and its diverse wildlife, together with her response to 'Nature's breathing life' in all its ceaselessly changing glory, and finally the portrait of herself.

One of Dorothy's most important contributions to the artistic life of the Wordsworth home was organising a framework of stability in which her brother could flourish as an artist. As a result she recognised William as the 'sole guardian of her future' and absorbed her own hopes and wishes in the wider purpose of ministering to him. In another letter to Lady Beaumont she confided:

> I have not those powers which Coleridge thinks I have – I know it. My only merits are my devotedness to those I love and I hope a charity towards all mankind.

Perhaps her strongest quality is a selfless and unstinting generosity and it was this that above all helped her maintain a creative environment (though many readers have claimed too that this is the real reason for her failing to assert herself as a poet in her own right). Yet this self-appointed duty was hardly light. As well as housekeeper, she busied herself in an astonishing workload of domestic roles, including nurse, secretary, painter, gardener, seamstress, shoemaker, tutor and carpenter. She was also a surrogate mother to William and, after he was married, a sister and best friend to his new bride, Mary Hutchinson whom the Wordworths had known since childhood days.

After the marriage she found another new role in caring for the subsequent children. De Quincey, a regular visitor at Dove Cottage, recorded that Dorothy herself had received several offers of marriage (including one from Hazlitt), but rejected them all decisively. Her need to love and be loved was satisfied by the affection of Wordsworth and later his family and her relationship was one of symbiosis – she provided and maintained the home in the belief that she was needed as much as others needed her.

As well as cataloguing the atmosphere of their daily life together her letters and journals freely declare her unshakeable conviction in her brother's genius. He seems constantly in her thoughts and one of the reasons for starting her Grasmere journal on 14 May 1800 is that 'I shall give Wm Pleasure by it when he comes home again.' They met almost every day and talked often about his poetry and though she was in no way a literary theorist she contributed the vital substance of his work and spiritual support, no less vital. His verse reveals a shared delight in the joy of earth, sky and all the life between and often she provided more.

Coleridge is a continual visitor and the Alfoxden journal mentions him as present almost every day. As with William, Dorothy continued to have faith in his often wayward artistic genius, even though she recognised that it was in part squandered. She saw too that it was diverted and diluted by his own weaknesses, especially the demoralizing frustrations connected with his love for Sara Hutchinson. Dorothy understood his deep sense of humanity and of the 'one-Life' but also of the things that threatened to destroy his genius, a deepening drug addiction, mysterious and debilitating ailments in addition to his notorious prodigality. On one occasion, her journal records how she wept to think of his vulnerability (9 October 1801). However, her writings vividly capture something of the delight he could engender in his encounters, such as one day when he announced his arrival by leaping over their gate.

> You had a great loss in not seeing Coleridge. He is a wonderful man. His conversation teems with soul, mind and spirit. Then he is so benevolent, so good tempered and cheerful, and like William, interests himself so much about every little trifle ... He is pale and thin, has a wide mouth, thick lips, and not very good teeth ... His eye is large and full ... but it speaks every emotion of his animated mind.
>
> (Letter to Mary Hutchinson, June 1797)

Although her journal was not intended for public scrutiny, Coleridge and especially Wordsworth were permitted to dip into her jottings for their own writing as an *aide-mémoire*, or for inspiration, or just for that particular detail. I have already mentioned her brother's plundering of some of the Ullswater journal for his guidebook, but his poems too are nourished by her descriptions. A good example of this is Wordsworth's 'I wandered lonely as a cloud', in part inspired by Dorothy's description of daffodils seen on a walk:

> I never saw daffodils so beautiful they grew among the mossy stones about and about them, some rested their heads upon these stones as on a pillow for weariness and the rest tossed and reeled and danced and seemed as if they verily laughed with the wind that blew upon them over the lake, they looked so gay ever glancing ever changing.
>
> (Grasmere Journal, 15 April 1802)

(in the next breath she memorably glorified this host as the 'simplicity and unity and life of that one busy highway'). Among Wordsworth's early lyrics, 'To a Butterfly', *The Ruined Cottage*, a 'Night-piece' and Coleridge's *Christabel* all owe at least some of their references to the Journals.

Dorothy's writings are also a revealing source for her brother's working practices:

> He composes his verses out of door, and while he is so engaged, he seldom knows how the time slips away, or hardly whether it is rain or fair.　(Letter, 25 May 1804)

She is frequently anxious at the intensity of his composing, often driving himself to illness:

> Wm was in the orchard. I went to him – he worked away at his poem – though he was ill and tired.　(Grasmere Journal, 28 April 1802)

and

> William had slept better. He fell to work and made himself unwell
>
> (Grasmere Journal, 9 February 1802)

She is occasionally a critic of his work. Discussing *An Evening Walk* and *Descriptive Sketches* she tells her friend, Jane Pollard:

> the poems contain many Faults, the chief of which are Obscurity, and a too frequent use of some particular expressions and uncommon

words for instance moveless which he applies in a sense if not new, at least different from its ordinary one.   (Letter, 16 February 1793)

and shares in their celebrations, adopting the communal 'we':

> The first volume [of *Lyrical Ballads*] sold much better than we expected … not that we had ever much doubt of its finally making its way, but we knew that poems so different from what have in general become popular immediately after their publication were not likely to be admired at once.   (Letter, 10 September 1800)

## (b)   *'more than half a poet': home at Alfoxden and Grasmere*

### Floating Island

Harmonious powers with Nature work
On sky, earth, river, lake, and sea:
Sunshine and storm, whirlwind and breeze
All in one duteous task agree.

Once did I see a slip of earth,
By throbbing waves long undermined
Loosed from its hold; – *how* no one
But all might see it float, obedient to the wind.

Might see it, from the mossy shore
Dissevered float upon the Lake,
Float, with its crest of trees adorned
On which the warbling birds their pastime take.

Food, shelter, safety there they find
There berries ripen, flowerets bloom;
There insects live their lives – and die:
A people *world* it is; in size a tiny room.

And thus through many seasons' space
This little Island may survive
But Nature, though we mark her not,
Will take away – may cease to give.

Perchance when you are wandering forth
Upon some vacant sunny day
Without an object, hope, or fear,
Thither your eyes may turn – the Isle is passed away.

Buried beneath the glittering Lake!
Its place no longer to be found,
Yet the lost fragments shall remain,
To fertilise some other ground.

This poem, written by Dorothy sometime in the 1820s and published in 1842 along with a miscellany of William's verse, encapsulates many of the concerns of her journals: detailed observation of a crowded natural scene with all life pulsing around her (in stanzas 1 and 4 especially); allied with this is a strong sense of realism, facing up to human mortality, symbolised here in the island, and the floating world of evanescent life-forms (which gives rise to a sense of eeriness here at the end) in stanzas 5 and 6; and underpinning these is her characteristic tranquillity, a wise passiveness unperturbed by any vital anxiousness of the ego (the 'I' of stanza 2 is only a sort of point in the poem's departure, towards 'they' in stanza 4 and eventually to 'you' in 6).

As always in the journals there is an unmistakable sense of Dorothy's affinity with the observed nature, an empathic involvement with it, without making proprietorial demands on it. So, on 18 March 1802, she records

> the lake was covered all over with Bright silver waves that were there each the twinkling of an eye, then others rose up and took their place as fast as they went away. The Rocks glittered in the sunshine, the crows and the ravens were busy, and the thrushes and little Birds sang.
>
> (Grasmere Journal)

She sits for half an hour watching a cow, afraid to pass it, but observes its responses to her. And then on the same date there is a marvellous account of her returning home alone at twilight:

> as I climbed Moss the moon came out from behind a mountain mass of Black clouds – O the unutterable darkness of the sky and the earth below the moon! and the glorious brightness of the moon itself! There

was a vivid sparkling streak of light at this end of Rydale water but the rest was very dark and Loughrigg fell and Silver How were white and bright and as if they were covered with hoar frost.

This is both a brilliantly evocative description and a glorious hymn to nature. As she finishes this section of the day's account she allows herself the hint of a vanity:

with that bright soft light upon it, it made me more than half a poet.

Yet even this is attributed to something other than her own powers, the resonances of the natural scene itself.

Her journals are a vivid picture of life and people in a small village at the beginning of the nineteenth century. Her writing is as vividly precise as any contemporary prose writer and, like John Ruskin much later in the century, her details teach us to see with a new eye. Grasmere in particular becomes a 'blessed place' where people, lakes, animals, the weather, butterflies, daffodils and God, all fuse delightfully in the 'busy highway' of her life.

It is no coincidence that her diaries furnish the living material for the poetry of William and Coleridge. The latter commended her 'exquisite eye', while De Quincey remarked on that 'sensibility of her visionary imagination' with which she brings alive her landscape and its people. The weather catches her eye most often, she was so often outside in it, and its subtle changes, too. She lives by the presiding rhythms of the seasons in a exaltation that we cannot easily relate to nowadays and chronicles the responses to it of other natural phenomena. So in November (1801) she records the appearance of 'our favourite birch tree':

It was yielding to the gusty windy with all its tender twigs, the sun shone upon it and it glanced in the wind like a flying sunshiny shower.

Then, six months later:

The Birch Tree is all over green in *small* leaf more light and elegant than when it is full out. It bent to the breezes as if for love of its own delightful motions. (Grasmere Journal, 6 May 1802)

Dorothy's journals clearly indicate that she was not much acquainted or concerned with the wider world beyond her local circles of interest in Alfoxden and Grasmere. She had accompanied William on visits to France and Germany and enjoyed tours of Scotland, but she was happiest in a simple country life among the familiar landscapes of her country. The great turmoil on the continent and the emerging revolution in literature have no reference in her writing. What most interests her are the 'common things that round us lie'.

She likes to catch transitory impressions, the ephemera of nature as they fall, aided by her wayward constructions and erratic punctuation. She has a fascination for the modulations of nature:

> Sat a considerable time upon the heath. It surface restless with and glittering with the motion of the scattered piles of withered grass, and the waving of the spiders' threads.   (Alfoxden Journal, 8 February 1798)

Anne K. Mellor writes that Dorothy's journals are a 'substantiated record of *relatedness*' and this idea of relatedness or communion extends both to the natural world and to its people. Children figure often in her concern and she has a deep compassion for the poor and oppressed. She also paints a vivid picture of participation in the busy life of a rural community. In addition to her immediate family she records the daily lives of the neighbourhood, registered in her homely intimacy with, for example, the Ashburner, Fisher and Bateman families, the Luffs and the Lloyds, little John Dawson plus the procession of visitors to their cottages, including the Hutchinsons, Tom Poole, Tom Wedgwood, poets, peddlers, beggars, leech gatherers, 'a half cray man', and those on the edge of her acquaintance, a 'little girl from Coniston', 'the poor woman who was drowned', 'the Man who stood like a Giant'.

The common image of the Grasmere area is one of a desolate and isolated enclave, but the pages of Dorothy's journals and letters project a great hurly burly of rural life and a panorama of its diverse emotions, from the sublime to, well, the plain earthy. So she could juxtapose almost in the same breath:

> At Breakfast Wm wrote part of an ode. Mr Olliff sent the dung
> (Grasmere Journal, 27 March 1802)

## (c)  *Dorothy herself: 'Come forth and feel the sun'*

My sister! ('tis a wish of mine)
Now that our morning meal is done,
Make haste, your morning task resign;
Come forth and feel the sun.                  ('To My Sister', ll. 9–12)

Wordsworth's exuberant encomium to spring summons Dorothy from her domestic retreat, outside into the light of attention. She had an abnormal shrinking from the 'limelight' too. She blanched at any hint of publicity that might have allowed her to think of herself as an author. In her surviving writing she is repeatedly self-effacing in terms of her literary talents but given the proximity to two of the giants of Romantic poetry, perhaps such modesty and passivity are inescapable. Wordsworth's 'exquisite sister', as Coleridge described her, made no claim to exceptional talents of any kind, in spite of the glowing tributes from her friends.

> And you persuade *me* that I am capable of writing poems that might give pleasure to others beside my own particular friends!! indeed, indeed you do not know me thoroughly; you think far better of me than I deserve.   (Letter to Lady Beaumont, 20 April 1806)

On the other hand, the identity in the journals and letters is within its own terms unmistakably self-confident (while managing to remain an intrinsic element of the observed scene). The 'I' of Dorothy the observer is much less William's 'egotistical sublime' than the organising consciousness, the genius of the meditations, and a point of orientation. While the public Dorothy is characterised by devotion to others and by refusal (i.e. to become the poet), the private Dorothy is one of affirmation of nature and her setting as well as of her place in them. Devotion and refusal were for her, however, both material assertions of her choice and a realisation of ambition.

Having discussed some of Dorothy's talents and her reluctance to be known as a writer, it remains to consider what sort of identity does emerge of her. We have 'Wordsworth's exquisite sister' from Coleridge and he expands on this in his letter of June 1797:

> her manners are simple, ardent, impressive, in every motion her most
> innocent soul beams out so brightly ... Her eye watchful in minutest
> observation of nature; and her taste a perfect electrometer.

Thomas De Quincey added:

> I may sum up in one brief abstract the amount of Miss Wordsworth's
> character, as a companion, by saying, that she was the very wildest (in
> the sense of the most natural) person I have ever known; and also the
> truest and at the same time the quickest and readiest in her sympathy
> with either joy or sorrow.   (*Reminiscences of the English Lake Poets*)

Wordsworth too noted her high sensitivity, that she once wept openly
on perceiving the sea. De Quincey remarks on her 'wild and startling
eyes' (John Thelwall called them 'too ardent') and Wordsworth himself, at the end of 'Tintern Abbey', draws attention to the 'shooting
lights / Of thy wild eyes' (119–20). Most of these admirers take this
physical element to be expressive of her quick brilliant nature and
what De Quincey termed 'freshness of intellect'.

De Quincey was relieved to find she was not a 'bluestocking' – but
added that he thought her poetry 'feeble and trivial'. The journals
reveal the sensitivity of her eye and ear and her receptiveness to a host
of phenomenon on the 'busy highway' that passes before her attention. Her unshakeable loyalty and service to her brothers, particularly
William and John, has been made evident, though before William's
marriage she insisted in her own financial independence by setting up
an annuity through another brother, Richard.

On the other hand it is clear that Dorothy's character is in large
measure formed by her relation with others. This alterity is closely
connected with the needs, personality and lifestyles of significant others with whom she chose to live in close proximity. This is made
apparent in her letters and journals by the vicarious joy she takes in
the successes and ordeals of others. At the same time the journals
especially have a strong exteriority in them, her delight and close
connection with objects, people she served and loved, the facts 'out

there'. As Anne K. Mellor has argued:

> It is a self built, as were many other nineteenth century women's selves, on a model of affiliation rather than a model of individual achievement.

Dorothy's writings are an invaluable resource in Romantic literary studies: for the lives and methods of the poets around her, the milieu and aspirations in which their poetry and writing was carried out, enabling us to date and contextualise the work of Wordsworth and Coleridge. They are a closely observed documentation of life served in a small rural community at a particular period in English history. Yet, while we may come to the letters to find out more about these elements we inevitably find them mediated through the biography of Dorothy herself.

However by their very nature, Dorothy's journal and letters offer the reader a different form of biography from the usual rounded and managed form (e.g., Wordsworth's *The Prelude*). Her purpose in beginning the journals was partly, as we have seen, 'because I shall give Wm pleasure by it'. Although they were not written for a public reading there does emerge an awareness of a sort of implied reader, other than herself. These fragmentary, happenstance notes, persistently interrupted and distracted, also exude a fluid, subjective construct of her character, of a personality continually unfolding within the narrative of her 'spots of time'. Her vital engagement with the real materiality of life, a complement to her brother's fascination with the sublime, anchors the 'floating island' of her narrative in a simple and positive affirmation of life.

# 10

# *Critical Responses to* Lyrical Ballads

In this chapter I would like to take a look at the way in which Wordsworth and Coleridge have been received by critics over the period since the first appearance of *Lyrical Ballads*. One reason for this is to try to show how their reputations have grown while another is to present some alternative critical attitudes towards these poets and their work. None of them is final or conclusive but are offered, as indeed the comments in this book are, as a challenge and a stimulus to your own ideas. The chapter begins with a survey of the critical reception of Wordsworth and Coleridge during the past 200 years, and then focuses closely on the views of four critics in particular: I. A. Richards, Robert Mayo, Geoffrey H. Hartman and Paul de Man.

From its very first appearance, *Lyrical Ballads* attracted critical debate, a debate that intensified after the appearance of Wordsworth's highly provocative Preface to the collection. At first, discussion was along two main strands: speculation about the identity of its authors, and argument about the experimental nature of the contents, their 'strangeness' and the 'charm of novelty' as Coleridge saw it.

The extent of the 'novelty' of the poems has been a matter of controversy ever since, though, as we have noted already, even the preface itself was distinctly something new of its time. In the opening decades of the nineteenth century, *Lyrical Ballads* suffered in the reactionary backlash against Romanticism as a whole, while attacks on the two authors of the collection tended to be personal and political, an expression of the established taste, apt to overlook the poems themselves, in any detail at least.

As we noted in Chapter 7, the appearance of *Lyrical Ballads* coincided with the emergence and rapid expansion of the literary periodical in the late eighteenth century. Given the massive rise in book publishing, readers sought instant views and advice on the array of material available, and the periodicals gave it to them. This was usually an expression of conventional taste and the political colouring of the magazine. Typically readers were given a raw opinion with little or no direct reference to the texts, which amounted to 'read this' and 'shun that'. The appeal or worthlessness of a new book was more likely to depend on the social circle of its author and the degree to which it sustained pre-established codes of culture.

Robert Southey was among the first to notice *Lyrical Ballads* and as a friend he had been expected by Wordsworth to be sympathetic.

> The 'experiment', we think, has failed, not because the language of conversation is little adapted to 'the purposes of poetic pleasure', but because it has been tried upon uninteresting subjects. Yet every piece discovers genius.    (*Critical Review*, October 1798)

Wordsworth himself was not grateful for Southey's feint approval, principally on the pragmatic grounds that it would decimate sales. Writing to their publisher, Joseph Cottle, he groaned:

> The bulk of the poems he has described as destitute of merit. Am I recompensed for this by vague praises of my talent?

Southey's singling out of *The Ancient Mariner* and 'The Idiot Boy', however, anticipated the predilections of later reviews. Most reviewers begrudgingly recognised the originality of the former's verse style but remained bewildered about its 'riddling' subject matter. 'The Idiot Boy', however, was often rejected out of hand on the basis of its 'unsuitable' subject. Southey lamented the 'worthlessness of its design'.

Wordsworth's pronouncements on preordained artistic attitudes were shown to be, with some irony, exactly right. Francis Jeffrey in

the opening edition of the *Edinburgh Review* savaged the collection
more out of fear of its author's levelling politics than for any literary
demerit:

> The poor and vulgar may interest us, in poetry, by their situation; but
> never, we apprehend, by any sentiments that are peculiar to their
> condition, and still less by any language that is characteristic of it.
>                                          (*Edinburgh Review*, 25 October 1802)

However, another close friend of Wordsworth, Francis Wrangham,
was responsible for the most glowing review of the collection at that
time:

> we think that in general the author has succeeded in attaining that
> judicious degree of simplicity, which accommodates itself with ease to
> the sublime.   (*British Critic*, October 1798)

Yet it was the *Edinburgh*'s attitude that prevailed for almost two
decades as *Lyrical Ballads* and other Romantic collections struggled
against the tide of a Neo-classical tradition of reason and conformity.
One of the reasons that early Victorian reviewers gradually came to
see *Lyrical Ballads* in a revised light was Wordsworth's own revisionary politics, the later poetry becoming less abrasively sociological.
The now-more respectable Wordsworth put the earlier material in a
favourable perspective. William Hazlitt noted that even if the poetry
was revolutionary, its author no longer seemed so.

> Mr Wordsworth's genius is a pure emanation of the Spirit of the
> Age ... He takes the simplest elements of nature and of the human
> mind, the mere abstract conditions of inseparable from our being, and
> tries to compound a new system of poetry from them; and has perhaps
> succeeded as well as any one could.   (*The Spirit of the Age*, 1825)

Exceptionally, Hazlitt's essay sets out to probe the detailed thematic
material of the *Lyrical Ballads* and other poetry – what Wordworth
actually wrote – and to evaluate it on its merits. More typically, the
reviews of the early Victorian period were quite nebulous on the

literary merits of a text and tended to admonish or approve on the basis of belles-lettrist taste or some indefinable aestheticist property (especially where political or religious controversy did not readily offer clear signposting to the predatory reviewer).

Conversely Hazlitt's reception reflected a growing tendency to see a division of attitudes about Wordsworth, namely, the polarisation of readings into the simple and the complex Wordsworth or as Hazlitt expressed it, the 'seeming simplicity and real abstruseness in the *Lyrical Ballads*'. Matthew Arnold represented the former view in his preface to *The Poems of Wordsworth* (1879), declaring the simple ecstasies in nature to be an assurance of moral power:

> Wordsworth's poetry is great because of the extraordinary power with which Wordsworth feels the joy offered to us in nature, the joy offered to us in the simple primary affections and duties.

In his *Oxford Lectures on Poetry* (1909), A. C. Bradley promoted the latter view, turning attention back to the visionary psychology and 'imaginative philosophy' of the poet, complexities, which he felt Arnold had purposely overlooked.

> My main object was to insist that the 'mystic', 'visionary', 'sublime', aspect of Wordsworth's poetry must not be slighted.

Most importantly, from the perspective of literary study, both Arnold and Bradley had consciously sought to set the poetry within a more reasoned framework of discussion, examining in particular the cultural implications of the work. Significantly, too, the seriousness with which Wordsworth was now greeted heralded his canonisation among the English poets by the start of the twentieth century.

Graham McMaster has charged the Victorian critics with systematically manipulating Wordsworth for their own cultural and political ends, exploited 'as a form of spiritual convalescence from the inhumanity of Victorian materialism'. The poetry was often seen as a form of escape from reality into the safe therapeutic haven of nature and its spiritual values. This was none of Wordsworth's own doing, of course, and twentieth-century analyses have, on the whole, endeavoured to get back to what lies within the poetry itself.

Where, in the nineteenth century, reputations and literary ideas had been shaped by the voices of the powerful periodical press, in the twentieth century these have been very much the product of university departments. The work of academic criticism has been advanced by two major developments in that century.

The first has been a proliferation of research into the life and contexts of authors. This development, drawing on the work of other scholarly disciplines, has powered the 'mind and art' approach to criticism that sees a close (and sometimes exclusive) connection between the biography of the poet and his or her writings. In the case of Wordsworth for example, the discovery by Emile Legouis and G. M. Harper of the love affair with Annette Vallon and the birth of daughter Caroline has broadened the field of critical vision in which the poet might be analysed. For some commentators, however, this slice of his life and the 'victimised-woman' syndrome have become the be-all and end-all rationale for all his 1790s verse.

This skilful piece of detective work has also had the result of presenting a more humanised and sexualised individual to counter the rather depersonalised image of a Victorian moral colossus. Linked in with this development has been the flourishing growth of primary biographical materials such as the collected letters of Wordsworth and Coleridge (Ernest De Selincourt and Earl Leslie Griggs, respectively), the journals of Dorothy Wordsworth, and the massive industry that is recovering the lectures, journalism, notebooks, sermons and marginalia of Coleridge.

The second major advance in the twentieth century has been important progress in bibliographical studies. The main thrust of this, textual criticism, has been the production of reliable, scholarly texts for the poetry of Wordsworth and Coleridge. Beset with the problems of, for example, Wordsworth's perpetual revising, merging and renaming of his verse, the result has been the establishment of workable chronologies, of parallel versions of poems and the mapping-out of the poet's artistic development.

Coleridge has been both a beneficiary and victim of the 'mind and art' tendency in the early part of the twentieth century. The major reason has been the fact that Coleridge the man is such a fascination as much in terms of his volatile artistic and philosophical theories as for his unconventional private life. In 1888 the critic Leslie Stephen (father of Virginia Woolf and Vanessa Bell) described him as 'certainly one of the most fascinating and most perplexing figures in our literary history'.

The moral paradoxes of Coleridge's biography have been, appropriately enough, both a stimulant and a frustration to rational critical discourse. For instance, *The Ancient Mariner* became the perennial and happy hunting ground of numerous psychological-symbol seekers, a trait that has consistently led to its being treated in isolation of the rest of the *Lyrical Ballads*.

## I. A. Richards

I. A. Richards's book *Coleridge on Imagination* was a landmark in both Coleridgean studies and literary studies as a whole. Published in 1934, this detailed examination sets out to analyse Coleridge's writing by close attention to exact words on the page. Richards is often held up as the inventor of 'practical criticism', which was the title of another of his books, although his student background was not in literary studies. As an undergraduate at Cambridge he had excelled in linguistic philosophy and later applied this and his research in psychology to the analysis of literary texts.

The Cambridge school of critics of the 1930s attempted to describe the particular imaginative effects of literature by *precise* study of texts. One crucial aim was to substitute a more scientific rigour for the hazy subjective waffle and vague biographical chit-chat then fashionable. This 'school' was greatly influenced by Freud and projected from this the view that since human behaviour is the product of hidden motives, poetry too must contain hidden meanings, the extraction of which necessitated close scrutiny of its words. Besides Richards, the chief proponents of practical criticism included F. R. Leavis, L. C. Knights and William Empson.

*Coleridge on Imagination* is a substantial analysis written in nine chapters that attempts two major projects: to establish new principles of literary criticism and to apply these to Coleridge's work. The Preface sets out clearly that his aim is not to explicate Coleridge's biography but instead to set down some hypotheses that might elevate literary analysis to the level of a science, by observing 'the behaviour of words in poetry'.

The book has a general attitude of tentatively building towards something, rather than starting from a solid prefabricated theory (though this is of course a screen). Progress is by a series of hard-fought steps, akin to constructing a scientific theory as the mountaineering title of the first chapter suggests: 'The First Range of Hills'. Here Richards reflects on the facts that Coleridge himself was a psychologist and philosopher, fascinated by the German metaphysicists, and deeply involved in the theory of criticism. As if to further justify his own methods Richards points out that Coleridge was engrossed in semantics (or 'semasiology' as Richards calls it), the connection between words as arbitrary signs and their imaginative effects on the reader.

The ensuing chapters make it clear that the book is to focus attention on how Coleridge's 'radically new' theory of the imagination determined his own poetry but also changed the course of literature and its criticism. The second chapter establishes a sort of base camp, by way of a historical survey of views on the imagination and concludes with Richards's statement of his aim:

> I hope to show that Coleridge was aware of, and actively at work on, problems and possibilities in the poetic and the ordinary consciousness ... and that Coleridge succeeded in bringing his suggestions to a point from which they can be taken on to become a new science.

The following chapter takes a step back at first by showing a paradox inherent to both philosophy and science. That while both disciplines strive for objectivity in reason and knowledge they both involve an 'inner sense': that is an internal, subjective component. Coleridge too was aware of this and transcended the issue by suggesting that all knowledge is ultimately self-knowledge or being, and is creative, synthetic not merely analytic (see *Biographia Literaria*, chapter XII). For this reason, knowledge for Coleridge is not limited to the usual cognitive material but includes feelings, desires, images, ideas, and so forth.

However, even if Coleridge resolves this paradox (to his own satisfaction at least) Richards identifies a more difficult one at the heart of his theory of the imagination. If past experience determines future experience, this conflicts with Coleridge's profound belief in free will. How could the imagination exist as a creative faculty? Surely it too must be controlled by this sort of determinism? Richards helps him out a little here with the response that, well, yes determinism is a law of nature but the human will is of a different order, is not controlled by it and therefore acts according to different laws. Therefore creativity, the capacity to break into new modes, is on these terms feasible.

Chapter IV is the hub of Richards's discussion of imagination and fancy, beginning with a survey of the two terms in *Biographia Literaria*, *Table Talk* and the *Notebooks*. As we have already noted, the fancy is an autonomic faculty with operates to combine images in a relatively accidental and inert manner whereas the imagination is emphatically creative, drawing together apparently disparate images but forging them in a richly stimulating, original juxtaposition (and for Coleridge 'image' includes feelings, ideas, concepts and so forth). This works for both the author and the reader, the latter as critic uncovering 'cross-connexion after cross-connexion'.

For Coleridge the imagination is always more valuable than the fancy. As a formalist, Richards too valorises the imagination, since he observes this as seeking and creating unity not just between images but between all elements in a text and on all levels, 'pulling together into some joint effect'. In effect the reader is making the text and at the same time smoothing over its discrepancies and tensions.

In the following chapter Richards changes his direction markedly to discuss what he terms the 'musical effects of rhythm' in verse. In particular he focuses on the nature of 'metre'. However, his use of this term is distinctly obtuse. By metre he understands not the sonic beat of a line (for example, iambic pentameter) but the 'very motion of the meaning'.

His point is to take up and argue Coleridge's contention in *Biographia Literaria* that poetry may exist without metre. His answer to this apparent paradox lies in his claim that literary criticism has been hindered by its emphasis on the *word* as the basic unit of meaning and poetic composition. Furthermore, it has focused on the semantics of the word and the word in isolation.

Richards wants to argue, alongside Coleridge, that the meaning depends on other factors. For example, on what the reader him/herself brings to the words and, more importantly, on the context. The context consists of a bond between the meaning of the individual words and the relationships between the words in a poem.

> The bond, in other words between metre and poetry – which remains unintelligible so long as we separate words from their meanings and treat them as mere signs fitted into a sensory pattern – becomes an evident necessity if we consider the words as invested with their meanings.   (114)

Although we should always be suspicious when a philosopher redefines our everyday terms to get out of a tight corner, his general theory seems plausible since beneath the verbiage he appears to be arguing that the effect of a poem depends on the complex dynamics of a text and not on separate components taken in isolation. Once again he discovers unifying forces 'coadunating' in the theory.

Richards next asks why we need a theory of literary analysis at all. One answer, disclosing his philosophy/science background, is that a reader would employ some sort of implicit theory anyway, so better to have a sound one. A sound theory is one rooted in reason and, with 1930s political upheaval in mind, he warns that there has lately been a 'revolt against reason'. Another answer rings more of the pompous paternalist:

> persons with literary interests today frequently suffer from lack of exercise in careful and sometimes arduous thinking.   (137)

You have been warned!

The book closes with some impressive analyses by Richards of two of the leading literary issues of his day, the role of myth in literature and of the direction of literary criticism. In 'The Boundaries of the Mythical', he considers the relationship between mythology and nature and concludes that myth is not a scientific description of truth but our artistic translation of it, its 'symbolisation'. The imagination is a central element in this translation, the raw bones of literature itself:

> The imagination projects the life of the mind not upon Nature ... but upon a Nature that is already a projection of our sensibility. (164)

Nature comes to us in the form of images but they are our own images shaped by our psychological needs (and eventually expressed in a form akin to the collective conscious). Coleridge would have approved of this definition of subjectivism and this has the merit too, for Richards, of subsuming Coleridge into the Imagist movement of the early twentieth century as well as reconciling him with current psychoanalytical speculation.

The strength of Richards's study lies in its close analysis of Coleridge's words and the ideas behind them, his methods to this end having been delineated in his *Principles of Literary Criticism* (1924). It is, thus, a valuable introduction to Coleridge's theory (though his prose is often windy and sometimes overbearing). His trademark passion is for meticulously paring down words to get a fixed meaning – even if the words do not always cooperate. In this he is a child of his philosophical time, bearing the influence of Wittgenstein and Austin's plain language ideals, but his attentiveness to linguistics anticipates some of the anxieties of post-structuralism.

On the 'minus' side, Richards also mirrors his period in presuming a consensus about what are Coleridge's good and poor poems. Another weakness is that, although he berates the 'fancy' from the author's side of the poem, he devalues the power of the reader's esemplastic imagination, the instinctive readiness to create original meanings from a text. His concern with unity, symbol and imagism are also very much of his age and yet by applying these aspects to Coleridge he necessarily demonstrates and explains the enduring appeal of the poetry and theory.

### Robert Mayo

The overriding theme in Robert Mayo's famous 1954 article 'The Contemporaneity of the *Lyrical Ballads*' is that the *Ballads* is neither

as experimental nor as innovative as Wordsworth makes out in his
Advertisement and Preface to the collection.

In the Advertisement to the first edition Wordsworth declared
that:

> The majority of the following poems are to be considered as
> experiments.

and reiterated this in the 1800 Preface

> It was published as an experiment.

Mayo wishes to demonstrate that while the poems are unquestion-
ably revolutionary in some respects, they are not so in all. The basis
for his claim is some fairly exhaustive research into the magazine
poetry of the late eighteenth century and popular taste, leading Mayo
to conclude that in many respects the poetry of *Lyrical Ballads* is
actually quite conventional.

He begins by revealing that in the latter end of the 1700s the great
explosion in demand for poetry encouraged a generation of poets,
now largely (and justly) consigned to oblivion. This group of poets,
however, was indirectly the progenitors of the canonical figures of
English Romanticism, including Wordsworth and Coleridge. The
gap in the supply of poetry was only partly met by these new writers
pandering to the popular demand and, where necessary, the poetry
sections of the magazines were filled up by lifting and plagiarising
published material.

Mayo reminds us of how Wordsworth and Coleridge had originally intended *The Ancient Mariner* as a commercial venture for
magazine publication and both had already used the popular press as
an outlet for their own poetry. In fact Wordsworth himself had (in
1794) planned to set up such a periodical himself, *Monthly
Miscellany*, along conventional lines.

While few would make literary claims for the contemporary popular verse, they can usefully be seen as a barometer of shifting taste by
which to gauge the appeal of *Lyrical Ballads* (a barometer with which
Wordsworth and Coleridge were closely acquainted). The 'common

taste' of the miscellany magazines not only accepted what Wordsworth damned as the 'gaudiness and inane' but, as conservative institutions, they consciously encouraged it. As a result, comments Mayo, they lagged at least fifty years behind the 'literary poetry', in what he calls the 'backwash of the Augustan era'.

The essay is now structured to analyse first the content of the *Ballads* and then the forms of its poems. Under 'content' the essay declares that Wordsworth's collection of verse seems an incongruous assemblage to us and was typical of volumes of popular verse in its day. Equally so is the quite narrow range of topics, that are likewise wholly commonplace in themselves. He groups these under three headings (nature, simplicity, and humanitarianism and sentimental morality) and tries to demonstrate how these categories were standard fare for the 1790s:

> the more one reads the popular poetry of the last quarter of the eighteenth century the more he is like to feel that the really surprising feature of these poems in the *Lyrical Ballads* ... is their intense fulfilment of an already stale convention.

Wordsworth's intimacy (and emulation) of the common taste contradicts the Victorian perception of him as a kind of prophet writing in the wilderness or swimming against the tide. Among the nature poetry Mayo highlights 'Tintern Abbey' as one poem that was remarkable only as a most traditional topographical poem presented conventionally as a rhapsodic, lyrical meditation. The true novelty of poem, however, lies in its 'vastly superior technical mastery'.

In the other two categories he identifies 'The Nightingale' (under 'simplicity') and 'The Female Vagrant' ('humanitarianism and sentimental morality') as projecting less a revolution than an 'excess of a new orthodoxy'. Furthermore he charges Wordsworth with employing conventional imagery and a procession of stereotypical characters. These are usually rendered with exaggerated sentiment. Among the *Ballads*, he finds only *The Rime of the Ancient Mariner* as creating any real surprise or controversy, chiefly because contemporary reviewers found it 'unintelligible' – in spite of the fact of its similarities to the traditional narrative ballad.

To readers in the 1790s outcasts were a readily recognisable type. At first sight and to modern readers, 'The Idiot Boy', usually strikes an exceptional or 'eccentric' note. But Mayo maintains that in fact contemporary reviewers did not treat it as anomalous but instead bracketed it with other 'rustic delineations' of the outsider. By the same token 'The Female Vagrant' fitted the existing pigeonhole of the outcast (rather than, as we might see her, the 'forsaken woman'). 'The Old Man Travelling' too was regarded on these terms and even the Ancient Mariner was fitted in with 'anguished and homeless sailors'.

Concluding this part of the essay, Mayo reluctantly accepts that there were several novelties and singles out *Goody Blake and Harry Gill* and 'Simon Lee' as offering a 'different kind and intensity' of rural life from that of the magazine pastorals.

So much for the subject matter of *Lyrical Ballads*. Mayo now turns to the 'forms' of the poems and by this term he intends poetic forms and genres. However, his verdict is extended into this area too:

> in general, it may be asserted that what is true of the contents of Lyrical Ballads, is true also of the *forms*. Except for the language and style of a few poems ... and a few limited experiments with metre, the *manner* of the volume cannot be regarded as extraordinary.

First of all the contents themselves, a heterogeneous assortment of poetic forms and subjects, was quite typical for the day. Ballads too were a ubiquitous form in eighteenth-century popular magazines and Mayo identifies two common types: the objective/narrative ballad and the subjective/lyrical. He argues that the term 'lyrical ballad' was in reality a hybrid term probably coined as a marketing ploy and to induce curiosity, though the result was just as likely to be a source of confusion.

In terms of prosody too *Lyrical Ballads* presents only limited evidence of experiment and does not exhibit revolutionary or surprising tendencies. With evident reluctance Mayo concludes that only about six of the twenty-three poems in the first edition could be understood as experimental with regard to form but adds that none of the contemporary commentators themselves drew attention to

this. In summing up his standpoint he reprises his opening contention but uses it to locate the *Lyrical Ballads* in their historical
context:

> From one point of view the *Lyrical Ballads* stand at the beginning of a
> new orientation of literary, social, ethical and religious values; and they
> are unquestionably a pivotal work in the transition from one century
> to the next. But from another point of view, equally valid, they come
> at the end of a long and complicated process of development, accord-
> ing to which a great deal in the volume must have seemed to many
> readers both right and inevitable.

In contrast to Richards's formalist study, Robert Mayo's objective
is to historicise the *Lyrical Ballads*. Where Richards sees the poems as
relatively isolated, to be analysed in terms of their internal imaging
and unities, Mayo is working towards a point at which the context
begins to bear on how we judge the verse and impressive quantity of
detailed research that the writer has undertaken in order to establish
that context.

Mayo's essay is justly celebrated as a landmark in its uncompro-
mising interrogation of the claims of experiment and innovation in
the 1798 Advertisement. Moreover his study has been especially valuable in extending the discussion of Wordsworth's work beyond the
traditional critical preoccupations with nature themes and into the
realm of his reading – or at least his astute awareness of the popular
reading of others.

Against this, however, it must be said that the range of (three)
themes that he discovers in the verse seems simplistic and reductive.
It could also be argued that Shakespeare too was not particularly
innovative in his choice of subject and form. Furthermore, an underlying assumption in the essay seems to be that contemporary magazine poetry was of a uniformly inferior quality. And even if Mayo's
conclusions about the literary context are valid the poems still have
to be encountered and analysed as poetry.

In spite of the objectivity of his research, Mayo's study has recently
been criticised for the subjectivity and impressionism of the *conclusions* based on the research. Critical fashions have of course moved on

since 1954 when analysts were expected to be judgemental in their conclusions. Other critics have adopted a slightly different take on Mayo's central issue. For instance, Stephen Parrish in *The Art of the 'Lyrical Ballads'* (1973) cautiously concurs with the research findings but adds that in spite of Mayo's disparagement of the progenitors or precedents of the collection it would be foolish to underestimate the potentialities of the traditional ballad. In this regard he posits the strong influence of Gottfried Bürger's German ballads and Thomas Percy's *Reliques*.

By contrast Mary Jacobus in her *Tradition and Experiment in Wordsworth's Lyrical Ballads'* (1798) takes Robert Mayo to task over both sectors of his thesis. She forcefully defends Wordsworth by maintaining that his experiments were, as declared, two-fold: actually adopting the 'non-literary idiom' of the lower classes, and transforming everyday subjects and stories 'by the Wordsworthian imagination'.

Ultimately the question of influence is by its subjectivist and relativist nature elusive of any final resolution. Because of the enormity of the superstructure of Mayo's research his thesis is necessarily confined to its findings. At the same time it is fair to say that while he discovers no great innovation in the content and form of the poems Wordsworth's technical excellence is luminously apparent:

> in their vastly superior technical mastery, their fullness of thought and intensity of feeling, the air of spontaneity which they breathe, and their attention to significant details.

## Geoffrey H. Hartman

The third critic I would like to consider is the author of the seminal study *Wordsworth's Poetry 1787–1814*.

Hartman, who was a professor of English and Comparative Literature at Yale University, was at first a proponent of 'New Criticism', the movement that flourished in America and Britain between about 1930 and 1965. Although in general terms New Critics accept that a fully scientific method of analysis is not possible they nevertheless support the rigorous rationalisation of literary criticism begun by commentators such as Richards. Advocates, who have included T. S. Eliot, F. R. Leavis, Allen Tate, R. P. Blackmur and John Crowe Ransom, emphasise the self-sufficiency and internal coherence of works. Stressing close linguistic analysis of texts, they tend to share the view that investigation should discover what they regard as the essential internal unity of the literary text, resolving its paradoxes, tensions and ambiguities in favour of this. Focusing on internal aspects they have played down the role of such external features as historical context and authorial intention (such as Wordsworth's Preface to *Lyrical Ballads*).

An earlier essay by Hartman, 'Romanticism and Anti-Self-Consciousness' (1962) attempted to show that poetry such as Wordsworth's logged the transition from sense experience in nature to knowledge about oneself as a sort of substitute for religion. Self-knowledge becomes a divine energy as the power behind the poetry. Yet in the absence of readily available and authentic myths Romantic poetry such as that of Wordsworth and Coleridge slips into subjectivism in which imagination prominently opens up issues of illusion, irony and deception in the texts but at the same time resolves them.

However, *Wordsworth's Poetry 1787–1814*, reveals Hartman's unease with the formal complacencies of New Criticism was well as his new sympathies in the direction of deconstructionism. His book tries to find a passage from nineteenth- to twentieth-century modes of thought, attempting to liberate Wordsworth from interpretations that have emphasised religious, didactic and 'growth of mind' approaches. Here Hartman focuses on the structures of consciousness reflected in verbal figures, literary modes and rhetorical forms. In particular he highlights two consciousnesses present in Wordsworth and regards the poetry as his coming to terms with them and the gulf between them. Wordsworth is divided between and tries to reconcile nature-consciousness and self-consciousness.

Unlike the formalist New Critics, Hartman has no commitment to discovering unity but is content to clarify and explore divisions in Wordsworth's vision especially the idea that the subjective imagination could intrinsically be opposed to nature. Hartman sees the division between nature-consciousness and self-consciousness, as symbolised by the trope of the abyss that is ubiquitous in the poetry.

Romanticism seemed to many to hold out the ideal of a merging of the mind and the physical object in which the knower would therefore be at one with the known. The history of British Romanticism's new enterprise is a journey from perception about the world to perception about self. However, the aggrandisement of the subjective consciousness quickly becomes problematic in the form of shame or guilt, a self-obliterating impulse demanding resolution through art.

Poetry for Wordsworth is therefore seen as a kind of cathartic therapy for rectifying the disintegration of the self-consciousness. The poet seeks to deal with this disunity arising from the fragmentariness of self-consciousness through a sublimation of the self-conscious into nature-conscious. In other words the imagination desires to become immersed in the mental image of the physical. Nevertheless, Hartman finds that the transition is repeatedly arrested or evaded and it is this perpetually deferred desire that motivates the poetry.

*Wordsworth's Poetry* was a highly influential study and – along with a series of Hartman's essays in 1960s – was important in setting the agenda for analyses of Wordsworth, and his writings have been widely critiqued. I would like to focus on his study of 'There was a Boy' (or 'Winander Boy' as it appeared in *The Prelude*) and then to discuss Paul de Man's important reaction to this study as the basis for his own deconstructive analysis of the poem.

After the boy's tumultuous mimicry of the hooting owls there follows a brief ominous pause that foretells a later state of mind. Nature begins to refashion the mind that interacts with it and the poem reveals:

> [how] the child is moved gently and unhurt towards the consciousness of nature's separate life, this being an early step in the growth of the mind.

In Wordsworth, though, the effect of nature on the consciousness is at a more complex level than the Rousseauesque programme normally permits. At the core of this process is the mild shock that the boy undergoes. Through this mild regulation, the boy approaches a sense of nature's and perhaps of his own, separate life. However he dies before his self-consciousness can fully develop.

Hartman then adduces Wordsworth's acknowledgement that the poem is autobiographical and that it deals with the 'transfer of internal feelings ... in the celestial soil of the Imagination'. He argues that the mysterious and supervening death of the boy (fulfilling its premonition in line 19) was included in the published version in order to satisfy demand for a narrative, so that the later form stresses incident over character, psychology over plot.

> The completed sketch, however, nicely rounded by converting a figurative death into an actual, yields to the prevalent taste and becomes a beautifully extended epitaph.

On the other hand, from Hartman's point of view the extension actually becomes another shock to popular taste. Additionally, the coda to the poem, with Wordsworth standing for a half-hour by the boy's grave, turns the physical events into an inward action, 'injects a new emphasis on inwardness'.

In this respect the poem accords with others in the collection:

> The timing of the boy's death and the tone in which it is narrated remind us strongly of the Lucy poems. Both Lucy and the Boy of Winander die before consciousness of self can emerge wholly from consciousness of nature.

And this points to the developmental impasse of death in the poem: growing further into consciousness would mean death (viz. of childhood unselfconscious, joyful being) as so would the failure to develop further (a physical death, absorption by nature). The space between the first and second paragraphs of the poem materialises this impasse, the abyss between the two consciousnesses. As Hartman argues, this childhood development represents a precarious transition, and 'no one crosses that gulf, at least not intact'.

The boy dies at a crossroads in life, a 'halted traveller', instead of waking from consciousness of nature into consciousness of self. Wordsworth himself shares in this because he shares the 'shock of surprise' that carried far into the heart of the boy. But, further, Wordsworth shares in the impasse too because although he knows that consciousness is always of death, he does not face up to this confrontation in the crisis of recognition. The result is that the shock of self-consciousness is 'once more elided'. Hartman observes that this impasse of transition in the poem is attended by two significant verbal tropes: the overhanging churchyard and the poet's lengthened pause.

## Paul de Man

Since the 1960s, literary studies has undergone a quantum revolution in its perspectives and aims. In the wake of European phenomenological philosophy the subject has and continues to reappraise its foundational paradigms; its presuppositions, intellectual groundwork, values, and even its texts and methods have been the subject of meticulous questioning. New Criticism was ousted by Structuralism, a revolutionary textual perspective grounded in semiotic theory, and this in turn has stimulated a host of theoretical approaches to criticism some inimical to Structuralism, including Deconstructive, Psychoanalytical, Marxist, Genderist and Neo-historicist movements.

Paul de Man (1919–83) was, with J. Hillis Miller and Harold Bloom (and later Hartman too), a leading member of the deconstructionist group of critics that made Yale a centre of the 'movement' in the 1970s. De Man himself was widely respected as a highly original and creative intellect and discovered Romanticism to be particularly responsive to the kinds of questioning distinctive in his form of deconstructionism.

Deconstructionism, inspired and informed chiefly by the linguistic philosophy of Jacques Derrida, is in part a reaction to the poetics of Structuralism, which valorises the broad role of 'cultural context' in the analysis of all types of text. Definition of deconstructionism would ultimately be impossible (and one of its 'tenets' has been resistance to the choking, logocentric impulse to fix and formulate). However it has presented a number of characteristics, including: meanings in language are continually in flux and arise through internal relationships; this fundamental instability of language implies that texts too are unstable; available meanings in a text are multiple, often ambiguous or indeterminate, frequently contradictory, evading final resolution or domination by particular groups. As de Man himself has written:

> Literature as well as criticism – the difference between them being delusive – is condemned (or privileged) to be forever the most rigorous and, consequently, the most unreliable language in terms of which man names and transforms himself.
>
> (de Man, *Allegories of Reading*, 1979)

But as this affirms, deconstruction is at the same time a method, a process and a relationship of interacting with a text. As used by Derrida and de Man, the term applies to the reader becoming alert to the multiplicity of meanings in a text and the tensions inherent in the linguistic interplay between its components. Like the New Critics, deconstructionists reject notions of intentionality (and penumbral contexts) in the working of a text but, unlike them, they stress the role of the reader in creating the meaning of the literary work. Thus there is no sense of a final (especially authorial) determinate meaning to be discovered in a work. Readings are thus always hesitated and continually undermined, readerly conclusions or closure being constantly deferred. Paradoxically, since deconstructionism essentially defies the notion of a consensus it must also evade any necessary or a priori definition of its own practices or status.

Paul de Man's writing on Romanticism has mostly been in the form of long essays, the best known of which is 'The Rhetoric of Temporality'. As I think the above quotation demonstrates, his work often attempts to expose the philosophical contradictions implicit in literary analysis. Literature, particularly poetry, by the process of parading its very literariness (or 'rhetoricity') draws attention to the complex shifting, evasive and subversive dynamics of discourse, even in the same moment that it pretends to present to the reader truths about the 'external physical world'. He advocates a close-reading approach but offers no concessions to any search for harmony or textual coherence.

De Man's essay 'Time and History in Wordsworth' is an explicit response to Hartman's comments on 'There was a Boy' in *Wordsworth's*

*Poetry 1787–1814.* It was delivered as a lecture at Princeton University in 1967 and then revised in 1971. In general terms it focuses on the relationship between Wordsworth's use of figures or tropes (in particular metonymy) and their relationship with the poem's meanings.

He begins by explaining that he has no disagreement with Hartman's methodological approach,

> Moreover, by interpreting Wordsworth from the inside, from the phenomenological point of view of his consciousness, Hartman can trace a coherent itinerary of Wordsworth's poetic development.

At the centre of his disagreement is Hartman's unquestioning acceptance of the traditional thematic problems in Wordsworth, namely the relationship between nature and the imagination (which can be traced back to the mid-nineteenth century at least). De Man wishes to argue that before we try to reach conclusions about themes and their problems we should examine the poetics, otherwise we end up with abstractions.

Quoting Wordsworth's Preface, that the mind of man and nature are essentially adapted to each other, de Man sees this as a somewhat tired idea and one that has dominated interpretations of 'There was a Boy'. Unlike Hartman he finds that the two parts of the poem do not sit easily together, though the word 'hung' is important in trying to connect them. It is a commonplace to say that the poem mourns the death of Wordsworth's own youth but de Man considers the poem more temporally complex than this, that it is a description of a future event (the poet's own death). The anticipation of this can only exist as a form of language, an anticipation ('prolepsis') or an epitaph written now but from beyond the grave. He turns the time scale on its head:

> The structure of the poem, although it seems retrospective, is in fact proleptic.

It is a 'preknowledge of his mortality' and

> [the] spatial heaven of the first five lines with its orderly moving stars has become the temporal heaven of line 24, 'uncertain' and precarious since it appears in the form of a pre-consciousness of death.

This uncertainty or anxiety is not allowed to go unrelieved but de Man sees in the poem a complex interplay between spatial and temporal awareness. 'Hung' is important because it works in both awarenesses, referring to a pause and to the idea of something hovering in space, each implying an unfulfilled movement. The second part of the poem also works like this because instead of the expected lament on the boy's death (time) we hear a eulogy on the location (place).

If Wordsworth is reflecting on the past, his own dead youth, then this objectification of the past is the apparent means to viewing his own future death ('that uncertain heaven', line 24), which is literally unimaginable. As this is so it can, again, only exist in a form of language (having no real correspondence with actuality). In support of this idea de Man refers to Wordsworth's *Essay upon Epitaphs* (in which the river is an emblem for the consciousness) where the poet closely connects the capacity to anticipate with the power to remember.

What divides the two parts of 'There was a Boy' is the fact that the first part relates to the writer of his own epitaph while the second relates to the reader. De Man calls this an attempted sleight-of-hand, because in reality they cannot be the same person. It is made possible only because the two co-exist exclusively in the form of language. This is 'metalepsis', a leap outside of thematic reality into the 'rhetorical fiction of the sign'. Thus, he argues, the poem does not reflect on death but on the rhetorical power of language that deceives us into viewing the unimaginable.

De Man wishes to say that the theme of the poem and its linguistic figures are in conflict. The key to coming to terms with this, and to understanding Wordsworth, lies in seeing his relationship not with nature (as Hartman does) but with time. He does not agree with the conventional notion that Wordsworth's imagination allows 'unmediated contact with a divine principle'. Instead his consciousness relates itself to a temporal entity, that is, history.

The subject of the imagination, however, lies at the heart of Wordsworth's themes of community and love. What bonds men together is the recognition of a common temporal predicament: mortality. De Man now refers to the sonnet 'River Duddon' to examine how Wordsworth deals with this predicament and finds that he resorts to the privileged status of the imagination since the language of the imagination is not dependent on correspondence with the natural world. The central figure now is the river, emblem of regeneration. But where Hartman sees and asserts the regenerative power of nature as transcending man's mortality, de Man sees the act of regeneration as a constant statement of man's mortality. From the point of view of Wordsworth's verse, this relationship between the mind and time rather than 'mere nature' represents a deepening awareness of the self. However, since this relationship is always mediated by death it cannot be marked as an actual experience but always as an experience of language.

The strengths of de Man's analysis tend to be the strengths of deconstructive readings in general. His brilliant revisionist account is stimulating and perversely provocative, rescuing and refreshing Wordsworth from the cul-de-sac of traditional critical discourse. His explorations are not easy to follow, partly due to the startlingly novel perspectives he discovers but also due to the terminology that this new approach necessitates.

# Further Reading

## Primary Texts

*Coleridge's Notebooks: A Selection*, ed. Seamus Perry (2002).
*Poetical Works of Samuel Taylor Coleridge*, ed. E. H. Coleridge (1912).
*Poetical Works of William Wordsworth*, ed. Ernest de Selincourt (1904).
*Samuel Taylor Coleridge: Selected Poetry*, ed. William Empson and David Pirie (1989).
*Wordsworth and Coleridge: 'Lyrical Ballads'*, ed. R. L. Brett and A. R. Jones, 2nd edn (2001).

## Biographical

de Selincourt, Ernest, *The Early Letters of William and Dorothy Wordsworth* (1935).
Griggs, E. L., *Letters of Samuel Taylor Coleridge* (1956).
Gill, Stephen, *William Wordsworth* (1989).
Holmes, Richard, *Coleridge: Early Visions* (1989).
Moorman, Mary, *William Wordsworth: A Biography* (1965).
Wordsworth, Dorothy, *Journals,* ed. Mary Moorman (1971).

## Critical Studies

Austen, Frances, *The Language of Wordsworth and Coleridge* (1989).
Campbell, Patrick, *Wordsworth and Coleridge: 'Lyrical Ballads'* (1991).

Danby, John, *The Simple Wordsworth: Studies in the Poems 1797–1807* (1960).

de Man, Paul, *Allegories of Reading* (1979).

Ford, Jennifer, *Coleridge on Dreaming* (1998).

Hamilton, Paul, *Wordsworth* (1986).

Hartman, Geoffrey H., *Wordsworth's Poetry 1787–1814* (1964).

Jacobus, Mary, *Tradition and Experiment in Wordsworth's Lyrical Ballads* (1976).

Kitson, Peter J. (ed.), *Coleridge, Keats and Shelley: New Casebooks* (1996).

McMaster, Graham, *William Wordsworth: A Critical Anthology* (1972).

Mayo, Robert, 'The Contemporaneity of the *Lyrical Ballads*' (1954).

Murray, Roger N., *Wordsworth's Style: Figures and Themes in Lyrical Ballads* (1967).

Newlyn, Lucy (ed.) *The Cambridge Companion to Coleridge* (2002).

Richards, I. A., *Coleridge on Imagination* (1934).

Trott, Nicola and Seamus Perry (eds), *1800: The New Lyrical Ballads* (2001).

Williams, John, *Critical Issues: William Wordsworth* (2002).

## Romanticism

Burt, E. S. (ed.), *Paul de Man, 'Romanticism and Contemporary Criticism'* (1993).

Chase, Cynthia, *Romanticism* (1993).

Day, Aidan, *Romanticism* (1996).

Everest, Kelvin, *English Romantic Poetry* (1990).

Mellor, Anne K., *Romanticism and Gender* (1993).

Watson, John, *English Poetry of the Romantic Period,* 2nd edn (1992).

# Index